CHINA REMEMBERS

CHINA
REMEMBERS

Zhang Lijia and Calum MacLeod

OXFORD
UNIVERSITY PRESS

OXFORD
UNIVERSITY PRESS

Oxford University Press is a department of the University of Oxford.
It furthers the University's objective of excellence in research, scholarship,
and education by publishing worldwide in

Oxford New York

Athens Auckland Bangkok Bogotá Buenos Aires Calcutta
Cape Town Chennai Dar es Salaam Delhi Florence Hong Kong Istanbul
Karachi Kuala Lumpur Madrid Melbourne Mexico City Mumbai
Nairobi Paris São Paulo Singapore Taipei Tokyo Toronto Warsaw

with associated companies in Berlin Ibadan

Oxford is a registered trade mark of Oxford University Press

British Library Cataloguing in Publication Data
available

Library of Congress Cataloguing-in-Publication Data
available

ISBN 0-19-591736-7

Printed in Hong Kong
Published by Oxford University Press (China) Ltd
18th Floor, Warwick House East, Taikoo Place, 979 King' Road, Quarry Bay
Hong Kong

For Grandmother Yang Huizhen,
who provided a sanctuary from turmoil

Acknowledgements

O ur foremost thanks to all the people who gave so kindly of their time to share their memories of China's past and their hopes and fears for the future. Their patience and candour have allowed us into their lives and under the surface of modern Chinese history.

Dr Lu Jianhua, Bian Yang, Shi Wei, Wu Qi, Cheng Tieliang, and Chai Jijun have all been generous with their advice and suggestions. Dr Laura Newby, Calum's tutor at Oxford, offered key comments, while a very special thanks is owed to Ian Johnson of the *Asian Wall Street Journal* for ideas, encouragement, and editorial help from the first drafts to the final proofs.

We are indebted to the staff of Batey Burn and *Newsweek*, who provided continuous logistical and moral support. In the course of researching this book, we have also benefitted from the goodwill of many individuals, even complete strangers and others who wish to remain anonymous, who were keen that the stories of the past fifty years be heard. Two such examples are Dong Huiying and Zhou Zhangyi from Shenyang, who showed such kindness to Lijia when, heavily pregnant, she visited their city.

Lijia would also like to acknowledge the advice, friendship, and fun offered by Carrie Gracie, Lucy Kynge, and their families, which really kept her going. Like our sometimes neglected friends, our families in China and the United Kingdom have been most understanding of the time pressures this project has brought. We are grateful for their constant encouragement, and in particular for the research assistance of Lijia's family in Nanjing. A final thank you belongs to our daughters May and Kirsty, for inspiration and patience beyond their years.

The authors and publisher would also like to thank the contributors to this book for providing contemporary photographs. Other photographs were taken by Cheng Tieliang (pp. 152, 258, 267, 293), Chai Jijun (pp. 77, 192, 283), Li Jianquan (pp. 106), and the authors (pp. 47, 56, 84, 91, 143, 201, 213, 220, 252, 273, 276).

Contents

Introduction

The fifty years of the People's Republic of China embrace some of the most remarkable social, economic, and political experiments in the history of man. Chairman Mao united a war-torn nation of some 500 million people, before dividing them by class and bidding the struggles begin. People's communes dictated rural life until Deng Xiaoping's reforms gave Chinese socialism a second lease on life, and his countrymen their first taste of prosperity. The retreat from Marxism towards a bustling free market over the past two decades has enabled the Chinese Communist Party to lift 200 million Chinese out of poverty, and confound all predictions of its demise. Few other nations, regardless of political persuasion, have ever attempted and achieved so much change within so brief a period.

By tracing the past half-century through the bitter-sweet memories of ordinary people, in whose name so many campaigns have been fought and so much blood spilt, this book reveals the human heart of modern China's many revolutions. From Shenyang in the industrial north-east, to Lhasa on the Tibetan plateau, the recollections compiled here give voice to the diversity of experience across the vast land that is China. Despite their different backgrounds, the interviewees demonstrate the unshakeable will to survive demanded by countless trials and tribulations. Together they illuminate every stage of China's search for strength and modernization.

The interviewees range from a land-reform activist who shot a village chief in the early 1950s, to a carpenter campaigning to become village chief in the late 1990s. China's rural transformation is further highlighted by recollections of backyard steel production in the Great Leap Forward, the tragic hubris of the famine that followed, the break-up of communal land, and the ongoing migration to the cities. There the witnesses of urban revolution recall the fall and rise of private business, the short-lived freedoms of the Hundred Flowers and Democracy Wall movements, and the euphoria-turned-terror of the Cultural Revolution and the 1989 protests in Tiananmen Square. While entrepreneurs relate their success stories in a society where money-making has eclipsed ideology, other interviewees voice contemporary concerns for the environment, religion, and women's rights that suggest the budding of a civil society.

The history of the highly politicized People's Republic of China defies classification by decades, so the five sections of the book are shaped instead by the major political turning points. Although many interviewees could have related the full half-century, we have asked each interviewee to concentrate on a particular period when his or her experience provides the greatest interest and insight for the reader. Yet since these are journeys told by real people, providing an account at once less rigid and more personal than conventional history, many interviewees recall events from across their lives and Chinese history. Where we have interviewed non-Chinese for their unique impression of the People's Republic, we have chosen people who have made China their home. Most of the interviews were conducted in Mandarin, plus some in English and Russian. We have attempted to ensure that our translations adhere as faithfully as possible to the original recollections. The system of Pinyin romanization is adopted for Chinese words bar familiar exceptions such as Yangtze and Hong Kong.

'Remember the bitterness of the past to savour the sweetness of the present.' For many years, political study sessions exhorted the Chinese people to open their hearts with gratitude at the benefits communism had bestowed on New China. On the eve of the fiftieth birthday of the People's Republic, and the start of a new millennium, the key to China's hopes and fears for the future still lies in understanding its past. The Asian financial crisis of the late 1990s has underlined the dangers of predicting an Asian-Pacific or Chinese century, but there is little doubt of China's growing regional and international role. By 2050 China could be a mid-ranking country in its gross domestic product, with the largest economy in the world and up to 200 million university graduates. While governments will guide this process, it is ultimately the ordinary people—the hardworking citizens whose stories are told here—who will struggle to realize these dreams.

Consolidating Power

1949–1956

To the cheers of 100,000 spectators, Mao Zedong ascended Tiananmen, the Gate of Heavenly Peace and entrance to the imperial palace, on 1 October 1949. A portrait of the Communist Party Chairman hung in place of defeated rival Generalissimo Chiang Kaishek. With the rousing cry, 'The Chinese people have stood up!', Mao declared the birth of a new China from the battlements of the old. For four millennia, those people had watched the Mandate of Heaven, the divine right to rule, pass from corrupt incumbent to vigorous conqueror. Chiang's Nationalist regime was a picture of imperial decay, while the Communists had emerged from the barren caves of North China steeled in guerrilla warfare and equipped with a revolutionary ideology tried and tested in China's villages, home to the vast majority of its 500 million people.

At first, most Chinese cared little for the political orientation of the new order. They were simply grateful for an end to the tumult of the previous century. A series of humiliating foreign treaties and devastating rebellions had long signalled the weakness of the ailing Qing dynasty. When the court finally introduced a package of reforms in the early 1900s, it was too little, too late. Yet to the distress of tireless activist Sun Yatsen, the eventual overthrow of the Qing in 1911 led not to the rebirth and strengthening of the nation, but the torment of fractured politics and regional warlordism.

Anger at the Treaty of Versailles, which in 1919 provided for the transfer to Japan of German concessions in China, was an important catalyst in the intellectual ferment that became known as the May Fourth Movement. The Chinese Communist Party (CCP) would in time prove the most significant legacy of the birth of Chinese Nationalism, yet it was Chiang Kaishek's Nationalist Party (the Guomindang) who succeeded in 1928 to Sun's dream of a national government claiming control of much of China. When not hounding the Communists, Chiang's administration was not without achievement—until the Japanese invasion of 1937 hijacked hopes of genuine unification and forced his retreat to Chongqing. At the time, Mao and his forces were holed up in the loess caves of Yan'an in northern Shaanxi province, after the Party's failure to launch a Bolshevik-style revolution among Chinese workers and the Long March to escape Nationalist 'extermination campaigns'. If neither side excelled in battle against the Japanese, the Communist-led People's Liberation Army (PLA) made greater capital from its patriotic stance and frugal ways. In contrast to the Nationalist focus on industrial and urban China, Mao sought peasant support through a Sinification of Marxism that exploited the revolutionary force of the countryside.

After the Japanese defeat in 1945, Mao and Chiang toasted each other's health in Chongqing, during US-led efforts to prevent civil war. This first encounter in two decades was to prove their last, for the so-called United Front against Japan had long lapsed into open enmity. Despite being outnumbered three to one in men and materials in 1947, the PLA reversed the odds through bold military leadership and widespread disaffection for the repressive, inflation-hit Nationalist government. Chiang fled with the country's gold reserves to found the Republic of China on Taiwan, leaving Mao the task of consolidating a war-torn and loosely integrated empire.

As the speed of conquest surprised even the Party, the newly established People's Republic of China (PRC) was until 1954 divided into six military regions to ease the passage to civilian rule. Lack of sufficient Party cadres with urban experience required most officials to remain at their posts. To the surprise of many nervous city dwellers, long accustomed to marauding victors, the PLA proved a model of discipline and courtesy. People were relieved to discover their wives would not be communized after all, despite the rumours, and it was safe to walk the streets. Cautious optimism was encouraged by early Party policy. The Common Programme, adopted by an advisory board that embraced the bourgeoisie and other non-Party elements, made no mention of socialism. Mao's New Democracy emphasized moderation and the toleration of private business. His new government fought corruption, prostitution, and opium-smoking, and by 1950 had hyperinflation under control and the budget balanced. This was a China to be proud of.

On 7 October 1950, as the PLA invaded Tibet, the last rebel province before Taiwan, China announced the dispatch of troops to the Korean peninsula. After decades of near-constant unrest and on the eve of an ambitious reform of land ownership, China was surely due a reprieve. Instead it faced forces of the United Nations closing on its north-east border, and the reasonable assumption that the United States and Taiwan would use Korea as a base for subversion in the PRC. The geopolitics of East Asia were fixed, as Communist China and the Soviet Union forged an uneasy alliance and the PRC's isolation from the West deepened: recovery of its United Nations seat was delayed by twenty years, while plans to dislodge the incumbent were put on indefinite hold after the US Seventh Fleet entered the Taiwan Strait.

Mao had warned Liberation was but the first step of a new long march. The outbreak of the Korean War (1950–3) sparked a shift from leniency towards a more radical domestic agenda. From 1951 to 1953, nationalist zeal fuelled an exhausting and violent series of witch-hunts against foreigners, counter-revolutionaries, capitalists, and other enemies, real and imagined. Intellectuals, initially wooed under a liberal united front strategy, underwent thought reform to mould their ideals to those of the Party. During a further thought-reform campaign in mid-1954, Mao stirred a wave of hysteria against the writer Hu Feng. Hu's brave call for greater autonomy in intellectual life earned him nationwide vilification and imprisonment as a warning against unorthodox thinking.

Although wealthy peasants had been tolerated after 1949, the redistribution of rural plots from landlords to the peasants that tilled them was fundamental Communist Party policy. With war, and the simultaneous campaign against counter-revolutionaries, land reform entered a more rigorous phase. Mobilized by Party activists, peasants exacted bloody revenge for centuries of servitude. By autumn 1952 up to 50 per cent of all cultivated land had changed hands, and perhaps one million landlords had been executed. The old rural élite had been crushed. Survivors and their persecutors alike found themselves labelled with a class status that determined their future fate under the PRC, from education and employment to marriage and even access to medical treatment. To be classified among the 'five dark categories'—landlords, rich peasants, counter-revolutionaries, bad elements, and rightists— was to join the dregs of society. These labels were the tools with which class struggle was fought for the next twenty-five years.

The quest to create the New Socialist Man began in earnest in the early days of the PRC through political study meetings, marches, and manual labour for the common good. Forced participation in nationwide movements countered the parochialism that plagued China's cities almost as much as her villages. The Party was able to mobilize the people by its success in penetrating Chinese society to a more complete degree than had any previous regime. In the countryside, the peasants were obliged to pool newly won land and equipment into mutual-aid teams that soon merged into cooperatives. In the cities, one's 'work unit' dominated professional and private life, ably supported by residents' committees that monitored every street and even today remain the ultimate grass-roots arm of Party control. In 1955, Mao noted with pride that almost all Chinese, individualists long described as 'loose sand', now belonged to mass organizations like the Communist Youth League or Women's Federation.

This framework of control, buoyed by the patriotic urge to 'build the nation', facilitated the repair of public works such as irrigation, the expansion of road and rail, and the growth of a nationwide food distribution system. The benefits were demonstrated in effective flood-fighting by massed volunteers in 1954, a marked improvement on the response to the disastrous 1931 floods. With fervour similar to that of the political campaigns, movements were launched to control disease and improve public health. Life expectancy quickly lengthened. To wipe out illiteracy, night schools were organized nationwide where simple lessons, songs, and plays taught many villagers to read, write, and understand the policies that were revolutionizing the Chinese countryside.

Socialist Transformation formally succeeded New Democracy from late 1953. In 1954, the Common Programme was superseded by the first state constitution, faithfully Soviet bar its appointment of a state chairman (Mao) to satisfy the Chinese need for a supreme patriarch. Agricultural cooperatives entered the 'higher stage', whereby entire villages toiled for collective goals, though the Soviet model of development left farming a low priority after heavy and light industry. In its First Five Year Plan (1953–7), China eagerly copied the Soviet elder brother, even outspending the heavy industrial investment of Stalin's own first plan. Taking too literally the slogan, 'Today's Soviet Union is tomorrow's China', town planners sacrificed traditional architecture for Stalinist monumentality. Beijing's old city walls gave way to Tiananmen Square and wide roads across the capital.

In the first four years of the 1950s, Mao had made no public pronouncements and rarely circumvented party and state. By 1955, however, his patience was exhausted by the slow speed of the transition to socialism. Fearful of capitalism returning to China's villages, he called in July for faster collectivization, ridiculing more pragmatic colleagues as 'tottering along like women with bound feet', and in December proclaimed the 'high tide of socialism' in the Chinese countryside. His millenarian visions would prove the planners wrong—'Chicken feathers really are flying up to heaven!' By 1956, almost all China's peasants belonged to rural cooperatives, and all private enterprises had been abolished.

The Eighth Party Congress in September 1956, the first since 1945, offered a platform to review achievements to date. From the party's view, the self-congratulation was justified: a centralized state and command economy had followed the successful consolidation of power. China had withstood American might and developed close ties with the Soviet bloc. Internal dissent was silenced, Party membership neared 11 million, and class struggle was declared to be over, for China had entered the socialist stage. Besides the purge of two senior leaders in 1954, there had been little disruption to the unity of the Yan'an élite, who had worked and fought at Mao's side for over two decades.

Yet strains within the leadership were becoming evident. In the light of Khrushchev's denunciation of Stalin in February 1956, Mao's personality cult was put on hold and his Thoughts deleted from the Party's constitution. Premier Zhou Enlai announced moderate economic plans that opposed the 'rash advance' favoured by his Chairman. It was not Mao but Vice-Chairman Liu Shaoqi who delivered the keynote speech to the 1956 congress. Although Mao himself appeared ready to 'retire to the second front', he remained frustrated by Party efforts to restrict mass mobilization. He served warning of his goals and the methods required to realize them: collectivization was 'a raging tidal wave sweeping away all demons and monsters'.

Traditionally, the Chinese have always been inclined to accept the cycle of dynastic change, asking only for a benevolent emperor who guarantees order and leaves them in peace. The new Communist regime had brought an end to the chaos, corruption, and inequities of old China. Most officials appeared genuine in their attempts to serve the people, but material improvement was not Mao's prime incentive. As China's citizens—bullied from one campaign to the next—were discovering, Mao led a party driven by the need to revolutionize society, when less brutality and more freedom of expression may have secured more willing cooperation. While Party prestige remained high, resentment at its overarching authority would soon ignite public debate.

Zhou Youguang
Return to the Motherland

As the PLA swept south during 1949, the total victory of the Chinese Communists was assured. Yet despite propaganda success in its 'base areas' during the civil war, the Party inspired no mass mobilization of the Chinese people behind its Marxist message. What occurred was the well-executed military defeat of a morally and financially bankrupt regime. While most Chinese were resigned to the passing of heaven's mandate to a new dynasty, thousands of intellectuals and entrepreneurs took their expertise, capital, and dissent to Hong Kong and beyond, or joined the Nationalists on Taiwan. More remarkable were returning émigrés like banker Zhou Youguang, inspired by the hope of national renewal after decades of disunity and abuse by hostile powers.

Born in 1906 to an intellectual's family in Jiangsu province, Zhou came of age, like the CCP, in Shanghai, a city of foreign concessions, élite high society, criminal underworld, and growing proletariat. The opening of Shanghai as a treaty port back in 1842, the spoils of the first opium war, had marked the start of China's 'century of shame'. Zhou was first attracted by communism at the missionary-run St John's University. In 1925, to protest against the May Thirtieth Incident, when British police killed student–worker demonstrators, he left to complete his finance degree at a more 'patriotic' Chinese institution, the newly established Guanghua University.

A career in banking led Zhou to New York in 1946, but China's call brought him and his wife back to Shanghai soon after Liberation. When the PLA entered the city of sin, the culture clash was extreme—city slickers enjoyed the tale of one soldier who encountered a Western-style toilet for the first time, guessed it was used for washing rice, and flushed his ration goodbye. The moderation of early policies ensured Zhou's abilities were fully employed and won widespread cooperation among Shanghai's capitalist classes. Their days, however, were numbered. The General Line for the Transition to Socialism from late 1953 signalled the Communists' intent, and by 1956, the nationalization of private enterprise was complete.

Zhou's interest in the Chinese language, which was spurred by his father, who had run a private language institute before 1949, lent him a second career. At university he had joined heated discussion among intellectuals about romanizing Chinese characters, an effort to narrow the gap between Chinese and the world's mainstream languages. After his transfer to the China Language Reform Committee in 1955, Zhou became the chief inventor of the Pinyin system of romanization, using the Latin alphabet in transliterations of ideographs in use for four thousand years. Pinyin opened an ancient language to the computer age, while another major reform, the simplification of characters, had purists weeping but proved a boon to educators spreading literacy nationwide.

A number of returned scholars and scientists made great contributions to the new republic, notably Qian Xuesen, who was fundamental in the building of China's atomic bomb. The skills of many others were sadly wasted, as suspicion and ignorance curtailed their work, and often their freedom. In Beijing, Zhou served as a member of the Chinese People's Political Consultative Conference (CPPCC), China's top advisory body, until he was 85, bar Cultural Revolution disruption. Still writing books on language at the age of 94, Zhou shares his retirement with his wife of sixty-six years, 90-year-old Zhang Yunhe, an expert on *kunqu*, the precursor to Peking opera.

MANY PEOPLE HAVE ASKED why I would give up a promising career and comfortable life in America to return to China. It may be difficult to understand for today's young people, rushing to get out of the country. Actually, it was the most natural thing to do at that time. The founding of the People's Republic of China sent shock waves across the world, Asia in particular. Ever since the opium wars, China had been bullied and invaded by foreign powers. Now, for the first time, we Chinese stood up independently on our own feet. Many people round the world saw hope in communism. Many Chinese, seeing new hope in their homeland, came back, one after another, when the Chinese Communists took power.

One has to admire their ability in organizing underground work. From 1946, I was running the New York representative office of a private Shanghai bank, Xinhua, and studying at New York University at night.

I also did some work for the
American Irving Trust bank, and
frequently travelled to Europe to
deal with the Bank of England
among others. Among many
visitors to my Broadway home
were Liu Zunqi and Yang Gang,
outstanding journalists, and,
unknown to me, both secret Party
members. From an early stage,
they were convinced the
Communists would win because
they enjoyed the support of the
masses, and communism was the
hope of mankind. I tended to
agree. They advocated that
patriotic Chinese must return to
help build the new China. In fact,
I needed little persuasion.

Wedding photo with wife Zhang Yunhe, 1933

I was christened when young,
but it was communism that attracted me after I grew up. St John's
University in Shanghai was run by American missionaries, yet a large
percentage of the students were left-wing. The library stocked many
Marxist books, translated into English, the working language of the
university, and I read them with interest. One classmate even left for
the Soviet Union before graduating. The Japanese invasion in 1937
pushed me closer to communism. The Japanese were imperialists, the
most despised by the Communists, and our whole family suffered at
their hands. In Chongqing, our little daughter died from appendicitis
when we were in the countryside, escaping Japanese bombing. It was
too late when we rushed her to hospital. Our son too nearly died from
shrapnel.

I went through the [Anti-Japanese] War, so I didn't believe the myth
that the Communists defeated the Japanese. They played a role, though
not a decisive one, yet by comparison the Nationalists lacked the
Communists' vitality, strength, and ability to mobilize people to work
together with them. After the Japanese defeat, the Nationalist

government's unwise policies lost any remaining trust. They should have controlled inflation, not let it soar, while some greedy officials made fortunes from our national disaster by pocketing property as they reclaimed Japanese-controlled areas. Corruption grew worse and worse.

Resisting offers to join large US banks, I decided to leave America after learning the Communists had crossed the Yangtze and taken Nanjing, the former Nationalist capital. It was obvious to anyone who would win. At that time, I must say a fair number of progressive Americans were also sympathetic to the Communists. Though the authorities might not like it, communism was tolerated, and [Senator Joseph] McCarthy's anti-communism began after I left. Later Chinese intellectuals had great trouble trying to return. Once I made up my mind, my wife and I moved quickly, flying to Hong Kong to await China's liberation. On 3 June 1949, a week after Shanghai was liberated, we boarded a boat from Hong Kong.

When we landed, I really felt I was back home. My bank even sent people to pick us up. I was excited and eager to make a contribution to the new government. I thought my skill in finance would be useful in China's construction, as the Communists had taken over a torn country. Returned scholars were generally treated very well, at least in the beginning. A committee was set up to look after us, and I was immediately made a senior manager at Xinhua. A friend on the committee arranged for me to teach at the economic research institute under Fudan University. I was very happy in the early days after my return, juggling various jobs and responsibilities. A year later, when the East China branch of the new People's Bank was established, I also became senior adviser to the private enterprise department, an indication of official trust in me.

On top of that, I became a member of Shanghai's political consultative council. Shanghai's mayor, Chen Yi, was a wonderful man, clear-headed, pragmatic, and open-minded, not the typical Party bureaucrat you usually meet. Every month he invited experts and celebrities to a symposium and listened to our suggestions. He made me feel I had not taken the wrong path by returning. I think he appreciated two of my suggestions: given that the vital task facing China was economic development, we should rely on economic not political methods to achieve it. Chen Yi nodded deeply. Secondly, I stressed the significance of industrial research. Ten leading professors and academics were organized to run the *Weekly Economic Journal*. Every weekend, we would write articles, discussing our views on issues related to the economy.

In those early days, policies were reasonable and the political atmosphere rather relaxed and tolerant. The government respected the private sector with little interference—at the People's Bank we even granted loans to private enterprises. Liu Shaoqi had a good policy called 'five types of economic coexistence', permitting state-owned and private companies, joint enterprises between the state and private sector, foreign-owned companies, and joint ventures.

At first, the government also interfered little in ordinary people's lives. People were still allowed to wear fancy clothes, but more and more began to wear the simple blue jacket and trousers. I was used to wearing Western-style suits, but soon found I was too embarrassed to wear one. So I too adopted the blue 'workers' suit', except at formal occasions. There were so many PLA soldiers in the streets, but they were so well-behaved and disciplined that the only jokes concerned their country bumpkin image. They took some very necessary measures against the city's social ills. One of the first was to wipe out the gangsters for which Shanghai was infamous. They closed all nightclubs with risqué sex shows or gambling, but most entertainment places stayed open. They also rounded up all the prostitutes, educated them, and arranged employment. Society was better controlled than in Nationalist times, and stricter control was not a bad thing, as long as the policies were right. Life instantly became safer and more orderly.

Like everyone else, I was impressed and welcomed such changes. I easily settled back in. Most returnees had expected a much poorer material life. I was not as comfortable as before, but my salary was high by Chinese standards. I occasionally missed Western food, but that was bearable. What I really missed was good newspapers, with all kinds of news and opinions. I wrote regular columns for the *Dagongbao* and *Wenhuibao*, published in Hong Kong, but I couldn't even read my own articles! On the other hand, it was probably just as well I couldn't buy them, or they might have been used as evidence against me in later campaigns (they were certainly politically incorrect!).

Gradually things began to change. From late 1952, the Soviet system was adopted in higher education. Then in 1953, as joint state–private ownership was introduced, Xinhua and all other private banks were merged into so-called state–private banks. The general manager was made the deputy head of the joint bank; the head, of course, was a Communist. At first, private owners' interests were not hurt. When the Communists took over, they confiscated the properties and shares they felt they had reason to take, like those belonging to the 'big four families', Jiang, Song, Kong, and Cheng, who had their fingers in almost everything. Those families' shares became state-owned, but others retained their stakes. As for management, the government sent someone to supervise, but businesses were still more or less run by their owners. Most of those concerned thought this quite acceptable.

The next stage, the 1955 Socialist Transformation campaign, was far more radical. Xinhua became totally state-owned, as the entire private sector was seized by the government and turned into state property. Private business people gained nothing and lost everything. Even their housing was taken away. One thing Communism hates is the economy. That's why all socialist countries are poor, without exception. Since Deng Xiaoping's reform, the situation has improved considerably, yet they continue with policies that make no economic sense. What's the point in keeping so many loss-making state-owned enterprises for so many years?

Anyway, it's no longer my concern. At the end of 1955 I was called to Beijing for a meeting on language reform. I had retained a strong interest in language and written articles on romanization. Afterwards, I was asked to stay on. It was a dramatic career change, and I might have been able to refuse, but by this stage I realized my financial knowledge and experience had little use in socialist China. Our newly formed committee was charged with standardizing the language (there are too many different dialects in China), simplifying the characters, and introducing a new spelling system, using the Latin alphabet. The last was the most important, without which we not only couldn't pronounce characters properly, but would be seriously disabled in modern communications.

Only a year after my move, the Anti-Rightist Campaign started. The head of Fudan's economic research institute committed suicide after falling victim, as did my favourite student, a bright, promising economist. If I had stayed in Shanghai, there was no chance I could have escaped attack, for I was famous for speaking out frankly. My friends half-joked that I ran away knowing trouble was coming. Both the journalists who befriended me in America suffered greatly. Yang Gang had been promoted to high office by Zhou Enlai, but she too killed herself after being attacked. Liu Zunqi spent twenty years in jail, before becoming chief editor of *China Daily*. All these vicious political campaigns not only shocked us returned scholars, but the millions worldwide who once had hope in communism. I myself only gave up communism during the Cultural Revolution. Inevitably, I was attacked like other intellectuals and sent into exile in Ningxia in China's north-west.

I've never regretted coming back, though the situation did not turn out exactly as I expected. Life is such a confusing business, determined by so many accidental factors. I've been lucky to work all these years on language, which has fascinated me since university. That I've achieved something is a great comfort. Of course, we would have been richer if we had stayed in America. In 1984, my wife and I visited some old colleagues who had become millionaire capitalist fat cats. It wouldn't have been difficult for me either. I was paid over US$500 a month in the forties. We travelled across the States by luxury Pullman car train, and to Europe on the Queen Elizabeth, first class. I've seen *Titanic* and honestly I think the Elizabeth was grander. In the evenings, we dressed formally for dinner, followed by dancing. My wife wore her finely tailored Chinese *qipao*, which always made her stand out.

But material life is not the only thing that matters. Today's young people are far more realistic and material-oriented than our generation. Pursuing an ideology like communism is not important to them; what's important is their practical, individual interests. Like Deng Xiaoping's grandchild, my own granddaughter has settled nicely with her family in Canada and has no intention of returning. She took the exact opposite path to mine, which is natural in today's China. Different times produce different people. I am an old man now, well into my nineties. Looking back on a long life, I really have no complaints. We have a saying in China: 'The fallen leaves return to the root.' I am where I belong and my heart is at ease.

Isabel Crook

Victory Days

C hairman Mao's head looms large over Tiananmen, as his troops march triumphantly underneath. A contemporary poster of the fall of Beijing, brought in by the Fourth Field Army, still adorns Isabel Crook's simple Beijing flat, fifty years after she arrived in the back of an army truck. The peaceful liberation of the capital in January 1949 sent positive signals nationwide, yet it posed the question of how a revolutionary force who had honed its fighting skills through decades of guerrilla combat would tackle the challenges of nationwide administration.

Undoubtedly there was irony in a Canadian missionary's daughter rejoicing in the hope of China's new, communist era. Isabel had returned from Toronto University in 1938 to pursue anthropological research near her birthplace, Chengdu, in south-western China, where she met Englishman David Crook. After marriage and wartime service in England, the Crooks returned to China in 1947 to study land reform in the Communist-controlled areas, an experience they documented in the 'Ten Mile Inn' trilogy. On reaching Beijing, they swapped the coarse cloth of the Eighth Route Army for Lenin suits and careers teaching English to New China's young diplomats. One student recalls the first phrase Isabel taught them: 'Workers of the World, Unite!'

The new dynasty enjoyed a promising start by reviving the economy and curbing hyperinflation. Of greater concern to Mao were the 'sugar-coated bullets' he saw the urban bourgeoisie aiming at his peasant cadres. The gradualist approach gave way to the mass campaigns, arrests, and executions that turned China into a nation of informers. True believers, the Crooks endured the first decade, leading classes to feed steel furnaces in the campus yard and plant trees on mountain slopes. As they completed their research in 1959–60, and prepared to leave for English universities, the Soviet Union withdrew its experts. The Crooks could not desert China in its hour of need. Nor did they leave after the Cultural Revolution, despite Isabel being branded a reactionary gang member and kept in isolation (or 'mass surveillance') for three years, when not forced to sweep the college yard, her husband imprisoned and their three sons labouring in factories to receive 're-education from the working class'.

Today, aged 84, Isabel remains busy as adviser to her university and active in Chinese women's issues, a lifelong passion. Loved by generations of students, many now in high office, the Crooks still adhere to the frugal spirit that first attracted them. They have been praised as 'living Bethunes', after the Canadian doctor and martyr Norman Bethune, immortalized by Mao in a famous essay: 'What kind of spirit is this that makes a foreigner selflessly adopt the cause of the Chinese people's liberation as his own? It is the spirit of internationalism, the spirit of communism, from which every Chinese Communist must learn.'

IN THE SUMMER OF 1948, we were invited to teach English at a small school near Shijiazhuang, in Hebei province. People refer to us as the founding members of the school that grew into Beijing Foreign Languages University. That's not exactly true, for English training classes were set up in the cave capital Yan'an. These were re-established, with just three dozen students, to prepare translators and diplomats for the coming victory. As soon as we arrived in the liberated areas the previous year, we knew the direction the war was taking. We weren't surprised at all. As an anthropologist, I had studied the terrible situation in rural Sichuan in the late thirties and could understand why the Communists, with land reform and other policies, enjoyed massive support in the north, where the situation was even worse.

At the very beginning of 1949, Beiping, as Beijing was then known, was about to fall, so the school was readied for the 160-mile march. I was pregnant and went by truck while David, all the teachers, and the students set out on foot. The Communists sought a peaceful take-over of the beautiful, historical city, but the negotiations with the Nationalist general Fu Zuoyi dragged on. We slept on the floor of a wrecked hotel in Tianjin. The city was badly damaged—that was why General Fu eventually surrendered the capital. He had thought Tianjin was unbreakable, but after his troops lost a twenty-seven-hour battle, he knew the Communists were going to win. Beiping was peacefully liberated on 31 January.

My truck drove directly to the headquarters near Qianmen. As I got off, I bumped into George Hatem, the American doctor. 'Come on, Isabel, we're all going to the victory parade!' It was early February 1949, and a day to remember. We climbed up onto the Qianmen gate. There were a lot of us up there, including Lin Biao, commander of the troops that liberated Beijing, but it didn't seem in the least strange that a few foreigners mingled among high-ranking military officials. We were all wearing the standard-issue military uniforms. When some resident foreigners in the Legation Quarter saw us, they stared in astonishment!

It was thrilling to be up there watching the parade. There was no Tiananmen Square then, and we could look both ways along the streets where people were dancing *yangkou* at the roadside, cheering and shouting, waving flags or home-made banners. Students from Beijing,

Qinghua, and other universities, workers like the women from Beijing's five textile factories all turned out, and they carried the day with their jubilation, parading proudly and happily. Soldiers showed off tanks and armoured cars captured from the Nationalists (and made in the USA). The Communists called Chiang Kaishek their 'quartermaster general' for supplying all these weapons. That was why the parade took six hours, to let everything pass through. Then came the Mongolian cavalry, the best sight of all, as each company had its own colour, so all the white horses cantered through, followed by all the brown. . .

At universities, factories, and similar places, people were looking forward to the take-over, as good underground work had been done by the Communists. But some people, like shopkeepers, remained nervous and apprehensive, from all the bad rumours spread by the Nationalists. On that day, however, you simply wouldn't know there were such people. They were either at home, or out there cheering like the rest because they felt they obliged to. Afterwards, a hundred of us went to the famous Quanjude restaurant, right next to Qianmen, for Peking duck. George told General Nie Rongzhen, a high-ranking military leader from Sichuan, that I was also born in Sichuan. He insisted on toasting me with white spirits. My missionary background meant I was a teetotaller, and I was pregnant with my first child, but how could I refuse General Nie, let alone on this special occasion? I drank the powerful liquor, and luckily no harm came to the baby.

When our school arrived, we were quartered in the barracks of the former Japanese embassy in the Legation Quarter. The students knew the building, which belonged to the Nationalist government, had been fully furnished so they were indignant to find it empty despite orders to return property intact. But we were instructed not to attempt to retrieve the furniture, or more rumours would spread that the Communists were confiscating private property. We made do as well as we could. I was given one of three remaining beds.

Only after we settled down did we learn how nervous some local people were. It was interesting to see how they came to feel secure. When we arrived, we remained under a supply system called military communism, whereby·you received food, shelter, and a little bit of money. We were not actually paid in money but in millet, or the equivalent of 70 *jin* of millet. The Communists stabilized the currency by moving from the gold standard to a 'commodity basket': they called for people to save money in state banks, with the value tied to the cost of a 'basket' of basic items—rice, oil, coal, flour, and cloth. When we first arrived, we paid 50,000 yuan for a piece of baked bread. After stabilizing the yuan, they just chopped off the six zeros and it became five cents! It was one of the earliest economic victories.

I was shocked that the whole police force was kept in place. I knew from the past how corrupt and even brutal they were, yet this clever policy stabilized the situation. It reassured people that not everything had changed. If local residents accused the police of violence or theft, the charges were dealt with one by one, and the policemen sentenced, or simply dismissed if the charge wasn't so serious. The same applied to the postal service, and all civil servants; the city employees got their pay and everything went on more or less as usual.

Another exciting event was of course the grand ceremony of the founding of the People's Republic of China on 1 October. Premier Zhou invited a small group of foreigners, including Russian experts, Western friends helping China, and teachers from our school, to sit at temporary wooden stands just beneath Tiananmen. There were so many people, though less than the great gatherings of the Cultural Revolution. As we watched the military and civilian parades, I made several trips back home to breast-feed my son Carl, who was only six weeks old. I hope no camera caught me sneaking backward and forward.

Luckily, I didn't miss the highlight: Chairman Mao's declaration from the top of Tiananmen. 'From now on, the Chinese people have stood up!' There was a great cheer from the crowds. Mao's words were unforgettable, partly because his voice was so unusual, his accent too. I have a vivid picture of Mao speaking, the cheering and excitement, though I'm not sure I gained it that very day or from all the documentary films I've watched. I could perfectly understand the joy and pride people felt. The Nationalists had gradually dissipated all the goodwill they enjoyed at certain periods. Corruption was so bad, while ordinary people's lives were miserable. At that moment, there was a real feeling that a whole new world had come about. The ceremony was a great event, a showcase for the Communists' managerial ability, but for me, the victory parade left a deeper impression. It was all so spontaneous and unrehearsed, yet so jubilant and spectacular.

I believe the Communists did brilliantly after they took power. The major problems they faced were poverty and unemployment. When we first arrived, the signs of poverty were obvious. People were poorly dressed, there were beggars and piles of rubbish everywhere that probably hadn't been moved for decades. It was decided that three jobs ought to be shared by five people, which immediately brought down unemployment. Yet having all these employees hanging around did foster inefficiency. It partly explains the casual, lax work attitude found in state-owned shops and factories to this day. But overall the policies in the early days were sensible and practical, and the pace was right, unlike later on. By the mid-fifties, Beijing and China began to prosper.

On the other hand, there was a highly vigilant side to early policy: China entered the Korean War, attacked Taiwan, and suspected secret

Isabel Crook and her family

agents were everywhere. There were various political campaigns every few years. Some of them made sense if undertaken correctly. Living in China, we inevitably took part. The slogan of the 1952 Three Antis Campaign [against graft, waste, and bureaucracy] ran, 'The leaders go into the water first'. As David was acting head of the English department, he had to criticize himself, then be criticized by our colleagues and students. Finally, his self-criticism was accepted and they went on to the next chap.

There was an ongoing struggle in English education between 'regularization' and 'guerrilla tactics'. The former stressed a regular timetable, language excellence, and a broad cultural basis achieved through the study of Shakespeare or even Chaucer. We belonged to the latter school: to become socialist diplomatic personnel, our students must take part in society when important events like political movements or harvests require time off from study. All my students joined propaganda teams to perform skits and songs to educate peasants in Beijing's outskirts about land reform. When a Soviet friend complained of the way these movements disrupted teaching, we argued, 'They keep us on the right track!'

In 1955 there was a further crackdown on counter-revolutionaries. At our school, everyone had to detail their personal history and faced pressure not only to report on themselves, but on others too. Some teachers were former Nationalist officers, but how to know who was innocent and who were secret agents sent to overthrow the Communists? Old Mr Zhang, a charming, scholarly gentleman and very dedicated to teaching, had served in the Nationalist army when a notorious massacre happened. It was difficult to determine his involvement, but after the movement he withdrew, as he no longer felt trusted.

That same year, my parents returned to China for the first time since leaving in 1942. But for seeing their grandchildren they wouldn't have come, since my father hated the Communists. We showed them around, but my father was not impressed, convinced everything was carefully prearranged. One Saturday night, he suddenly announced, 'I want to go to a church tomorrow.' He knew we couldn't possibly arrange anything beforehand. Both of us had long forgotten about religious matters, but David remembered vaguely there was a church in Wangfujing, a shopping district near Tiananmen. When they found it, the doorman explained morning mass was over, but the next service would begin at 11am. Despite being a devout Protestant, my father was pleased to see a Catholic church still functioning.

The doorman told them where to find a Protestant church. In those days, people went round by rickshaws, not taxis. The rickshaw driver asked where my father was from. As a missionary for thirty years, fluent in Chinese with a Sichuan accent, he replied, 'My miserable country is Canada.' 'Oh, that's where Norman Bethune was from!' cried the driver. David described the Canadian doctor who came to help the Communists. After the service, my father asked the congregation, 'Have you heard of Norman Bethune?' Of course, everybody replied, as Bethune features in all school textbooks. My father's view of the Communists changed. He was overwhelmed by the immense

improvements the new government had brought. As a missionary in China, he said he was determined to achieve progress on six fronts: eliminate illiteracy, begging, prostitution, gambling, opium, and alcohol abuse. In the short spell of six years, the Chinese Communists had achieved what he and other missionaries failed to do in thirty. Before he left, he told me, 'If only the Communists believed in God, the world would be perfect!'

Zhang Da

Resist America, Aid Korea!

On 25 June 1950, North Korean leader Kim Il Sung dispatched a massive force over the Thirty-eighth Parallel and into South Korea. The Korean War had begun, a conflict whose impact spread far beyond the peninsula and the three years of engagement. If the Soviet Union had precipitated the invasion, which the United States felt duly obliged to repulse, it was the young PRC which bore the greatest suffering, losing up to one million men in its first major test of sovereignty and ideology. Chairman Mao, whose son Anying died in an American air raid, was convinced of the need to 'lean to one side'. For the United States, China's stalwart defence of the North confirmed the need for containment, and active involvement wherever communism threatened to infiltrate.

Swept up in the globalization of this civil war was 17-year-old Zhang Da, son of a warlord army officer from Meishan, Sichuan. The spirit of revolution saw Zhang denounce his 'counter-revolutionary' family and set off for a battlefield far from his father's local skirmishes. Premier Zhou Enlai had warned of Chinese intervention if UN forces entered North Korea. When they crossed the border in October 1950, aimed straight for the Yalu River and China's industrial heartland, Marshal Peng Dehuai led the 'Chinese People Volunteers' in three brilliant campaigns that pushed the enemy beyond the Thirty-eighth Parallel. Tales of Chinese valour inspired a heady patriotism at home: the former Sick Man of Asia, source of countless coolies for US railways and gold-mines, was standing up to Yankee aggression.

During the fourth and fifth campaigns in early 1951, logistical weaknesses and lack of air cover exposed the Chinese to the full brunt of American firepower. Zhang was captured and held as a prisoner of war for two years until the armistice long delayed by Chinese demands on repatriation. Spurning exile in Taiwan, Zhang returned home to a changed China. New Democracy had given way to mass campaigns and witch-hunts. Like most of his fellow patriots, Zhang was cast as a traitor, expelled from the army and the Communist Youth League. He fell victim to every subsequent political movement, forced to confess the details of his capture and 'betrayal'. Petty jobs were all he was permitted—for over a decade he repaired roads on the harsh Tibetan plateau in western Sichuan. Rehabilitation came only in 1984. Zhang saved enough money to start the successful Sichuan restaurant he currently runs in Beijing. Of his two children, one now studies in Europe.

Official regret at the appalling loss of Chinese lives in the Korean War is offset by success in preventing the establishment of a unified, pro-American neighbour. While international isolation hurt the PRC, the war was exploited domestically to consolidate the new regime. Military disasters highlighted the need to modernize the PLA, today the world's largest land army. US naval protection of Taiwan lent the Nationalists time to lay the foundation for today's democratic republic. As for the catalyst, almost fifty years later no peace agreement has been signed. Starving, heavily armed North Korea continues to threaten East Asian stability.

I WAS ONLY 17 when I went to Korea. It all happened so quickly. Only the year before, I was still a student, dancing in the streets of Chengdu to welcome the liberating army. I was so drawn by the revolution, I gave up normal schooling to join the South-west People's Revolutionary University. This military institute led by Marshal He Long offered short-term training to revolutionary cadres. I joined the Communist Youth League there and after half a year was sent to work for the county government in my hometown, Meishan. Our main task was to clear out the residual warlords and bandits and prepare for land reform.

The nationwide campaign, 'Resist America, Aid Korea', had begun. I remember long reports in the newspapers, attacking the South for invading the North and the Americans for using North Korea as a stepping-stone to invade China. The United States even sent a fleet to the Taiwan Strait in an open challenge to our territory. Today, with so much information coming to light, I know who invaded whom. But back then, I was so angry with America and badly wanted to join the army to fight for justice. When a high-ranking officer from Meishan was called up, he took me and another enthusiastic young man with him.

In October 1950, I joined the 539th Regiment of the 180th Division of the Sixtieth Army, then based in the outskirts of Chengdu. After only over a month's military training, our regiment was moved up north. We understood fighting had intensified. We were briefly stationed at Changzhou in Hebei, where we were given mobilization talks. And we were asked to write a statement saying we voluntarily went to war. In fact, few of us needed any persuasion. We were all more than willing to go and wrote many times asking to be sent. Some even wrote in their own blood to show their determination!

At the very beginning of 1951, we reached Dandong, on the Korean border. Our weapons were changed for better models made in the Soviet Union. The atmosphere of war at the border was already very strong. Whether or not America really intended to invade China, I saw with my own eyes US aeroplanes that flew over to the Chinese side and dropped bombs. As we crossed the bridge over the border, we too were bombed. We were mostly virgin soldiers with the barest training and no war experience. We also knew that the Americans were better equipped. But we had no fear of them. Chairman Mao called the American imperialists 'paper tigers', so that's what we thought of them. And there were just so many of us, maybe 200,000 to 300,000, sent there as the second batch of volunteers.

I had the nerve-racking experience of combat for the first time when we were caught in the middle of the fourth campaign, which took place in the North, near the Thirty-eighth Parallel. I know now that all new soldiers are frightened of the loud crash of artillery fire, while veteran soldiers fear gunshots. Luckily, we were not at the front line and didn't engage the enemy at close range. That didn't mean we were spared any danger, though. The Americans had great aerial advantage over us and bombed us so heavily it made little difference where you were. They also used advanced artillery that could fire shells miles away. By this time, we understood what good equipment meant. Still, our regiment survived our first battle with limited casualties. We didn't enjoy such good luck in the fifth campaign.

In terms of equipment, we were luckier than the first batch of soldiers hurriedly called up and sent to the battlefield, where some suffered severe frostbite to their hands and feet. At least we received new uniforms, and soon after our arrival the weather grew warm. As you can imagine, the food was poor: our main staple was baked dry flour with rice, sorghum, or ship biscuits. Canned food was an occasional treat. Once, I was walking a few metres behind a staff officer, when he saw a small box on the ground like a tin of shoe polish. We were instructed not to pick things up, but he had previously picked up some delicious canned food left by the Amercians, so he kicked it for a better look. In the loud explosion his right leg was blown away! I was badly traumatized by that moment.

After the fourth battle, we took a welcome rest. One of my legs was so swollen I could barely walk. Memory is a funny business. Small things still stick in the mind. One full moon, the officer from our county came to my foxhole for a chat. He had become head of the regiment. 'Little fellow'—I was both young and short—'what do you want to do after we win the war and go back to China?' I wanted to further my studies. He seemed pleased with the answer. 'It's good you have a plan. I have mine too.' I never got to fulfil my dream when eventually I returned to China. Nor did he, whatever it was. I learned from one of his assistants that he met a horrible death in the fifth battle. They never found his body.

The fourth campaign gave us the upper hand—the battleground moved further south—and the first half of the fifth, begun in late April 1951, also went in our favour. I remember we confiscated many trucks and asked the American prisoners to drive. But they firmly refused, even after death threats, as they knew driving such obvious targets was inviting trouble. The latter half of the battle was hard and bitter. Around 19 May, when the fifth was declared over, our 180th Division was holed up at a hilly place around Chun Chon in the South. Our food and ammunition had run out. We were told that morning we would be pulled back. In the afternoon, we were instructed to stay on for three to five days while the flanking divisions 179 and 181 withdrew. As a mere trooper, I didn't understand the manoeuvres but guessed reinforcements couldn't be sent in time, or had difficulty getting there. We experienced terrible hardship and casualties during those few days.

Pretty soon, the leaders decided to let two other regiments go first. Our 539th Regiment, hardly a full regiment by this time, was left behind on its own to maintain a fighting force. We hadn't eaten properly for weeks; many of us suffered various degrees of malnutrition. All we could eat were wild weeds and grass, like horses. In fact, there were quite a few horses and some soldiers suggested killing them for meat. However, the leaders opposed the idea, as these were 'revolutionary horses' that had made great contributions. I contracted night-blindness and couldn't see a thing after dusk. We had lost more than half of our original 4,000 soldiers and were surrounded by well-equipped Americans and South Koreans.

Now, I fully understand the old saying, 'the rout of an army is as fast as a landslide'. Our soldiers were killed with such speed, or chased by the enemy out of their positions. They sent planes to circle over our heads, persuading us to surrender. The regiment leaders decided we should each try to break out of the encirclement and march towards the north-west, from where reinforcements were expected. That decision was later considered a mistake, for if we had stuck together more of us might have escaped. Secondly, it was too difficult to determine the north-west, as none of us had a compass. I started off with other soldiers, but at night we ran into some Americans. We scattered in different directions and lost touch with each other.

I was completely on my own for seven days before my capture. I carried one hand grenade I had picked up somewhere (for myself in case I was caught), but my bullets had long before run out so there was no point keeping my gun. I was lucky to stumble upon a small bag of raw rice. Soaked rotten in the rain, it was black and smelly but it saved my life. Whenever I was hungry, I would chew a handful, washed down with stream water. I thought I was quite clever to figure out which direction to take—the same as the enemy's artillery fire. I was convinced our troops were behind a high hill ahead of me. At dusk, I began to climb but was spotted and dense cannon shots were fired. Luckily, only the calf of my right leg was hit. I crawled into the woods and pulled out the shell fragment with my hands. I tore a piece of my trousers to bind the wound.

I don't understand why I wasn't in any kind of panic. I just kept going. Yet there was no sign of our army from the top. I hid during the day and moved only at night. Once, I bumped into a foxhole, but with my bad eyesight it took a while to realize some large American soldiers were sleeping there! Startled, I ran for my life, but the noise disturbed them and they fired. I ran as fast as possible, totally forgetting my injured leg. How narrowly I escaped death! After that hair-raising experience, I had another skirmish with death when I fell from a rock cliff. I lost consciousness for a long time. I don't know where I got the strength and energy to do what I did then. Some might call it bravery, but it was really survival instinct.

I was determined to keep on marching until one day I saw a run-down cottage deep in the mountains. I observed it for a long time from my hiding place and could only see a middle-aged Korean woman, looking calm and harmless. I was sure she wouldn't refuse me if I asked for help. We volunteer soldiers came from China to Korea to liberate these poor people from the hands of the American imperialists.

Near lunch-time, I gathered up my nerve and went up to her as she busied in the kitchen. We had been taught some basic Korean, so I explained that I was an injured Chinese soldier who had not eaten cooked food for a long time. Could she kindly cook my rice while I rested? She seemed to have understood and left with the rice, I assumed to get more fuel. After maybe five to ten minutes, as I was blowing the fire, I heard a harsh voice: 'Put up your hands!' One American and two Korean soldiers were aiming their guns straight at me!

I froze. They swiftly entered and grabbed me. I was totally unarmed. Even my grenade was long lost in the woods. The moment I was captured, my whole world collapsed. I thought I might die heroically on the battlefield, or return to my homeland in triumph. I had never contemplated a third possibility. I couldn't understand why the Korean woman would betray me—a Chinese volunteer who was running the risk of my life? Until that point, I functioned more or less as normal, running around in the mountains. But now I lost the strength even to walk on my own. They had to carry me out. I guess that was not a heroic scene.

Soon, I was transferred from a field hospital to a prisoner-of-war camp in Pusan, where I had the sad comfort of meeting numerous people from the same division. I later heard that about one-third of the 180th Division was captured, another third survived, and the rest were dead.

I am sure casualties in our regiment were the heaviest of all. After Pusan, we were moved to Koje Island. It took negotiators a long time to settle the repatriation of over 20,000 Chinese POWs. The Americans insisted only those willing to return would be sent back, but China demanded them all. In the end, 14,000 went to Taiwan and 6,000 of us returned to mainland China. Another couple of thousand died from illness or torture. I had a harder time in the camp than on the battlefield. For example, in order to celebrate the third anniversary of the founding of the People's Republic of China in October 1952, we raised the red flag. But our little uprising was brutally put down by the Americans and around one hundred of us were killed.

Why did so many soldiers not want to come back to China? I don't think all of them were traitors, though most worried they would be regarded as such, particularly after being warned or threatened by the Nationalists or real traitors. Yes, some did turn tables to oppose the Communists. When I made it clear that I didn't want to go to Taiwan, several traitors forced a tattoo on my left arm: 'Oppose Communism, Fight the Soviet Union'. I had to scrape it off with a razor. These people were often used to persuade prisoners not to return home. The Americans didn't ask so openly but would come and preach to us with Christianity or humanitarian theories. Honestly, there were lots of things going on in the prison, a very complicated time and place.

For people like me who clearly stated our intention to come home, they even offered us passage to a third country. One American told me: 'I know you prefer the Communists to the Guomindang. That's okay. But you can go to Brazil or Singapore, where you'll be treated nicely and have the freedom to do whatever you want.' It all sounded very attractive. But I was determined to return. Once when I was talking about my experience with some university students in China, one asked, 'Are you a Party member?' I am afraid I am not. I desperately wanted to be one, even in my dreams, but I never applied back then, because I thought I wasn't qualified. I chose to come back basically because I was patriotic.

Looking back at the Korean War, I still don't understand why the top leaders decided to participate. It's a question far beyond a little character like me. But I do have some different views now. The war has always been regarded as a victory in China. Yet today, I tend to agree with one

American general's view: 'You did not win and we did not lose.' More importantly, it was not worthwhile. We lost so many lives—the official figure was 30,000, but I know the real figure is far greater. And the war planted such deep hatred between the ordinary people of China and the United States, creating a negative impact which is not over even today.

When the peace agreement was signed, I was being held at a camp on Cheju Island. Thirteen of us hard-core prisoners were put together in a tent encircled by metal nets. The American responsible for us was a friendly sergeant who never tried to impose his ideology. In the early morning of 27 July 1953, he came to our tent and shouted excitedly, 'Zhang, quickly!' I rushed out and saw him violently shaking the metal nets. 'The armistice was signed today! You'll all be going home soon!' He had a big smile on his face and was genuinely happy for us. I was moved to tears. He was supposedly our enemy, but how could I hate such a man?

I plan to join an organized tour to South Korea in the near future, to take a look at the place where I fought nearly half a century ago. Sadly, I don't think the North Koreans have learned their lessons properly. They still seem to be aggressive. China has done so much better than North Korea. Recently, when the film *Saving Private Ryan* came to China, I watched it with great emotion, as it reminded me of my own war experience. The true face of war is ugly and cruel. As a veteran of war, I just want to say, 'No more war, please.'

Sheng Chong

Speak Bitterness

'A revolution is not a dinner party,' wrote Mao in 1927. 'A revolution is an insurrection, an act of violence whereby one class overthrows another.' He was reporting on the peasant uprisings against rural gentry that entrenched his unorthodox belief in a non-proletarian Marxist revolution. Twenty years later, land reform remained a central platform of party popularity in the areas of North China under Communist control. Policy swung from radical to moderate during the years of conquest, and even after Liberation rich peasants were initially condoned, particularly in southern China, where the party enjoyed little penetration with either propaganda or peasant associations. Much of Guangdong province had barely changed when Sheng Chong was dispatched in early 1951 to rouse villagers into grabbing the fruits of revolution for themselves.

The eighth of nine children, born into a Beijing teacher's family in the year of Mao's report, Sheng grew up in Malaysia opposing the Japanese. She joined the Malay Communist Party at 18, and in 1949 was arrested in Singapore for seeking its independence from colonial rule. Her refusal to confess saw her expelled in June 1950 and escorted back to China. As her ship sank off the coast of the Mainland, she was fortunate to be rescued by the PLA, who offered an excellent first impression of New China: 'We are the People's Liberation Army led by Chairman Mao and the Communist Party. We do not take even a needle from the people.' After a crash course in revolutionary basics, she joined 62,000 Party cadres and PLA soldiers sent to mobilize the peasants of Guangdong.

Mao had left little doubt of the need for terror—'proper limits have to be exceeded to right a wrong'—and the assault on China's landlords offered conclusive proof. As the Korean War signalled an end to moderation, a concurrent campaign against counter-revolutionaries sealed the landlords' fate. Across China, work teams like Sheng's determined the class background of every villager before organizing public 'speak bitterness' meetings against the landed classes. Executions were followed by land and property distribution. By autumn 1952, land reform had been completed in areas occupied by over 90 per cent of the rural population, though the results were not overwhelmingly egalitarian. The position of the poorest undoubtedly improved, and landlords (or their survivors) suffered dramatic reductions in income, but 'middle' and 'rich' peasants continued to enjoy a standard of living far above average.

Mao correctly reasoned that the poor would be the most revolutionary force in land reform. The violence with which they redressed their many grievances achieved the campaign's political purpose: elimination of all potential enemies of Communist rule. While advances in productivity were debatable, the emergence of a new élite in the countryside—poor peasant activists, intensely political and ambitious—paved the way for rapid and remarkably peaceful collectivization in the mid-1950s.

After land reform, Sheng was transferred to a county cultural hall, becoming its deputy director before she moved to the provincial capital in 1960 to teach at the Guangzhou Finance and Politics College. During the Cultural Revolution, she grew tea at a May Seventh cadre school in Conghua, until a heart problem obliged a return to the city. She now enjoys a comfortable retirement with her extended family in Guangzhou.

I DIDN'T KNOW WHAT TO EXPECT when I was deported to China in mid-1950, let alone that I would be involved in a dynamic movement like land reform. Back in Beijing, the central government's united front sent me on a course with one hundred other patriotic Chinese from South-east Asia. For six months we studied Marxist theory, Party history, and China's current situation. We were then organized into a 'youth land-reform work group' and in March 1951 sent down to Guangdong province. My understanding was the government meant to train us as future cadres, so it would be good for us to gain some firsthand experience. Most were returned students from well-off backgrounds who knew nothing about the countryside. Nor did I, though in my favour I was an expelled political prisoner and my family was poor.

As soon as we arrived, we were sent to Huizhou for a week's training, where the land-reform policy and its significance were explained. I listened very attentively, terribly keen to perform the important task I was given. I was assigned to Boluo, an impoverished county 130 kilometres east of Guangzhou. There I became a member of the county land-reform work team, made up mainly of PLA soldiers, local government cadres, and university teachers. After being briefed about the local situation, five of us walked to Tunli village in Botang township. It was a small village with under forty families and 160 people. They harvested rice from their paddy fields twice a year and also grew wheat.

We worked like this: first, we selected a *genzi* (root) family, with whom we lived, ate, and tilled the land. We worked on these *genzi* first, asking them about the evil behaviour of the landlords, teaching them about the benefits of land reform, and inspiring them to struggle against the landlord class. After the *genzi* were roused, they would mobilize fellow villagers. As we were outsiders, reform would simply not work if we had tried to approach the ordinary peasants directly. Moreover, unlike the liberated areas in the north, there were no peasant unions with whom to cooperate. The township government was already Communist, but village-level rule was the same as during the Nationalists' time, for Boluo was only liberated in October 1949. The Botang township head suggested a few genzi, though he did not know the detailed situation in the village. On his recommendation, I stayed with a man called Zhou Youdi. Although Zhou was a strong supporter of the Communists, his family was not very poor. I politely asked if he could suggest a poorer family.

I'll never forget the moment I entered the home of A Lan, a poor widow. It was a simple brick house of about 20 square metres, with a mud floor and no windows. It was so dark I could hardly see anything. The powerful smell of the fermented urine the family kept for fertilizer went straight to my head. I couldn't breathe. I put down my luggage and ran outside for a long breath of fresh air. Then I began to criticize my petty bourgeois sentiments and lack of compassion to the poor peasants. I forced myself back in. Having lost her husband a few years before, A Lan lived with her mother-in-law and two sons aged 8 and 6. The lack of able-bodied men meant their family life was desperately poor. Though only in her thirties, she already looked old. She was a kind and gentle woman but in the beginning really did not know what to do with me. She daren't ask me to leave for fear of offending the Communist workers, but she was hardly inclined to be friendly either. Like all the villagers, she was afraid of us. The head of our little group was a soldier who carried a gun that he soon lent to me as the only young female in the group. The Nationalists had spread all kinds of rumours that the Communists would share peasants' property and even their wives. There was talk in some places that the Nationalists returned and killed anyone who helped the Communists.

I didn't pay A Lan for my food and lodging but gave them my 30-*jin* rice allocation from the land-reform team. The family almost totally relied on my rice: spring was the worst time of the year, as the old grain stock had long gone and the crops were not ripe. The family normally just ate wild vegetables and left-over yams from other people's fields. My first meal with her family was one of the most awkward moments in my life. We drank some very thin porridge. The only dish on the table was a few chunks of pickled radish, rotten with mould. As soon as I popped one in my mouth, the taste and smell brought tears to my eyes. I felt I was eating a human stool. I couldn't swallow, but if I spat it out, that would indicate my lack of sympathy towards the poor peasants. If discovered, it would leave a black mark on my record. I forced it down and nearly vomited.

The first week with A Lan wasn't easy. My own family was fairly poor, but we always had enough to eat and decent sanitation. I was shocked by the primitive conditions here. The large metal wok fixed to the stove was used for cooking, making pigfeed, and washing ourselves! But I was determined to put up with it all. I helped A Lan collect grass and wood in the hills to sell at market. That was how she kept her family going. Only during harvest time could she find temporary work in the fields. I didn't mind the hard work so much as the constant hunger, for I felt obliged to give more food to the grandmother and two children. Every week, we went to the Boluo county town for a meeting and work report. It was the only time I could fill up with rice and even meat dishes!

Gradually, I won A Lan's trust. She began to tell me which family was poor and who had suffered at the hands of the landlords. Encouraged by me, she went out to mobilize other poor villagers and helped to form the core land-reform team. I cried when she told me the miserable story of A Juan, a servant of the local landlord. When his wife, the daughter of another landlord, proved barren, the landlord took pretty A Juan as his concubine. She gave birth to three sons, but was then locked in a small dark room by his hard-hearted wife, who was worried her husband would ignore her. Sometimes A Juan was fed leftovers. When they gave her no food, she scavenged food from the dog's bowl. Worse still, the wife raised the children as her own and taught them to spit on A Juan, their real mother. She looked like a skeleton when A Lan took me to see her. She was a typical victim of the exploiting class. We set her free and later gave her a plot of land. We wanted her to 'speak bitterness' at the struggle meeting against the landlord's wife. But not having spoken for twenty years, the poor woman could hardly talk. Zhou Youdi spoke for her. The landlord only escaped public humiliation because he had died a few years back. From all accounts, he was an evil man who brutally exploited the poor peasants and labourers.

People were divided into five categories: landlords, rich peasants, middle peasants, poor peasants, and [landless] labourers. The policy was to rely on the labourers and poor peasants, unite with the middle peasants, suppress the rich peasants, and overthrow the landlords. Tunli was so impoverished that up to 70 per cent of families were poor peasants and labourers. There were half a dozen middle peasants, a couple of rich peasants, and two landlords. The rich peasants were not struggled

Sheng Chong (right) with colleagues in 1953

against, but any land exceeding the average amount was confiscated, while middle peasants were very much left alone.

There was no strict policy on how many *mu* of land made you a landlord. In Guangdong, where arable land was so precious, you could hardly find a landlord with a few hundred *mu*, yet that was common for northern landlords. Down south, once a landlord accumulated any wealth, he would invest it in a shop in the city and leave the land to be managed by relatives. The family of Tunli's main landlord owned over 60 *mu* of land, the largest plot in the village. Another smaller landlord had under 40 *mu*. He had grown rich quite recently and had not committed as many crimes as the other landlord. We still struggled against him.

Before each struggle session, we would find *kuzhu* (victims) who had suffered at the hands of the accused, to ensure that someone would get up and 'speak bitterness'. Moreover, we needed to inspire their hatred and coach them in what to say. Almost all the peasants were illiterate, and so accustomed to the system of exploitation they just accepted it as the way life was. For example, a poor peasant would rent a few *mu* from a landlord to grow rice. The harvest was usually divided between the landlord and the peasant at a ratio of 7:3, or 6:4 if the land was less fertile. The peasant often borrowed grain from the landlord early in the year, which he had to return four- or five-fold after the harvest. The whole family worked so hard on the land, but at the end of the year most of the rice ended up with the landlord, who had done absolutely nothing. We would teach the poor peasants, 'Look, this is unfair, you are being exploited by the landlord.'

Struggle sessions were held at an open space in the village. A simple stage was set up where we would sit. The landlord would stand before us with his head bowed. His victims would ascend the stage one after another to accuse him of evil deeds. Before leaving the stage, the victims often shouted, 'Down with the landlord!' The audience echoed, 'Down with the landlord!' Sometimes ordinary peasants, without prior arrangement, became so excited they jumped on-stage to reveal their own bitterness. The landlord being struggled against had to nod and reply 'yes' when asked, 'Is it true?' Sometimes he was beaten if he tried to deny anything, yet the policy was to treat landlords in a civilized fashion. Personally, I tried to observe the policy. Land-reform workers who suffered under landlords back home might interpret the policy differently. I heard of landlords being beaten or stoned to death by angry peasants. There were actually guiding principles as to when to kill a landlord, and approval from county leaders was needed. Three landlords from the neighbouring township were put to death.

Though we didn't execute any landlords, the Tunli village head was killed. After all, ours was a keypoint village—carefully chosen as an example to others in the region. Several struggle sessions had been held against him. On the day of his execution, a final session was held. Several hundred people turned up from nearby villages. He stood on the stage with his hands tied behind him and his name stuck to his back. Firstly, his crimes were announced one after another. He admitted some and denied others. Whenever he denied a crime, a witness went on-stage to confront him with the facts. He was accused of 'wallowing in the mire' with the landlords and the Nationalist government; he always took a cut of the grain tax for himself, and beat those who failed to pay, some of them to death; he practised usury—if he lent you 1 yuan, the debt became 2 yuan if you didn't pay within six months, and 4 yuan within a year; and he never showed any mercy, even when desperate peasants were forced to sell their children. 'How could a human being be so terrible?' I thought. He was indeed 'rapacious as a wolf and savage as a cur'.

After the village head eventually confessed to all his crimes, he was ordered to kneel down. Two men from the people's militia stepped up and shot him. It was the first and only time I witnessed an execution, but I wasn't afraid, as my heart was filled with hatred. I took out the gun I had been lent and shot him in the back as he sprawled against the ground. White papers flew out of his breast pocket as the bullet exploded through his chest. I'm sure he was already dead, but I was so outraged I just had to do it. There were cheers from the crowd, who pressed against the stage for a better look. Some spat on the corpse.

After the struggle sessions, a new village head was chosen, and a peasant alliance loyal to the Communists was formed. All land and property owned by the landlords were redistributed. We worked tirelessly in those days, measuring the land and calculating how to give each person an equal amount of land, taking into consideration good and bad plots, and distance from the village. Ultimately, everyone received

about one *mu*. The landlord families were given a fair share too, while their houses were given to those without, like their hired labourers, or peasants living in hovels. The landlord families were allocated small houses with basic cooking utensils like a pot and a few bowls.

As for other items like furniture and clothes belonging to landlord families, we called them *fucai* (floating property), and again divided them among the villagers, including middle peasants. Floating property was divided into different grades according to its value, just as people had grades according to their class status. The poorest people enjoyed the first-grade *fucai*, picked by drawing lots. You can imagine all the work involved, but we felt it was meaningful and rewarding. When the peasants received certificates for their plots of land, some burst into tears. 'Thank the work team! Thank the Communist Party! Thank Chairman Mao!' Many had not owned land for generations. Women were also given equal rights in owning land, which was something quite new to them. Some women cried even when handed an old jacket or bamboo chair. They just couldn't believe their luck.

Problems frequently occurred where landlords had transferred or hidden property before land reform began. We had a little drama with the number-two landlord in Tunli, as we couldn't find any jewellery or valuable items in his house. So we struggled against him. He couldn't get away, as fellow villagers had often seen his family wearing jewellery. He admitted he had buried his treasure next to so-and-so's grave over such-and-such a hill. We went to the spot but found nothing. Returning in anger, we struggled against him more intensely and ordered him to kneel down. We threw a spade at him and ordered him to dig, or the struggle against him would continue. Finally, he dug up the jewellery and gold ingots he had buried in his own backyard. We exchanged them for cash at the bank and handed it over to the local government.

When we left Tunli a few months later, the villagers walked along with us for miles before tearfully waving goodbye, pressing eggs and bread into our hands. We moved on to another village in the region. We were more experienced now, and our work went very smoothly. I worked over a year on land reform, but my experience at Tunli left the deepest impression.

In the past fifty years, there have been so many movements and campaigns, some of them unnecessary or even wrong. But land reform was a correct, wise, and crucial strategy. Firstly, it effectively finished the feudal system in rural China and greatly liberated the productive forces. By owning their land, farmers had incentive to work hard. The following year, production in the areas that had undergone land reform increased considerably. Secondly, a grass-roots government which supported and loved the Communist Party was established. The ordinary peasants were so grateful for the Party and Chairman Mao, who gave them the land. This is one of the reasons why so many old peasants still love Mao.

On a personal level, my land-reform experience taught me what real China was like and convinced me of the greatness and correctness of the Chinese Communist Party. Afterwards, when I was assigned to the library of the county cultural hall, I remained eager in my work and desperate to join the Party. Sadly, the Party turned to the left. People like me who had returned from abroad were trusted no longer. Only one of the returnees with whom I studied achieved a senior rank. All the rest were commoners like me, and most have now left China again thanks to their foreign connections. I had even less chance of joining the Party, since my imprisonment in Singapore was described as 'unclear' on my file. In the mid-sixties I eventually gave up trying, to stop hurting myself. Only when I neared retirement did the Party finally ask if I was still interested. 'No!' What was the point? I wanted to join the Party to make a contribution. What kind of contribution can an old bag like me make?

I was delighted when Deng Xiaoping's rural reforms gave the land back to the peasants. Having worked with them, I knew that owning a plot of land was the only dream a farmer had. It worries me when I read reports about the heavy taxes on peasants and other problems. I can only hope the government will resolve them. As I learned from land reform, the peasants deserve to be treated well. They are vital for the country's stability.

Zhang Tong

The Blank Page

With the saying, 'Socialism is paradise but you can't get there without literacy', the Communist Party promised to break down the barriers that trapped the peasant masses. For centuries, education in China had signified memorizing the Confucian classics and mastering a writing system little changed since 200 BC, in the hope of passing civil service examinations and entering imperial employ. Amid belated moves towards a modern curriculum, the examinations were abolished in 1905, yet it would take the vernacular movement that began in 1919 to break the stranglehold of the literary élite. Educational establishments proliferated nationwide— Mao's first proper job was as headmaster of a primary school—but beyond the cities and the county towns, village boys still learned the basic Confucian values, and at most a few hundred Chinese characters, while their sisters were almost entirely ignored.

After Liberation, the party faced a daunting task: some 80 per cent of China's people were effectively illiterate, 90 per cent of them in rural areas. By adapting the methods of the Communist base areas in the 1930s and 1940s, a 'winter-study campaign' during the slack season in 1949 taught characters to over 12 million peasants, and increased that number to 25 million the following year. From December 1950, these winter schools were expanded into year-round, spare-time study schools, run by ordinary people such as Zhang Tong, who abandoned his apprenticeship as a carpenter to teach fellow villagers. Zhang was born in 1928 in Daolingjiang village, in the shadow of the thirteen tombs of the Ming emperors 50 kilometres north-west of Beijing. Like many a hot-blooded youth, he was stirred by hopes of revolution and in 1946 had become a guerrilla with the Communists' Eighth Route Army fighting the Nationalists on the Hebei plain.

In October 1955, Mao first likened China to a blank page on which fine words could be written. Over the next two years, as he developed his thesis that peasant poverty and illiteracy guaranteed their appetite for revolution, China boasted of eliminating illiteracy by the early 1960s. The problem would prove rather more intractable. The goal of a school in every village was dropped, and distractions such as the Cultural Revolution caused literacy growth to slide. Zhang's limited education and considerable initiative were put to use as a production-team head in the Ming Tombs People's Commune, the height of egalitarianism in the heart of an imperial cemetery.

The 1982 census revealed almost 30 per cent of Chinese remained illiterate or semi-literate (defined as knowing under 1,000 characters). Efforts since have reduced illiteracy to under 6 per cent of China's young and middle-aged people, with hopes of full literacy in this category by the year 2000. As registration in primary schools approaches 99 per cent, the government's stated goal is to extend nationwide by 2010 the nine-year compulsory programme: six in primary, three in middle. Critics charge that education spending of 2.5 per cent of gross domestic product (GDP) is not only below the government's own target of 4 per cent, but below that of many poor nations. Urban schoolchildren may surf the Internet, but basic conditions still prevail in rural areas, where there are high drop-out rates among girls.

Zhang remains in the village, a respected wise man and proponent of the importance of education. It has served his family well—four of five children completed senior middle school, while two daughters even achieved university degrees (one is an official at Beijing airport). His sons are only part-time farmers, at weekends and harvest time, as they supplement their income working at the county town, Changping, as doctor and mechanic.

IT WAS LIKE A FESTIVAL when the night school first opened. Drums and gongs were played and almost all the villagers, men and women, the young and the old, came out to take a look and join in the fun. Children shouted excitedly and dogs ran around. It was late 1950 and New Year was approaching, so there little to do in the fields. Everyone in the village had heard that the night school would offer free education and was curious what it would be like.

Our village had been liberated at the end of 1948. In the autumn of the following year, when the land-reform work team first arrived, meetings were held about the winter-study campaign to 'wipe out illiteracy'. The authorities instructed every village to organize a night school for the peasants. I could understand the importance of the campaign. Most Chinese at that time were illiterate, especially in the countryside. With the work team's help, we used the private village school and appointed its old teacher. Lacking any textbooks, he had to make everything up himself, yet despite a long career teaching Chinese classics, he was quite progressive and willingly taught us the popular slogans like 'Overthrow the landlords and divide their land!' and 'Long live New China!' The night school was held every night. Drums and gongs were no longer needed after the first few nights, but the *yangkou* dances and folk-songs after each class continued to attract more people.

When the initial excitement calmed down, almost a third of the adults of suitable age stayed on, and children came too, as the government school had not been set up. Women outnumbered men, since very few had any education in those days. Only families without sons or unusually open-minded families previously sent girls to school—my class had two dozen boys and only two girls. In a conservative village like ours, young women, particularly if married, were not allowed out of their houses, let alone at night. Now women were told they were liberated, and they wanted to taste the freedom. Going to the night school offered them a good excuse, and women like to get together for a chat anyway. My wife happily seized the opportunity. Otherwise, living in a big family like ours, she would hardly dare set her foot outside the threshold without good reason.

After the Spring Festival in 1951, the private school resumed teaching until the government school was established later in the year. As the old teacher had to give up his night duty, I and two other lads took turns to teach. I was an active member of the village youth league, in charge of propaganda work, and all three of us had been lucky to have a few years' education at the private school. None of us was highly educated, but probably good enough to teach people who didn't know a single character. Perhaps only 10 per cent of the village had ever attended a class.

By this time, we felt we had learned the basic tricks of teaching. More importantly, we were enthusiastic and determined to make the class more lively. We taught a dozen characters a night, then after class we performed local songs or crosstalk. We taught the students to sing too—revolutionary songs like 'The East is Red' and 'Overthrow the Landlords'—or folk-songs with new lyrics: 'Whoever plants the crop, harvests it; whoever grows fruit trees, gets the fruit; we fight and bleed, but no one will take the fruit of victory from our hands.' We expanded the after-class performances into small plays to make them interesting and educational.

I first heard of the revolutionary play *The White-Haired Girl* from a land-reform worker. Knowing she will be sold by an evil landlord, a servant girl hides in the mountains. When she is rescued by the PLA, her hair has already turned white. He used it to inspire the peasants' class hatred against the landlords, develop their love for the Party, and encourage young people to join the army. As we improved, I thought it would be fun to perform longer and more serious works. I thought its message was appropriate, so I went to the county bookstore and bought the script with my own money. I was the director, the white-haired girl's father, and filled in roles whenever necessary. For a play like this, we performed one act each night, with up to thirty people in the cast. It was a great success and a lot of fun for everyone.

Our night school took off just as land-reform work in the village was nearing completion. Among the 400 villagers, there were no landlords but a couple of rich peasants. They were not struggled against, though their extra land was confiscated. We were also given land belonging to landlords from neighbouring villages. Some peasants thought: Those landlords might have exploited others, but they didn't exploit me. Why should I keep his land for nothing? They were only half-hearted in cultivating the land, as they were uncertain they could collect the harvest. Some even rented land out to others. We repeatedly explained that they were indeed entitled to the plot, that the government had confiscated the land to distribute to the poor peasants. When they realized they could keep the land, they started work enthusiastically.

After complaints about fairness, another work team arrived later that year to re-adjust the distribution: those who received too much had to return the surplus, those with insufficient land were given more, and resettled families were also allocated a share. Most people were overjoyed at receiving their plot of land. Each family was given a certificate, which the owner was required to sign or mark with his fingerprint. Literate or otherwise, everyone knew a formal piece of paper carried some weight. Many peasants felt it was a pity they couldn't read what the certificate said, and that inspired some illiterate villagers to attend night school.

We moved the school into a large room in a family home with desks, benches, and a massive *kang* [a heated brick platform for sitting and sleeping]. Classes averaged fifty to sixty people, but on fine summer nights the floor and windows were crowded with people. Even on rainy days, there were plenty of students, for there was little entertainment at night, and no such things as radio or TV. Some women brought needlework to class. Each student brought a few sheets of coarse paper onto which they copied new characters from the blackboard. Some discarded the sheets right away; more diligent students bound them together with thread.

We eventually received some textbooks, which made teaching easier, though there were no extra copies for the students. The textbook explained basic information about China and great detail on how other areas were implementing government policy. Apart from teaching characters and arithmetic, it was our duty to publicize these policies, not only land reform but issues like equality between men and women and prohibitions on bad marriage practices like polygamy. We also taught villagers about the planting seasons and new farming techniques. A teacher would draw a sweetcorn on the blackboard, and explain how it grows and how to make it grow better. Before, we only knew to follow the traditional way of growing crops, without ever understanding why, and we never thought about improving output.

We also had to teach people not to believe in superstition. Siling, a tomb near our village, is where the last Ming emperor Chongzhen was buried. He hanged himself on Jinshan, the hill behind the Forbidden City, as troops of the rebel Li Zicheng approached. Early this century the tomb was destroyed by lightning, and later one of its ancient trees was struck. Locals believed it was because Chongzhen's lot was so bad. They also said the tomb was haunted, as peasants claimed to see lanterns dancing in circles. We persuaded them that it was impossible for lanterns to dance without anyone holding them, while lightning is a natural phenomenon, and the strike on the tomb was accidental, unconnected to the emperor's fate.

After two or three years, villagers' lives were visibly improving. Some built new houses to replace their run-down homes. In a way, the early mutual-aid teams began when we were busy with the night-school performances. If an actor apologized that he couldn't make the day's rehearsal because of work in the fields, we would reply, 'Come on, we'll all help you,' as we didn't want him to miss the play. We also helped each other with tools and animals. The next day, we might help another actor. Based on this system, more formal teams were organized in the spring of 1953. I

had left the village at the end of 1952 to work as a carpenter in another county, though I came home for the spring seeding and autumn harvest. I left mainly because of poor relations with the new village head, who cared little for the night school.

It had shut down in 1954 when I returned for good. The agricultural producers' cooperatives were introduced that year. Villagers were divided into three production teams to which we contributed animals and tools. If I had a donkey, the accountant would write it down at the market price: Zhang Tong, one donkey, 100 yuan. I never received 100 yuan, as the account was soon balanced. When each peasant had to pay, say, 10 yuan for seeds, the accountant took 10 from my donkey money. When the production team decided to buy a tractor, everyone paid 30 yuan, and so on. It was like an investment, to borrow a modern word. We tilled the land together, and since everyone had the same amount, no one owed anything to anyone. The peasants welcomed these changes, as the village output remained low and the people fairly poor. None of us could possibly buy a tractor, but by pooling our resources everyone could enjoy the machine. Again, the peasants had such trust in the government that no one opposed the jump to people's communes in 1958: collectivization was meant to increase production.

Despite the name of the campaign, it was impossible to wipe out illiteracy just like that. Some students had no interest in learning, and even for those who did, I don't know how much they mastered. Yet the campaign did benefit peasants in their lives and their work. At the very least they learned to write their own names, and the names of their village and province. The better ones could even read newspapers! More significantly, by attending night school villagers gained a better understanding of government policies and increased their own political consciousness. For the women in the village, learning even simple skills had a great impact. Few women previously went to shop in the market for fear they would be cheated. Once we taught them how to count, no one dared to cheat them, and they were no longer stuck inside the house. Some women were even elected group leaders of the production team, which was unimaginable before.

I was so happy and excited to see New China founded. It brought such hope to the ordinary people that I wanted to make my contribution. Of course, there is no need of a night school anymore. Apart from the very old, all the villagers are more or less literate. My own reading improved considerably from attending the night school, and I still read newspapers, sometimes even novels, though my vision is a bit blurred nowadays, and I'm afraid my wife's forgotten most of the characters she learned. All children of school age, boys and girls, now attend the local school fifteen minutes' walk away.

Still, I don't believe people are paying sufficient attention to education. Particularly in recent years, some peasants have begun to engage in business and let their children give up schooling early to help out. This is a very short-sighted view. I am glad all my five children received a fair amount of education, especially the three girls. They all have good jobs in the cities now. The Chinese government knows the importance of education, but they just don't have enough money to invest.

Tashi Tsering

Honeymoon on the Roof of the World

The fledgling CCP had made bold promises of self-determination for the Tibetans, Mongolians, and other non-Han Chinese minorities, but by 1938 Mao dropped these tactical slogans and adopted anti-imperialism as the cornerstone of Party policy. Whereas Lenin and Stalin required non-Russian support, and granted the Soviet republics the constitutional right to secede, the Chinese revolution was strictly a Han affair: China's other nationalities comprised just 6 per cent of her population. Yet this figure belies their strategic significance in dominating the borderlands and at least 60 per cent of China's land mass. These peoples had not been stirred to revolution by agrarian reform and anti-Japanese nationalism. Their transition to socialism would require time and tact on the part of the CCP.

On the roof of the world, a centuries-old theocracy continued to rule the splendid isolation afforded by the Tibetan plateau. Monastic and aristocratic estates terrorized their serf tenants with violence in this world and the threat of multiple hells in the next. The Tibetan court paid lip-service to the Chinese Republic's claim of suzerainty and maintained their antipathy towards foreign influence. But unlike the Great Game manoeuvres of Britain and Russia in the preceding century, Tibet now faced a revolutionary ideology of social, political, and economic reform, backed by powerful land forces. As the PLA closed in, Lhasa's monks held public prayers and displayed rare amulets as additional protection. Given the military disparities, divine intervention was as solid a hope as any.

For 20-year-old Tashi Tsering, a clerk at the Potala Palace, the Chinese entry opened a world of new ideas. The Party's united front organized propaganda teams to co-opt progressive Tibetans and 'democratic personages'. Openly volatile elements were removed, including two prime ministers in 1952, but expediency required a generally liberal approach and the maintenance of existing power structures. The Tibetan god–king, the Fourteenth Dalai Lama, remained the secular and ecclesiastical ruler. Tibetan Buddhism affected every aspect of local culture, and was initially left undisturbed. Traditional values held sway: as was customary, Tashi lived with a senior monk who was his mentor and lover, yet he was free to fall in love with a noble woman who bore a son. Tashi's lowly background meant marriage was impossible. One remark by Mao to the Dalai Lama in 1954 epitomized the tensions that underlay such tolerance: 'Religion is poison.'

It was agreed that 'democratic reforms' be postponed in Tibet until at least 1962, but the 1959 Lhasa Uprising marked an end to the honeymoon period of Chinese rule and the start of life in exile for the Dalai Lama. Eager for the education denied him in Lhasa, Tashi had left Tibet for India two years earlier and subsequently moved to the United States. In 1964, disregarding his friends' warnings and an offer to join the government-in-exile, he returned 'to build socialism, democracy, and happiness in Tibet'. At the start of the Cultural Revolution, Tashi even joined the Red Guards glimpsing Mao at Tiananmen, but, as predicted, he was soon accused as a counter-revolutionary and American agent. After six years in a Shaanxi prison, and a long fight for rehabilitation, he was assigned as English professor to Tibet University in 1981. In his long absence, his brother had starved to death in jail, while their parents barely survived in an old monastery, one of thousands destroyed in Tibet.

Marxist nationality policy has long espoused national fusion, the disappearance of national characteristics as the world unites in an as yet unattained truly communist phase. The steady influx of Chinese settlers into Tibet during the reform era threatens greater impact than any other Han-sponsored change this past half-century. Such encroachment only deepens Tashi's conviction that the written language is the key to Tibet's cultural heritage. After completing the first English–Tibetan–Chinese dictionary, he has financed fifty schools in his home county Namling, near Shigatse, through his own efforts and foreign donations, providing education to over 5,000 children.

IN AMERICA IN THE EARLY 1960S I heard an African leader say, 'If a nation or people do not know how to make revolution for themselves, revolution will be forcibly imposed upon them.' I thought back to my own country, where a theocratic government, linking church and state, was controlled by a handful of aristocrats, lamas, and government officials. Politically, economically, and ruthlessly, they oppressed and exploited the great masses of the people, the peasants and the nomads. We ordinary Tibetans did not know how to change things or make revolution. The Chinese revolution was imposed on us. We had no choice but to accept.

I was born in 1929 in Guchok village, a seven-day horse ride through the mountains to Lhasa, or twenty-five days by yak. When I was 10 years old, I was chosen to become a *gadrugba* dancer in the Dalai Lama's ceremonial troupe. My family was then exempted from land tax. All twenty novices were selected from different provinces by high officials: we had to be good-looking and of clean birth—sons of butchers or blacksmiths, regarded as low caste, were ineligible. *Gadrugba* performed dances and songs for the Dalai Lama and government officials. None of us was literate, not even the head of the *gadrugba*, and they never cared to teach us. I got my first three months' education aged 14, and even that only by fleeing the host family who mistreated me. In 1944 an English school for upper-class students was briefly set up in Lhasa, but monks from Sera monastery feared it would bring modern changes and harm the interests of the monasteries. The threat of kidnap by deviant *dobdo* monks forced parents to withdraw their children. Yet I was thirsty to learn and gradually learned enough to pass a calligraphy exam and become a clerk at the Potala Palace treasury in 1947. Besides my ability and enthusiasm, someone was pulling me up—the monk official who kept me as his *drombo* [a passive homosexual partner].

In July 1949, all Han Chinese connected with the Nationalist government were expelled from Lhasa. I saw it with my own eyes, but this move had little impact on me. By 1950, my *gadrugba* term had ended and my social life expanded. The only entertainment places in Lhasa were teashops selling sweet tea and cookies, and Muslim restaurants selling mutton curry. I went with other young people, chatting and drinking, playing games, sharing the gossip from the market. This was an exciting time, when we first felt free of family restrictions. The sons of aristocrats and merchants studying in India made me envious with their tales of school life.

One day in 1950, I was in a teashop when a Muslim translated the news from a Chinese radio broadcast: China had decided to send troops to 'liberate' Tibet. The announcement was not a complete shock, given reports that the poor people of China had risen in revolution, and all the rumours that these Communists would come to Tibet. But still there was panic. The people of Lhasa felt so uncertain, yet certain something was bound to happen. Some teased we should *invite* the Communists to liberate us; others really meant it. On the other hand, the high officials were uneasy and fearful. As a minor government clerk I neither feared nor cared—surely it had no connection with me—yet I too began to feel change was coming.

The Tibetan government was asked by the central government to send a delegation to Beijing, and in May 1951 the two sides signed the Seventeen-Point Agreement. I was literate by then, so I read this document and thought it was a good arrangement. The Chinese wanted to avoid violence—that's why they signed—and apart from the Tibetans, no other nationality signed an agreement with the central government.

Tashi and son, Lhasa, early 1980s

It's clear from this that there *are* basic, significant differences relating to Tibet and its relationship with the central government, compared with the other 'minority nationalities'. I really hope the central government accepts this fact.

In October 1951, the PLA marched into Lhasa in neat, uniformed lines, 'left, right, left, right!', each soldier with pack, gun, water bottle, and rubber shoes. More and more arrived. They conducted military exercises in the monk officials' park right in front of the Potala. We would often go to watch them living in tents and cooking outside. They were very efficient, not wasting or leaving anything behind. I never heard they took as much as a needle from the ordinary people. In their spare time, they fished in Lhasa's small rivers by putting small worms on hooks. As a religious person, I was shocked when I saw this. In our old society, some people had fished but not like this. I felt the Chinese were truly atheist, without sympathy for living creatures—such behaviour was cruel and thoroughly unacceptable.

Where we lived, there were piles of human excrement in the street— honestly we were so dirty, and there were no public toilets. All this waste became frozen in winter, when I saw the PLA take baskets and spades, scrape it up and carry it away. Then they mixed it with water into a porridge, and poured it onto their vegetable fields. It made me want to vomit! I didn't have any concept that it might improve the soil, and felt it was so dirty I would never eat Chinese vegetables!

Chinese discipline was a sharp contrast to my job at the Potala treasury, a real robbery shop. The duty of us *chola* [clerks] was simply to obey the officials, doing housework, collecting money, keeping a ledger of daily accounts, and supplying the Dalai Lama with *khada* [white scarves], tea bricks, money, and brocades for official meetings. There was so much borrowing, not only by our officials but by other officials and their relatives, and hardly anything was returned. I knew I had clean hands, but many old *chola* resented my pointing out the corruption. It was like an eggshell, intact on the outside but rotten within.

A loudspeaker was set up in the Barkhor, the heart of Lhasa, broadcasting daily propaganda in Tibetan. I kept asking myself what were all these new ideas, these 'isms'—socialism, communism, capitalism, imperialism. We had never heard of them before. Youth leagues and study groups were formed to educate Tibetans about them. Friends would say, 'What fun we had last night, dancing and singing until late, when the party secretary gave a lecture.' Many young people went to China to study; some sons and daughters of aristocratic and merchant families were even called back from India and sent to China. Chinese government workers, in collaboration with Tibetan activists, sought candidates for political, social, and propaganda posts. One friend who was a youth league member asked me to become a teacher at a new primary school, on a very attractive salary. I declined. The school is still the best in Lhasa.

These were the honeymoon days. The Chinese government did not have full control, so the two political systems and powers existed side by side. The Chinese used silver coin diplomacy so effectively, not only paying students to study, but hiring serfs to labour for good money. The PLA too worked unbelievably hard, building the Tibet–Qinghai and Tibet–Sichuan highways, completed in 1954. There were only paths before, where man and animal walked. They built schools and hospitals too, where once there were hardly any. I myself enjoyed good treatment from a Chinese doctor who cured me with what I now know was penicillin. All these new ideas and comparisons made me conclude the Chinese could bring positive change. I came to believe that the Tibetan social and governmental system *should* be changed, more common people should have a voice, but I didn't know how, and I strongly felt religion should not be affected.

Other friends were completely opposed to change, like my patron Gyentsenla, a monk official whose house I shared. It was ironic that he and a lay official became the guides of Zhang Jingwu, the highest-ranking official sent by China. Gyentsenla was very conservative and totally disagreed with the Chinese style of revolutionary change, but they were instructed by the Tibetan government to provide everything Zhang and his party needed. Perhaps the majority of the élite felt like Gyentsenla, or were even more reactionary and conservative. He was one factor why I couldn't decide either to join the Chinese workers or go to study in China.

When the Dalai Lama went to Beijing in 1954, I was not worried about his safety, though countless rumours said he would be kept there. On the whole, the Dalai Lama was quite progressive at that time. I saw this in his dealings with Chinese officials. In March the following year, the Preparatory Committee of the Tibetan Autonomous Region was inaugurated. I played the six-string mandolin at a welcome banquet the Dalai Lama held for Foreign Minister Chen Yi. I was too lowly to participate, but I knew there was debate on what changes were acceptable and what was too fast a pace.

In 1949, the Dalai Lama had set up a reform committee, but it was too late and would have been too difficult for him to push through real reforms. His predecessor, the Thirteenth Dalai Lama, set up military forces around him during his reign and had plans for modern, democratic changes. They were never realized, due mainly to opposition from the great monasteries, Drepung and Sera. Progressive Tibetan officials were arrested and jailed, some even lost their eyes. The Fourteenth Dalai Lama too would probably have failed with any plans for major social change, under pressure from the great monasteries, aristocratic families, and vested interests of government officials.

Social and agricultural reforms in Tibetan parts of Sichuan and Qinghai in 1956 pushed many rich Tibetans to carry their fortunes to Lhasa, and finally India. Why? They were in great fear of a revolution that would remove their political and economic power. Their fear aroused great anxiety among the upper classes and landowners in Tibet proper—what happened there yesterday will happen to us tomorrow! It was a logical conclusion. I too faced a choice: to study in China or go elsewhere. As my mind and conscience were not ready to accept the Chinese revolution and Communist system, I chose India in 1957, to study English and through it to know the history and meaning of the 'isms' I was exposed to. News of the 1959 Lhasa Uprising came as a great and unexpected shock as I studied in Darjeeling. Looking back, it seems inevitable: stubborn monk officials opposed any form of change as they had for centuries. The uprising was crushed within a couple of days, and then the upper class was helpless. What else could they do but run.

Until 1959, most of the decisions on Tibet were made by Mao, and generally they helped the masses. Among all the Chinese leaders, I found him quite magnanimous in dealing with sensitive issues like Tibetan religious and nationality concerns. He was obliged to: the central government did not fully control Tibet until the crushing of the Lhasa Uprising. After 1959, the situation totally changed.

The last twenty years, coinciding with the Open Door policy and my own rehabilitation in 1978, have been successful ones. Everything came together and was favourable for my development. I am helping not only the sons and daughters of peasants and nomads, but also the government. Overall, the Chinese Revolution has brought advantage to the bulk of the population, and their living standards have improved. Comparatively speaking, since 1950 Tibet has established a modern educational system, nearly 4,000 schools enrolling over 300,000 students in a population of 2.4 million. In my own forty-six schools, I respect the rules and regulations but always emphasize the great importance of learning Tibetan. Language remains such a stumbling block—at college level in Tibet, scientific subjects are all taught in Chinese. Yet without being taught in Tibetan, the great majority of Tibetans are unable to master scientific subjects. Without acquiring scientific knowledge, the construction of a modern society is out of the question.

When I met the Dalai Lama in America in 1994, I said the Tibetans must know how to oppose the Chinese when their policies seem unreasonable, but also how to live with them. Policies must be guaranteed by the rule of law, not the rule of man as so often in the past. Full implementation must be guaranteed, such as equality of language-learning. Modernization is my generation's duty. I am not interested in other, unreachable goals. My body and soul is in my rural-schools project, something concrete I can contribute to benefit the people. My success is the fruit of my struggle these past fifty years, and my ongoing struggle for modern education in Tibet. The pillar of Tibetan culture is the written language. When that is finished, the basis of our culture is finished. That will not happen. But there is weakening— willingly or unwillingly, consciously or unconsciously—and particularly among our young people. I say to them, 'This is your forefather's language, to be learned and respected. If you can't read or write Tibetan, I consider you only semi-literate!'

Leaping into Famine

1957–1965

Khrushchev's 1956 attack on Stalin shocked the entire communist world. The Hungarian uprising in October of the same year further convinced many in the Chinese Communist leadership that strict internal controls must be maintained. Yet Mao himself was arguing for open discussion with non-Party intellectuals, to encourage their collaboration in overcoming China's problems. Confident of China's overall unity, he finally overcame nervous hardliners in May 1957 and called on the nation to 'let a hundred flowers bloom'. It was a testament to the hopes and frustrations the new regime had engendered in the Chinese people that, seven years after the founding of New China, so many dared speak out.

Where Mao anticipated a 'gentle breeze' of criticism, the Hundred Flowers Movement blew up a storm of protest against abuses by the Party and its monopoly on power, while non-Chinese minorities complained that regional autonomy was 'as useful as ears on a basket'. Whatever his ultimate objectives, beginning in June 1957, Mao sided with the conservative backlash. Deng Xiaoping, a veteran of the Long March promoted to Party general secretary in 1956, proved an able lieutenant in sifting the 'poisonous weeds' from the 'fragrant flowers'. Over 300,000 intellectuals were targeted as 'rightists' and removed from society.

The honeymoon was over. The Party's trap betrayed the trust of the intelligentsia and silenced potential voices of opposition to Mao's increasingly radical policies. The 'disloyalty' of the intellectuals also turned Mao back to his oldest constituency, the peasants of China. Average growth of 8.9 per cent in national income between 1953 and 1957 was in stark contrast to pre-Liberation chaos, but agriculture posted under 4 per cent growth, and the 1957 harvest was poor. To realize his dream of writing socialist prosperity on the 'poor and blank' Chinese people, Mao opted for all-out attack, taming nature by force, just as he had won the country.

Under the rallying banner 'politics in command', the Great Leap Forward (1958–61) was the Chinese Communists' first significant break with the Soviet model of development. By mobilizing underemployed labour into vast water-control and irrigation projects, China hoped to compensate for a lack of capital in both industry and agriculture. Mao's leap of faith inspired the nation to sweat for utopia—technological weakness was no obstacle to will-power on this scale. 'A million men with teaspoons', remarked a visitor to one of the countless earth-moving projects changing China's face at the time.

From the summer of 1958, the frenzy for grass-roots industry saw backyard steel furnaces mushroom across China, consuming the peasants' pots and pans and deforesting the countryside, to smelt household metals into useless ingots. Misdirected energy knew no bounds: during the elimination of the 'four pests' (rats, sparrows, flies, and mosquitoes), Chinese everywhere drummed up a cacophony of noise to prevent sparrows alighting until they dropped exhausted from the skies. The resulting plague of caterpillars saw sparrows rehabilitated and replaced as official pests by bedbugs.

Mao's vision found its ultimate expression in the people's communes, after an autumnal 'communist wind' in 1958 swept China's peasants into production units averaging 25,000 members. Private plots were abolished during the amalgamation of agricultural cooperatives into communes that interfered in the minutiae of farming life to an unprecedented degree. Communal kitchens symbolized the public spirit and economy of scale Mao believed would release peasant energies: 'The output of the land is as great as the people's courage.' Money appeared destined for obscurity, since one's commune met almost every need, from haircuts to childcare. The dawn of true Communism was declared imminent.

On 1 October 1958, *The People's Daily* rejoiced, 'Today, in the era of Mao Zedong, heaven is here on earth.' Steel and grain production miracles kept stacking up, such as wheat crops so dense children were photographed walking across them (on carefully concealed benches). Beijing announced ten grandiose projects to be completed by the PRC's tenth birthday in October 1959—including the Great Hall of the People, raised in just ten months by volunteer armies. Such spectacular feats were made possible by the fervour of the times and the military-style organization of the communes: people's militia units under commune control were said to embrace some 220 million people, or one third of China's population, at the height of the Leap.

The People's Daily could not have been more wrong. The year's grain harvest was reported as 375 million tonnes, almost twice its actual size, and the pattern was set: false statistics from the provinces escalated requisitions for the cities just as actual production slumped. The communal kitchens soon ran out of real food, yet peasants were ordered to leave land fallow from misplaced concern over inadequate storage space for the anticipated surplus. When Mao learned of food shortages, he declared hoarders were responsible and ordered brutal searches for 'hidden' grain stocks.

Only one of China's leaders emerges with any honour from the horrors of a famine that took 20 to 30 million lives. At the Lushan Conference in 1959 (a senior Party meeting, the Eighth Plenum of the Eighth Central Committee), Defense Minister Peng Dehuai, one of the few leaders of true poor peasant stock, wrote to Mao with concern over misreporting of harvests. For his honesty, this long-time ally was branded the head of a 'right opportunist clique' and dismissed. The other leaders cowered into accepting Mao's line, and the famine went on unchecked. Lushan marked the end of any semblance of democracy at the apex of the leadership. Where once policy issues had been openly discussed before uniform implementation, Mao chose to interpret Peng's argument as a personal attack and used it to bring him down. This betrayal of trust sowed the seeds of factionalism with which he and the country would become obsessed.

On 1 October 1959, Mao proudly displayed the new Great Hall of the People, but anniversary celebrations were hollow throughout China, a nation in crisis. Poor harvests continued into 1960 and 1961, amid rumours Chiang Kaishek would return to take the Mainland at its weakest hour. A further blow came in July 1960 with the withdrawal of all Soviet experts. The troubled Sino-Soviet relationship had long been heading for divorce. Mao was already frustrated with Soviet methods and arrogance, and Khrushchev had been openly condemning Mao's initiatives since 1958. By 1960, both leaders had had enough.

After the collapse of the Great Leap Forward, Mao 'retired from the front line' in 1960, leaving Liu Shaoqi, Zhou Enlai, Deng Xiaoping, and the economic planner Chen Yun to resuscitate the devastated economy. Retrenchment was the only option. The impositions of the people's communes were relaxed and China's emaciated villagers permitted small private plots and sideline production for reopened rural markets. In January 1962, at a meeting of 7,000 top officials, including Mao himself, Liu blamed nature for only 30 per cent of the Leap's failures, and human error for 70 per cent, a bold reversal of Mao's own verdict. In July, Deng quoted the Sichuanese saying that became his catch-phrase: 'Whether white or black, a cat is a good cat so long as it catches the rat.' Such ideological flexibility would spur China's economic miracle in the early 1980s, but at the time it clashed with Mao's September 1962 warning: 'Never forget class struggle!'

The Chairman was down but far from out. He had ceded the state chairmanship to Liu in 1959, yet remained head of both party and military. While intellectuals from 1961 began to publish oblique criticism of Mao through historical allegory, Marshal Lin Biao, Peng's successor, was busy turning the PLA into a political force guided by Maoism. Alarmed that the spread of material incentives heralded the return of capitalism to China's villages, Mao engineered the Socialist Education Movement from 1963 to 1965. Cadres and intellectuals were dispatched to the countryside to clean up grass-roots corruption and learn from the masses.

This movement was launched with a grave warning: 'Who will win in the struggle between socialism and capitalism . . . between Marxism–Leninism and revisionism?' Even in the highly politicized PRC this was no hyperbole, given the growing factionalism among the leadership. All recognized the problems of low Party morale and corrupt tendencies. But while Liu and Deng wished to resolve them, as internal administrative matters, Mao characteristically sought to rouse the masses. Liu dispatched work teams to dominate the Four Clean-Ups—in politics, economy, organization, and ideology—yet when investigators in 1964 exposed the lies behind Mao's model commune Dazhai, the Chairman promoted its illiterate peasant leader to the National People's Congress and the work team was dismissed. The conflict between visionary politics and pragmatic management was coming to a head.

In 1964, Mao called on China to 'learn from the PLA'. Army personnel were transferred into new political departments in government and Party units. If this strengthening of the military's role in civilian life contradicted the primacy of the Communist Party, Mao clearly believed only the PLA offered his desired blend of 'red and expert'. There was no doubt of its political loyalties once Lin Biao had compiled the text of Mao's growing personality cult: over 350 million copies of *Quotations from Chairman Mao*, Mao's 'Little Red Book', were published between

1964 and 1966. As for technical prowess, the army had fought well in the 1962 border war with India—the highest in the history of warfare. The nuclear test of 1964 also offered a bold example of self-reliance.

The economic damage from the Great Leap Forward had been repaired by 1965, when China's agricultural output almost matched pre-Leap levels, and most industrial products doubled their 1957 yield. Of far greater consequence were the divisions among the leadership. Party democracy had so weakened that no formal meeting of the Party's central committee convened between 1962 and 1966. Mao could secure decisions through the ad hoc series of work conferences he called, but implementation was often frustrated through a bureaucracy led by Liu Shaoqi and Deng Xiaoping. 'The officials of China are a class, and one whose interests are antagonistic to those of the workers and peasants,' Mao complained in 1965. It was time to rectify those 'Party persons in power taking the capitalist road'. The stage was set for Mao's final struggle to reinvigorate the Chinese revolution.

Dai Huang

Righting the Wronged

'Let a hundred flowers bloom, let a hundred schools of thought contend': Mao's invitation in the spring of 1957 encouraged intellectuals nationwide to open their hearts for the sake of a better system. As a conscientious Party member and committed communist, celebrated war correspondent Dai Huang felt obliged to highlight both the inequalities he saw and the risks that lay ahead. Thus did the veteran of both the Thirty-eighth Parallel and the demise of French Indochina at Dien Bien Phu seal his own fate. The consequences were all too predictable for those schooled in Party methods from the formative years in the loess caves of Yan'an. In the vicious Anti-Rightist Campaign that began in July 1957, a generation, including future Premier Zhu Rongji, were condemned to wear 'rightist hats' that many would only shed in the late 1970s.

Born Dai Penglin in Jiangsu province in 1928, the young boy was so inspired by the new ideas expounded in the journals of his father, a doctor, and elder brother, a schoolmaster, that he almost joined a passing communist troop at the age of 12, but for his family's last-minute intervention. Four years later, Dai joined the New Fourth Route Army, where writing talent and performances in revolutionary dramas soon won him Party membership. Beginning in 1947, he covered the civil war for Xinhua (New China) News Agency and made his name in front-line dispatches from Korea. One tale of sacrifice, 'International soldier, Lou Shengjiao', remains a patriotic school text to this day. A posting to Vietnam enabled him to report the defeat of the French imperialists.

The reward for Dai's honesty was a one-way ticket to Beidahuang, the Great Northern Wilderness, an immense wasteland in China's north-east, where temperatures drop to 30 or 40 degrees below zero in the long winter months. By the time Dai and other rightists arrived, well over 100,000 retired soldiers, officers, and countless prisoners were already settled there to cultivate and populate the Soviet border. Beidahuang had become China's Siberia. It was Dai's first step on a journey of twenty-one wasted years, despite lobbying from friends like Ho Chi Minh, the leader of Communist Vietnam, who refused to accept the rightist charge.

Dai's bitter experiences, and his passion to improve a system he still believes in, find expression in his writing on China's 'wrong cases'. From the late seventies, Dai's small Xinhua flat became open house for petitioners seeking justice in Beijing. He reported their cases and gave material help when possible. Moved by the determination of Hu Yaobang to 'reverse the verdicts', Dai has struggled to rehabilitate the former Party secretary's reputation, blackened after student unrest in 1986. Even today, aged 71, Dai continues his self-appointed task, to help people remember China's painful history and draw lessons from it. 'Before Liberation, the mission for party workers was to "awaken the masses". I hope my books can also awaken the masses.'

I FELL VICTIM to the Anti-Rightist Campaign in 1957. While the majority of the victims were labelled 'rightists' during the Hundred Flowers Movement, I only gained my 'rightist hat' when the Party had already launched its counter-attack. I had not spoken out earlier, because I felt a Party member ought to obey discipline. The Party had not yet called for its members to take part in the Rectification Campaign, (the June 1957 crackdown on the Hundred Flowers movement). Indeed, in June 1957, following the article, 'What is this for?' in *The People's Daily*, the lively campaign changed suddenly into a terrifying anti-rightist movement. All the newspapers who once warmly invited criticism from intellectuals, patriotic personnel, and other non-Party people, began to criticize many of them as 'bourgeois rightists who oppose the Party and Socialism'.

At this crucial moment, Party secretaries from all of Beijing's universities and colleges were summoned to a speech by the Beijing Party Secretary, Peng Zhen. I attended as Party secretary of the Party members seconded to Beijing Diplomatic College from the central government. Peng, energetic and with a powerful voice, gave a passionate speech inviting Party members to continue to offer suggestions and criticism. He explained that we Party members were totally different from 'outsiders'. 'We are all one big family,' he stressed.

'The Party needs your help in order to be perfect.' He promised again and again there would be absolutely no punishment for whatever we were about to say, even if it was wrong. Later we realized his was a false promise, a trick called 'luring the snake out', which he learned from Chairman Mao. But at the time he really fired everyone up. Any suspicion at all disappeared in the long applause after his persuasive speech.

On the same night, we held a symposium among the committee members of our college's Party branch. I was the first to give a speech in which I vented what had been brewing in my mind for over a year. I argued the biggest threat to the Party and our nation lay in 'deification and privilege'. If the two were not controlled or demolished, the whole nation would become isolated and people narrow-minded, which would inevitably lead to great disaster. I suggested the best way to eliminate these threats was to listen to criticism, implement real supervision, improve elections, and let the people's representatives speak. Also, real equality ought to be implemented throughout the country. All policies or systems that would promote privilege openly or otherwise ought to be demolished, and the gap in living standards between cadres and the ordinary people ought to be narrowed. Others also gave enthusiastic speeches.

Why did I raise the issue of 'deification and privilege'? Back in March 1956, a so-called secret report by Khrushchev denouncing Stalin was read to Party members above a certain rank at Xinhua. No explanation was given; all those who attended the meeting were asked only to listen, without writing notes or discussing it with others. During the whole morning, the only sound was the voice of the person reading the report. Underneath the calm surface, the report sent a shock wave through people's minds. We all asked: How come? How could a great leader like Stalin, whom we thought perfect, make such great mistakes? How could he so abuse the people's love and trust to seek fame through a personality cult? I then began to ask: Is there a personality cult in China? Was the overwhelming praise for Chairman Mao right, particularly slogans like 'All the glory, all the credit, goes to our great leader Chairman Mao'?

Three months later I was sent to Shanghai to report on the visiting Soviet fleet. After my foreign assignments, I was happy to have a chance to see what was happening elsewhere in China. During this trip, and a home visit soon afterwards, I discovered to my surprise widespread corruption and injustice, such as cadres enjoying lavish banquets and privileged access to desirable goods, at very cheap prices, that ordinary people didn't even know existed. In the countryside, most peasants' living standards were little better than prior to Liberation, but village leaders still built fine houses for themselves. Further shocking news in October—political turmoil in Poland and Hungary—convinced me that without taking positive measures catastrophe could befall China too.

As a Party member, I felt obliged to give suggestions to the Party. So, from November 1956 until April the following year, on and off during my spare time, I wrote a long letter to Chairman Mao and the central committee members—it later became known as the 'ten thousand word letter'. I talked about the problems I saw and my thoughts on them. My speech in June 1957 at the symposium took the same line.

Who would know that only a month later I would be accused as a 'rightist' for my speech, the first Party member in our agency to gain such a title? Catching me as a 'rightist' was hailed by Wu Lengxi, head of Xinhua and chief editor of *The People's Daily*, as a 'major victory in our agency'. Big-character posters criticizing me shot up everywhere overnight. Even my own wife put one up.

I felt I was misunderstood, and therefore handed in the unfinished letter, which I did not even show to my wife. The letter, which I had hoped would put things in perspective, was instead used as evidence against me. On 18 March 1958, my fate was eventually decided: second-grade punishment, labour under supervision. I was deprived of my post, my party membership, and military rank of senior captain. My monthly salary was reduced from 157.75 to 28 yuan. There were six different grades of punishment for rightists. I never expected my few heartfelt words would earn the second severest punishment available. By that time, about a dozen journalists or editors from our domestic section, about 20 per cent of all staff, had been labelled rightists.

Trouble never comes alone. As I was suffering the heaviest set-back in my life, my wife, who had already cut off her ties with me politically, filed for divorce. I agreed, as I understood her position. I only felt sorry for our two daughters, aged 3 years and 10 months. My only hope was in the future our two daughters would understand neither of their parents was responsible for the family tragedy.

The destination of internal exile was a farm in Mishan county, Heilongjiang province. It was here I sweated, bled, and suffered for two years and eight months. In our batch was a *Guangming Daily* journalist called Xu Ying, the wife of a colleague of mine, also a fellow rightist. She had just given birth prematurely to a baby girl in Beijing; as soon as the infant was out of intensive care, the young mother was dragged away. Others I came to know included famous painters, playwrights, poets, economists, engineers, doctors, actors. . . . The youngest rightist was a 17-year-old typist, Dai Juying, whose only crime—the casual remark, 'The American-made shoe polish is really good!'—left her guilty of 'admiring foreign things'.

At the beginning, we were not treated too badly, at least without deliberate humiliation. There was also a hopeful atmosphere among the rightists, who naïvely thought if we worked hard we could 'wash away the dirt in our souls' and rid ourselves of our rightist hats. We got up just after 4am and only rested after 7 or 8pm. We were made to do all kinds of hard labour, seeding, ploughing, cutting trees . . . but we didn't mind, particularly since we had a very reasonable team leader called Liu Wen. After work, we talked, sang, and joked.

Dai Huang at his labour camp, Beidahuang, 1950

This 'civilized' exile came to an abrupt end half a year later, when Liu was accused of being 'sympathetic to the rightists' and was promptly removed. He was replaced by an evil person who did not treat us as human beings. In all the various places I worked in the farm, I never had a decent leader like Liu again. We were subject to physical and psychological abuse at any time, by the team leaders and a few vicious people, also rightists, whom they appointed as 'little bosses'. The trend was the more vicious you were, the more likely you had given up your rightist hat.

Our food ration was cut again and again. By 1960, when China was severely hit by natural disasters, supplies were reduced to the bare minimum. Normally, we had two small bread rolls for breakfast and lunch, and some terribly runny porridge for supper—it was so thin one could use it as a mirror to see one's own gaunt face. During the worst time, we were only given two 'meals' a day. Driven by survival instincts, we ate rotten vegetables, rats, or anything we could find. Almost everyone, save the leader's favourites, suffered various degrees of malnutrition. Many died from starvation plus serious mistreatment. One promising lad named Lou Xiangcheng, previously an official at the Education Commission, died right in front of me. In Lou's case, as in many others, if any consideration or humanity had been given, he would not have died.

It was October 1960, when Lou had already reached the critical swollen stage of third-degree oedema. His whole skinny body puffed up; his long thin face turned from pale to yellow, from yellow to grey. He could hardly walk on his own. Some kind person reported his case to the doctor and team leader, who both agreed to let him rest for three days. The next day, however, Sheng Guilin, a fellow rightist and our 'little boss', forced Lou up. Sheng was an evil character under whom I too had often suffered. 'There are not enough hands in the fields. You must go, lazy bones!' It was snowing heavily on that day. Poor Lou, wearing an old raincoat and a worn bed sheet around his neck, set out with the rest of us. In a minute, he lagged behind. On that day, our job was to gather and pile up the wet rice stalks from the fields. By 2pm, when most of us had finished the day's quota, the horse-drawn cart arrived with lunch. So did Lou at almost the same time. Just as he was about to fill his lunch box, Sheng stopped him. 'You want to eat? No f*****g way!' 'Please pity me. I am dying,' Lou begged. 'If you kindly give me a mouthful of food, I might be able to make my way back.' 'Shame on you! No work, no food!'

The tearful Lou came to find me in the field. I was so outraged by his humiliating experience, but all I could do was help him return to our 'home'. By this time, he was no longer able to walk unassisted. I tried to carry him on my back but fell after only a few steps—I myself was not the big strong man I used to be. I tried to crawl on through the snow but I found Lou had already lost consciousness. I buried him under a pile of beans and ran back for help. After emergency treatment, he recovered a little. He thanked me and asked me to stay with him. But then he was left in the care of an unsympathetic person.

Lou Xiangcheng died two days later, leaving behind his old mother in a lonely courtyard in Beijing. Becoming a widow when pregnant with Lou, she had raised him single-handed and sent him to prestigious Qinghua University. A talented youth was ruined just like that. During the early 'civilized' days at Beidahuang, he had even tried to carry on his research on education! His death saddened and angered us. One man said, 'Even animals are better treated than us—at least they have enough to eat.'

Lou was not the only one never to return home. Shortly before this, seven people died on a single, freezing day when a dozen rightists were dispatched without food to harvest beans in a distant field. How many died overall? The farm never made it public. According to one accountant and secretary of a 110-person team, he himself wrote out over thirty death reports, or one-third of his total workforce. I narrowly escaped death a few times. I suffered oedema twice, and often fainted. Once I was lucky—someone found me when lying unconscious outside on a winter day. Another time I fainted inside a brick kiln. The guy I was working with quickly realized what had happened, pulled me out with the help of others and gave me mouth-to-mouth resuscitation. A few minutes later and I would have died of suffocation.

As the death-toll was rising, the second investigation team from the central government arrived to remove 'hats' from a second batch of rightists. Naturally, I was not among them, as I had too many bad marks and remarks on file. It was also then decided to let all rightists originally from various departments of the central government go back to their units. We were spared! But the tragedies did not stop immediately. On hearing the news, one young man was so overjoyed he died in his sleep that night, leaving behind a beautiful Russian wife and their baby daughter. When another learned his rightist hat was lifted, he let out a great laugh and dropped down dead.

There's one other experience I ought to mention. At the very last minute at the farm, I discovered my biscuits, my only food on the four-day journey home, had been stolen. In a panic, I went to headquarters to beg for more. The leaders were enjoying a meal with numerous meat and fish dishes, and bread rolls made from white flour. Party secretary Xu, chewing a large mouthful of pork, replied, 'Right now, grain is a big problem in our country. Everyone should take his own responsibility for his food ration.' Left empty-handed, I thought even the capitalists might not be as hard-hearted as these cadres of a communist country!

In the last days of 1960, I made my way back to Beijing. People hardly recognized this thin, sickly looking man. No wonder—my weight had shrunk from 98 to 41 kilograms. Once at home, I discovered more personal tragedies. My sister, who suffered from tuberculosis and relied on my money for medical care, died three months after I was banished. One nephew, a young teacher, was denied RMB200 in help from his school for a heart operation, because his uncle was a 'big rightist'. He died too.

I did petty jobs here and there at the agency. Then, in early 1962, when the political atmosphere relaxed somewhat, I was encouraged by my bosses to write a self-criticism, hoping to remove my rightist hat. I did so truthfully. Only months later, however, Mao reminded the nation, 'Never forget class struggle!' My self-criticism was once again used as evidence against myself. For two years I was under investigation and repeatedly struggled against.

In April 1964, I was finally taken in handcuffs to a prison in Changping on the outskirts of Beijing to serve two years of reform through labour. I had been 'persisting in my reactionary stand of rightism, even trying to overturn the verdict', I was told. I had prepared for the moment, yet I was still shaken, particularly as I had to leave my new wife, who was about to give birth, to fend on her own. I did not expect in my worst nightmares that this two-year term would extend to fourteen! After completing my two-year sentence, I ought to have been taken back by my work unit. Unfortunately, the Cultural Revolution had just begun and everything was chaotic. I was employed by the prison and continued to live there in marginally better conditions. In 1969, as the political atmosphere worsened, I was transferred to another prison in Shanxi province, where I stayed until 1978.

In December 1978, I was rehabilitated, though still with great difficulty, for some Xinhua leaders argued, 'Dai Huang opposed Chairman Mao; if he's not a rightist, there isn't a single rightist in the whole country!' Justice was done in the end—the 'rightist hat' I wore for twenty-one years was finally lifted. From the age of 29 to 50, the twenty-one best years of my life were wasted. During that time, I suffered incredible hardship, humiliation, and pain. Without experiencing it personally, I might not believe the story could be true. Even a reactionary novelist from a capitalist country might fail to imagine such horrid, evil, and unjust events could occur in a socialist country! On the other hand, my rightist experience deepened my understanding of society; it taught me things I would never have learned from books.

In my view, the damage caused by the 1957 Anti-Rightist Campaign is too great to calculate. Firstly, it represents the sharp turning-point when the popularity and prestige of the Chinese Communist Party fell from its height to the abyss. Later rehabilitation, due to efforts of righteous comrades like Hu Yaobang, eased some damage. But the wounds in the rightists' hearts were incurable. The campaign also led to other disasters, for without it there would be no Great Leap Forward. After seeing how the whole nation responded so enthusiastically to his call to 'catch the rightists', Mao felt he had succeeded again. At the time, there was chaos among socialist countries after Khrushchev had disgraced Stalin, and Mao wanted to be number one in the international communist movement. He launched the impossible tasks of 'catching up to Britain in three years and overtaking America in five'. He introduced the people's commune and ordered everyone to eat from a communal pot. He wanted be the first to reach the true 'Communist society'.

Without the Great Leap, there would have been no famine in which so many innocent people died, nor the downfall of honest general Peng Dehuai. Without such political disasters, there would have been no

Cultural Revolution. Most of the victims of the Anti-Rightist Movement were intellectuals who were later deprived of the right to work. Can you imagine a country making progress without scientists, artists, teachers, engineers, economists, and so on?

But the greatest damage of the Anti-Rightist Campaign was the fact that people lost their trust in the Communists. The lesson our party and government should learn from this part of history is to implement real democracy and grant people freedom of speech. This is the only way to ensure we never repeat our history. I still have my belief in communism, which is the greatest ideology of humanity. Under a communist system, society should be equal, free, and democratic. The current government has improved compared to before, but it still falls short of the requirements of the Constitution.

Bu Yulong

The Battle for Steel

At a conference of the communist world held in Moscow in November 1957, Nikita Khrushchev declared that the Soviet Union would overtake the United States in fifteen years. Not to be outdone before his socialist brothers, Chairman Mao then announced that Chinese industry would overtake Great Britain within the same time frame. Privately, Mao was growing impatient with Soviet methods. His model of revolutionary development was the mass mobilization of peasant forces that harked back to Yan'an practice. The Eighth Party Congress in May 1958, a supplementary session of the Eighth Party Congress in 1956, approved his slogan: 'Stir up all energy, aim high, build socialism; more, faster, better, cheaper.' The ill-fated Great Leap Forward had begun.

The Chairman's utopian dreams intoxicated the nation. By 'walking on two legs', the transformation of both agriculture and industry through sheer will and infinite manpower, China would overcome the Three Great Differences: between mental and manual labour, city and countryside, worker and peasant. Steel production in 'backyard furnaces' became the rallying cry and epitome of unrealistic targets. The goal for 1958 jumped from 6.2 million tonnes in January to 10.7 million in August. By the end of the year, 100 million people, one-sixth of the total population, were fighting the 'battle for steel' in 1 million makeshift iron foundries nationwide. As the Leap galvanized his people, and the 1959 goal was set at 30 million tonnes, Mao revised his time table to leapfrog Britain down to seven, five, and eventually only two years.

As a cadre in a Henan village, Bu Yulong felt the full weight of Maoist excess. Born in 1937 into a prosperous farming family in southern Henan, Bu attended senior middle school and thus qualified to act as village accountant from 1955. In summer 1957, Provincial Party Secretary Wu Zhipu, a former student of Mao, launched a regime of terror to ensure that Henan was a front runner in collectivization and small-scale industrialization. Chayashan, China's first people's commune, was established near Bu's home in April 1958. Another first was the 'production satellite', in which peasants were coerced into twenty-four-hour working days to achieve miraculous output levels: daily output of 1.2 million tons of iron in Xinxiang county alone.

When Mao inspected model communes in Henan and elsewhere, local leaders queued up to deceive the head of state. Wu Zhipu claimed a 1958 grain output that was triple reality, yet many fields went unharvested as Bu and millions like him were busy smelting steel or engaged in local industry. The results were inevitable: Henan suffered heavy requisitions by the central government, and up to 8 million people died in the province alone. While his people starved, including over 30 per cent of the members of the Chayashan model commune, Wu constructed seven luxury villas in his capital, Zhengzhou, for the Politburo Standing Committee. He was demoted before he could host them, yet still earned Party praise at his death in 1967. The expensive villas were left to rot.

By August 1959, most backyard steel was declared unfit for industrial use. Mud-and-brick furnaces simply could not match large-scale, professional production, and a loss of RMB5 billion was admitted. After Bu's iron-making duties concluded, he taught at a local school until his retirement a few years ago. China finally exceeded Britain in output of major industrial products in the early 1980s, ironically at a time when some peasant entrepreneurs were profitably reviving backyard-furnace production. In spite of past excesses, China became the world's largest steel-maker in 1996.

AT VARIOUS MEETINGS we learned that the Great Leap Forward meant a leap in steel production. China was going to overtake Britain and catch up with America, and to do so we needed lots and lots of steel and iron. But making it was not just the task of steel-factory workers. The whole nation was to be mobilized to participate in the 'overwhelming central task'. We were called on to make our contribution: 'Those who have strength, give your strength, and those who have things, give your things.' The atmosphere at these gatherings was so lively and exciting. Hey, China would catch up with Britain and America! Our country needed our help. Right on the spot, some women handed over silver earrings, bracelets, hair combs, and even their children's pendants. Most were silver, and a few items gold. My wife gave away my mother's wedding present, a handsome pair of bracelets.

Like millions of other Chinese, I was involved in the iron-and-steel campaign. It began in August 1958 and led to an eventful autumn. A commune named Shaodian had recently been set up in our Shangcai county, following the establishment of China's first in Suiping county, some 50 li away. Almost at the same time, the communal canteen was introduced. As a member of the Communist Youth League and a village cadre, I was excited by the changes and keen to take part in whatever we were instructed to do.

Iron became the hottest item at the time. We all picked up scrap metal to hand in to our production brigade, now fashionably renamed the Rocket Brigade. Some vigorous lads were put in charge of collecting scrap. By then, since everyone was eating at the communal canteen, we were urged to hand in all metal cooking utensils, like pots and knives. Naturally, some people tried to keep a few things at home. But the metal hunters searched every household. When a wok or kettle caught their eye, they would smash it with an iron rod. 'Now it's no use, we'll take it as scrap metal.' They didn't even spare doorknobs or scissors, for the more metal you collected, the more revolutionary you were.

We gave away everything metal at home. I had no silverware, only strength and plenty of energy. Each commune was given a quota of people to send to the iron and steel refinery in Queshan county, some 110 li to the south. We were asked to volunteer and I did, since I was young and a brigade cadre. Others were less willing. The saying, 'born in Shangcai, die in Queshan', made clear we were forbidden from returning during our assignment. No one had any idea how long that might be. Once you were chosen, you couldn't get away anyway. One late August day, after shouting loudly, 'Born in Shangcai, die in Queshan!', a dozen of us from the same village set off on foot like soldiers going to war. There were a few hundred from the same commune, each carrying their own bedding. We reached Queshan in the afternoon of the second day.

We were stationed in Dawangzhuang village, 12 li from the county town, yet when we arrived there was nowhere to stay. The people sent to locate the iron mine in this mountainous area had makeshift houses of straw and mud, but not enough for everyone, and more came after us. A couple of thousand farmers from Xinyang laboured at Queshan to produce iron. We were divided into companies of 180 people, like a military company. Indeed, everything was a copy of the military system. We were soon given green military uniforms and the running of daily life was also militarized. Every morning, a bugle blew to rouse everyone. We received 3 yuan per month, a decent amount given a soldier's allowance was 6 yuan. Apart from myself as a group leader, there was a political instructor and company commander. As I was in charge of company logistics, I was given 50 yuan to buy cooking facilities, straw, and wood to build simple housing. The very next day, we started construction. We slept on the hard ground on bamboo mattresses. Only when winter came did we fashion some wooden beds.

My own job was not difficult, organizing supplies and food, but required someone who knew how to do accounts. The task of supplying fuel was given to another company. Although some wood was bought from the county, people mostly went into the mountains to cut down trees, any type, precious or otherwise. At that time, steel production was the number-one priority and everything else was secondary.

Our company was given two tasks: mining iron ore and making limestone from the ore. Local miners briefly showed us how to blow up ore with powder. After the ore exploded to pieces, we broke up the larger pieces with hammers. The second group worked on making limestone in a brick kiln. People had to work around the clock when fire-bricks were being made. Everyone laboured tirelessly for long hours every day. Given our total lack of experience, we worked quite well. Life was hard, but nobody minded much. We all felt we were making a contribution to the construction of our great socialist country. To be fair, conditions were not too bad at first. We had enough to eat, and occasionally even enjoyed meat dishes, which was not always possible back home.

When we arrived, the steel furnace was not yet built. People were sent to consult the technicians at the proper steel factory in Xinyang, and only a month later, five or six home-made furnaces got going at Zhugou, the headquarters of the iron-and-steel campaign in Queshan. I often had to walk the hour to Zhugou, for meetings or to ask for more rations. I'll never forget the excitement when I saw my first furnace. Half the sky seemed to be red. I spotted it from afar, as the flame shot

up into the sky—quite spectacular to look at! Not counting the base, each furnace was 3 or 4 metres high, built with fire-bricks. It was another month before we saw any molten iron emerge.

Whatever they did, they succeeded in producing some iron. It was fun to watch the red hot molten iron flow onto the cinder-covered ground. The solidified iron became pig iron, or raw iron as we called it, and was taken to the factory to be further refined. In the early days, the furnaces produced as little as one to two *jin* a day. But our leaders were always encouraging and optimistic. 'Even one *jin* is an achievement! It means we are closely following Chairman's Mao's general line of the Great Leap Forward!' The week of real production coincided with the nationwide 'week for the high production of steel and iron' in September. Our output was hardly high, yet a big celebration took place in Zhugou. Firecrackers were let off and drums beaten. Some read out their poems: 'Our spirits rise higher than the rockets; our will is stronger than the iron and steel; we are counting the limited days until we overtake Britain and America.'

Life in Queshan was certainly not dull. The priority given to iron-making was clear from all the song-and-dance troupes sent down to entertain us amateur iron and steel makers. Yet some people still tried to sneak back home for a visit. Those who were caught were badly beaten. I sorely missed my young family. Once, with the excuse of organizing food supplies, I returned home with a caravan of fifteen horse carts, only to find an empty house. My wife had been sent to work on a reservoir project 15 *li* away. Since she was breast-feeding our baby daughter, my mother-in-law went with her. Only because I knew our brigade leaders was she allowed home for a few days. In those days, many households in the village were empty, since all the able-bodied people had to work on irrigation channels or dig deep to increase grain production.

Towards the end of the year, as the amateur iron workers became more experienced, iron output rose considerably. On better days, pig-iron production per furnace could reach 500 *jin*. Then it was New Year, which became marked by the 'one-hundred explosions'. It was decided that we would celebrate a 'revolutionary festival'—meaning we worked throughout the festival. But since it was a special occasion, we had to do something special to lift people's spirits. Miners were divided into groups and given a specific time to blow up the ore. On 1 January 1959, a hundred explosions were made, starting from eight in the morning till six at night. So exciting! I guarded the entrance of the village to prevent people going into the mountain area, for stone was blown into the sky and shot all over the place. Luckily, everything went smoothly. In the evening, we were treated to a feast. Pigs and sheep were slaughtered, white spirits drunk, and many songs were sung.

That was probably the highlight of our iron-making days. Yet the loud and happy beginning did not bring good luck to the year 1959. It turned out a disastrous year that took away so many lives. The situation took a turn for the worse after the New Year. Food rations, as well as quality, were shrinking fast. Every month, each person's ration was 50 *jin* of rice and 55 *jin* of flour. Since our company's tasks were physically demanding, I usually asked for more and was granted it, but not anymore. It was cold, people were tired and homesick, yet we couldn't go home, even for Spring Festival, and we didn't have enough to eat. Shortly after the festival, the authorities decided to halt the iron-making. It was obvious that despite the effort and cost, we weren't producing much iron at all, and any output was poor-quality. A final meeting was called, at which the leaders declared, 'Starting from scratch, purely relying on our own hands, under the guidance of the spirit of self-reliance, the task of making iron and steel is now triumphantly completed!'

We were glad to come home, though the situation there was no easier. There was just no food. The provincial leaders falsely claimed such a high grain output that most of what we really produced was taken away from us, leaving little to live on. So many farmers died of starvation. For forty-eight days I saw no flour whatsoever, but I was the lucky one: before heading home, my boss asked if I would like to work in the commune or in the county as a cadre. I replied I just wanted to go home and it was arranged that I would teach at the local school. Thanks to the monthly salary, my family and I managed to survive.

How naïve we were to believe we could make iron and steel just like that, without proper facilities, training, or skill, yet so many people took part. Future generations may not believe what we did. People of our generation were simple, even silly. People nowadays are more clever. They will not make the same mistakes.

Bian Shaofeng

The Three Bitter Years

The numbers are almost too startling to comprehend. If his revolution began by emancipating the peasants, Mao's natural base of support, how could he let up to 30 million die in the worst famine of the twentieth century? In its long and troubled history, China was no stranger to famines born of flooding, drought, and dynastic upheaval. Yet by the time starvation reached every village in the land, New China was a decade old, at war only with nature itself, many granaries were full, and food exports reached record levels.

Equally disturbing is the way China has buried this darkest of secrets. While the Cultural Revolution is tagged the Ten Years of Chaos, the Three Bitter Years from 1959 to 1961 are officially known as the Three Years of Natural Disasters. Yet in many areas, like Bian Shaofeng's region of Anhui province, there was enough grain to eat. Why, then, did half of her village, including nine members of her family, starve to death? Bad weather and the mid-1960 withdrawal of Soviet technicians were terrible blows, but this was a man-made, Mao-made disaster. Its causes were political, as the misplaced fervour of the Great Leap Forward spiralled into fantasy harvests and excessive state procurement of grain.

If Bian was unlucky to live in one of the worst affected provinces, led by a tyrant desperate to impress Mao, she might still have escaped what was overwhelmingly a rural catastrophe, but for her politically incorrect background: daughter of a doctor who had once served Nationalist troops. She was born in 1930 in Fengtai county, but the Communist take-over saw the whole family banished from the relative comfort of the county town back to her father's home village. Bian married a teacher in the village, who in 1957 was himself disgraced as a 'rightist sympathizer'.

The Lushan Conference in August 1959, when Mao dismissed Peng Dehuai's concerns, literally tolled the death knell; there would be no relief from the vicious cycle of deceit, nor emergency relief from home or abroad. While city dwellers also endured rationing, the climate of secrecy, and strict internal passport controls, ensured ignorance of the rural holocaust.

Bian's younger brother, at university in Hefei province just five hours away, was unaware of his family tragedy. China's leaders closed their eyes and ears and foreign observers played down the crisis. Partial land redistribution in 1961 heralded a retreat from utopia and the return of sense.

Given the province's dreadful experience, it was perhaps no coincidence that, in the late 1970s, Anhui would pioneer land use reforms, begun in secret near Bian's home, that would provide China's best defence against famine and underpin the economic take-off of the eighties and nineties. Bian still lives in the same village, where her younger daughter farms and another works as a teacher. Bian herself remains illiterate, unlike three younger siblings who followed their father to university, yet few would doubt the courage and resourcefulness without which she would not have survived.

OUR PRODUCTION TEAM was called Xiaomiao, under the Liuji commune set up around August 1958. In the first few months of the communal kitchen we could really 'open our bellies' and eat as much as we wanted. Towards the end of the year, the kitchen started rationing, and food grew less and less. I didn't understand why there was a grain problem, as we had a good harvest that year. It was only much later I learned how different levels of leaders exaggerated our harvests so everything we produced was handed over.

Before the communes were set up, they gave us grain according to the work points we earned. After the communes came, we no longer had our own grain. It was even forbidden to grow vegetables or crops in the small plot of land behind our yards. We were told there was no need to store grain at home anyway, as the communal kitchen would look after our stomachs. Even our cooking pots were taken away for steel production in the 'backyard furnaces'. It was okay at the beginning, but the food grew less and worse, until it could barely be called food for humans. The little bit of flour mixed in the porridge with vegetables and wild grass soon disappeared altogether. The daily diet became sweet potato powder or yellow bean powder and grass soup. It was so runny and thin, almost like water. The daily ration per person should have been half a *jin*, but the production leaders and cooks kept some back for themselves. My job was to grind dried sweet potatoes or yellow beans for working days. Thanks to this job, my family and I survived.

Villagers began to die beginning in spring 1959. By that time, all the leaves and bark on the trees had been eaten. When you were hungry, you would eat anything. We ate all kinds of wild grass, wild roots, pumpkin leaves, and peanut shells; we ate worms, baby frogs, toads... it was disgusting to eat toads, as they made you feel sick. We ate rats if we could catch any, but often we were too weak. Animal bones became a delicacy. When we found one, we would smash it into small bits with a stone or hammer, and either boil it or stuff it straight into our mouths! We ate leather belts or anything leather. Once I boiled a leather strap used to bind the cow to the plough and shared it with my husband and our children. We lived together with his family, thirteen of us in the same courtyard compound. Everybody except me and my husband, our two daughters, and my niece died in the famine.

My father-in-law went first, followed by his wife. One morning, in late spring 1959, I came home from digging wild grass—every day we had to hand in some wild grass to the communal kitchen or they would not let you eat. I went to granny's room and saw she looked awful, with her mouth wide open. My elder brother-in-law managed to get a little yellow bean powder that I mixed with garlic shoots. But she was too sick to swallow. When I returned that afternoon, I found her already dead. My husband was away at the commune working on steel production, and no one else at home had the energy to move her. Her corpse stayed in that room for over two months until it grew rotten and smelly as the weather turned hotter. Only then, I begged the team leaders to send people to carry her out. When my second brother-in-law died, his wife was already bedridden with their younger child, a 5-year-old. I went to the communal kitchen to get their rations for them, but of course it wasn't enough to keep them alive. Their 13-year-old daughter was given as wife to a family in another village; otherwise, she would have met the same fate. Just like that, a large family of three generations living under the same roof shrank to a family of four.

By this time, all of the villagers had learned not to report deaths, in order to get the dead people's food rations. Then the production-team leaders demanded everyone show up personally for their ration. Sometimes they came to each house to check the number of people.

Still, it was easier to cover up the death of children. We kept secret my 5-year-old nephew's death for weeks until his corpse became too rotten. The dead bodies were just dumped in fields, ditches, or anywhere. There were too many deaths; no one bothered to bury them any more.

These corpses nearly cost me dear. During the harvest in 1959, hunger drove me to sneak out at night to steal from the fields, but the night-watchman found me. I ran and ran for my life—you could be beaten to death for stealing—but I stumbled into something and fell. It was a body. I got up and ran again. After a few steps, I stumbled into another body. The watchman, whom I knew, caught up with me. I told him I had tried and failed to steal some wheat. I begged him on my knees: 'My younger daughter fainted today. I just wanted to give her some food.' He let me go without reporting me. When my younger brother returned from university for summer vacation a few years later, he asked, 'Weren't you frightened to bump into a corpse at night?' But no one was frightened any more. There were too many deaths. We had already got used to it.

I said it was my job at the kitchen that saved me. Every day, as I was grinding the yellow beans or sweet potatoes, I would pop a handful in my pocket. The woman who worked with me also stole, as did the cooks. It was almost an open secret. As long as we didn't steal too much, no one minded. But a handful was only enough to save my immediate family, not everyone else. At that time, two families shared one cooking stove, but only for boiling water or cooking grass. If any leader saw smoke coming from your chimney, they would come to check. Thanks to my position at the kitchen, I enjoyed good relations with the leaders, who didn't check me too strictly. Every night I cooked the powder with grass in a metal pot that I had to keep secret. My other job was to collect about 10 *jin* of river weed, which we came to rely on. If I didn't collect enough, they wouldn't let me eat, but if I got more, I could sell it. Once, on the way to sell weed at Liuji market, I saw a man's body, but only the head and chest remained. When I asked a woman tending a cow nearby about it, she said, 'They chopped off the rest to take home to eat.' I noticed there was a chunk of meat in her own basket! Later on, when I saw dismembered bodies, I knew what had happened.

My brother in Beidahuang sometimes sent us grain coupons. Not very much, maybe 20 *jin* a year, but a huge help. With a coupon, we could go to the Liuji grain shop and buy desperately needed grain. We had to be careful, though, as there were several campaigns to search for hidden grain. We had a cabinet at home with a secret drawer where I hid our precious food. When the leaders came to search the house, I offered them peanuts and sunflower seeds brought by my brother. With such small bribes, they didn't search too carefully. I also dared to do things I wasn't supposed to. One rule stopped us picking up loose ears of wheat left in the fields after harvest. It didn't make sense, but it was an order. Anyone caught disobeying would be badly beaten. I secretly picked up ears of wheat whenever possible and hid them in my underwear. When I walked home, I bled between my legs.

This was why the famine was a man-made one. People often talk about it as 'the three years of natural disasters'. But there were no natural disasters in Anhui during these years—I don't know about anywhere else—and there *were* good harvests in 1958, 1959, and 1960. Why take away all the grain we grew? Why stop us picking up leftover wheat? They'd rather let it rot than let us eat. The leaders made the rules but didn't have to suffer by them. In our village, there were about 330 people; in the end, only about 150 survived. Most died between spring 1959

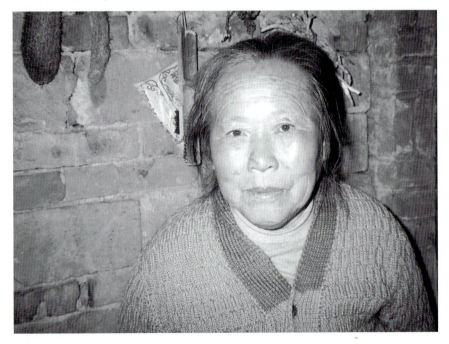

and summer 1960. Big and small leaders, their families, relatives, and good friends survived. The leaders not only had enough to eat but also *good* food to eat, like meat and fine white flour. When livestock died, even our own dogs, we weren't allowed to eat them, but had to hand them over to the production-team leaders.

There was a popular saying then: 'A man with a big face and strong legs is either a cadre or a cook.' Cooks became important characters. The leaders at the kitchen watched closely, but it was the cook who actually doled out the food. If you were on good terms with him, he would give you the thicker porridge from the bottom, not the runny stuff on the top. More people died on rainy days. As the rain stopped work in the fields, the team leaders saved the daily ration of yellow bean powder, which was slightly more nourishing, and served only dried sweet potato.

No one thought to revolt. We just put up quietly with whatever we had to endure. Not long ago, a few bold peasants from a village in this area detained the county Party secretary. They were upset at corruption and excessive taxes and organized the whole village to fight the policemen and burn their cars. The leaders ended up in jail, but at least they had the guts to do something. Back in those days, people were just so dumb. Few even thought of escape. Our leaders specifically ordered us not to leave the village, even if it meant waiting for death. The food rations for the whole family would be stopped if anyone dared not obey. One or two who tried to run away were caught and beaten.

At the time of the famine, people were not only dumb, but also numb, without feeling. No one cried when a family member died, even if the dead one was the dearest spouse, child, or parent. You just carried on as usual, going to the fields, or whatever. No fear of death, no emotion for the living. Maybe we were just too hungry to think straight. Hunger also drove people to be selfish. One scene still sticks in my mind. We shared a cooking stove with our next-door neighbours. On the day her husband died, 'Dacai's mum', as we called her, didn't report his death in order to get his share of food. I saw her lift up her head to gulp down the runny porridge. Her three sons rushed up to fight for the bowl, but she used a bamboo stick to keep them off until she finished!

From that day on, she refused to give them any food, though somehow, miraculously, they all survived. Dacai, at 11 the eldest son, joined my husband tending the production team's cows. I tell you the animals had better things to eat than us. We needed the cows to plough the land, as all the people had grown weak; my poor husband was so badly swollen with oedema he couldn't jump over a ditch. Dacai's middle brother went to stay with a relative. Most incredible was how the youngest boy, a mere 5-year-old, survived. He disappeared for a long time and no one knew exactly how he lived. It was believed he just stayed in the pea fields, eating the green shoots, drinking water from the river, and sleeping there at night. Since he was so tiny, no one accused him of stealing.

I shouldn't accuse Dacai's mother of being cold. I didn't feel that sad when my 1-year-old boy died. My milk simply dried out. At first, I gave him mashed carrots and peas when I remembered—I was so busy I often forgot him. But he was too little for such hard food. He would die anyway, as many infants and small children died in the village. But strong men died too, since they were used to eating a lot. They couldn't cope when there was no food to fill their big stomachs. I heard that in some villages all the inhabitants died. No one knows the exact figures. No one was allowed to say 'died from starvation'; all these deaths were supposed to be from disease. Among all the deaths, my own father's really made me sad. I was there when he passed away. He lived in a village 2 *li* from mine. Though he was very weak, he kept saying, 'Bun, give me a bun.' I said to him, 'Where can I get you a bun, Dad?' 'Bun, I'm hungry,' he moaned. My father was a doctor who saved many lives. I knew what could have saved him—a bun or some decent food. But I didn't have any.

After the harvest in 1960, the situation in our village gradually improved. Later that year, the communal kitchen was abolished. By 1961, land was given back to each family, so people worked hard again. The famine was over. Once you've lived through a famine, you never forget the feeling of hunger. It taught me to cherish grain, every single pellet. I often teach my grandchildren not to leave any food in their rice-bowl. When they throw soya beans at each other, I tell them a handful of beans at the time of the famine could save a life, but they think it's only granny's silly talk. Luckily, they don't have to understand what famine means.

Zhong Xunzheng
Bridge-Building

By 1957, infrastructural development under the Soviet-inspired First Five Year Plan had linked all China, bar Tibet, by rail. Only the mighty Yangtze, the longest river in Asia and the artery that cuts China in two, still held back the flow of people and goods between north and south. With no direct road and rail link between Beijing and Shanghai, passengers went by ferry across what seemed an unbridgeable expanse. It was a bold demonstration of Communist confidence when plans for a bridge at the old Nationalist capital Nanjing were announced. Like many ambitious projects of the time, it enjoyed the promise of help from Soviet experts—yet in July 1960 they withdrew en masse from China, taking their designs with them. Undaunted by the dramatic turn of events, nor the famine that was devouring China's villages, the government pressed ahead.

The spirit and necessity of self-reliance was an opportunity for home-grown talent like the young architect Zhong Xunzheng. Born in 1929 in Wugang county, Hunan province, Zhong was the eighth of ten children from a middle-class family. After graduating from Nanjing Engineering University, he stayed on as a lecturer, and in 1958 won the nationwide competition to design the four identical bridge towers. But just as construction work suffered frequent delays, so was Zhong's own career disrupted by Maoist distrust of educated people who were not Party members—the growing preference for 'red over expert'. From 1964 to 1965, Zhong and the entire architecture department were dismissed to the countryside for the Socialist Education Movement. Only as the bridge finally neared completion in 1968 was Zhong drafted in at the eleventh hour to realize his design.

In December 1968, to commemorate Mao's seventy-fifth birthday, the bridge was inaugurated, moving the Great Helmsman to compose a poem, 'One bridge flying over north and south; heavenly gully becomes a smooth road.' It took 100,000 tonnes of steel and 1 million tonnes of cement to create a 6.8-kilometre railway and 4.6-kilometre highway. Zhong received little reward for his efforts. From 1969 to 1970, he and the other members of his department laboured with the peasants at a May Seventh farm school. Teaching recommenced in 1972, but only to students selected for their model 'worker, peasant, soldier' backgrounds. The end of the Cultural Revolution, and the return of relative normality, was over four years away.

Zhong remains an active university professor, convinced his best work is still to come, though perhaps none will boast symbolism equal to that of the bridge towers. Both his sons are involved in design, while his daughter is an architect for the provincial government. The red flags their father designed, still illuminated at night atop the bridge towers, have welcomed over 1 million trains and 300 million vehicles during thirty years of service.

THE CONSTRUCTION OF the Great Yangtze River Bridge in Nanjing, one of the largest engineering projects in the country, was to be a triumph for socialist China. It was not the first bridge over the Yangtze, but the Wuhan link finished in 1957 had Soviet assistance. The Nanjing bridge, designed and constructed entirely by ourselves, became a shining example of how the principle of self-reliance could work wonders.

In 1958, as the bridge design was more or less decided, design work on the tower began. Most large bridges worldwide have towers, to connect road and rail and the ground level down on the river bank, and for administrative offices or viewing platforms. They are decorative too, adding colour and character or the whole construction may look flat and dull. The design task naturally fell on us at the architecture department of Nanjing Engineering University, due to its location and reputation as a cradle of Chinese architects. Our department head and two senior professors took up the work—I was too junior to be included. Somehow, the authorities were not pleased with their proposed designs, so a nationwide competition was organized. Our whole department was mobilized. After the initial failure, only a win second time around could avoid a great loss of face for the university.

Some thirty-eight designs from 200 proposals nationwide entered the last round of bidding. They varied from traditional Chinese styles with pointed spires and curved roofs to Western-style castles and modern combinations. I submitted three designs: one rather traditional, topped with pavilions—nothing creative or original about it, to be honest—and another featuring an arch of triumph—I knew the idea was borrowed from abroad, but we could add Chinese characteristics. My other design featured red flags. Though not a Communist Party member, I was young and strong and enthusiastically participated in the Great Leap Forward, feeding the backyard furnaces or helping out in the fields, whatever we were asked to do. In the middle of the Leap, 'red flag' became such a popular term and symbol of revolution it was simply everywhere. In the countryside, a red flag would be placed wherever we laboured. Since I was active in steel production, a little red flag was placed under my name on the university blackboard. Thus the idea of using a red flag to represent the time came into my mind. Moreover, the red-flag pattern, like statues, can easily be incorporated into architecture.

Top experts from a special committee for the competition reviewed the designs again and again, finally selecting a short-list of three to present to the central government. To my surprise, and delight, the first two were both my work. The third was similar to my flag design, with the addition of sculptures designed by Beijing Architecture Institute. I travelled to Beijing for the final decision, while the three proposals were being reviewed by the top leadership, in case any modification was necessary. However, in an indication of the importance addressed to the issue, it had been decided that Premier Zhou must have the final say. As he was abroad, I returned home and only later learned he went for my red-flag design.

Naturally I was pleased, but not as excited as my university! I believe several aspects made my bid successful. Firstly, the strong political message: red flags went down very well at a time when politics were emphasized. I must admit I only had two in my original design, and added a third at my colleagues' recommendation. Three flags made more sense, given the three slogans of the time: the General Line for Socialist Construction, the Great Leap Forward, and the people's communes. Secondly, my design was practical and easy to implement—others were too complex, such as utilizing train-track vibrations to generate power, while another hoped to harness solar energy. Thirdly, my tower design matched the design of the bridge. I had studied the huge model and liked its simplicity, yet it still looked magnificent and powerful. I tried to keep my design simple too, yet emphasize that sense of strength.

After the Soviet withdrawal in 1960, everyone in Nanjing thought, 'We'll show them!' Regardless of whether we could build the bridge well or not, on our own, there was great confidence that we could build it. Formal construction began in 1961, yet little work was done on the bridge towers, apart from simplifying the design from fear of Soviet attack—it would be a pity if highly sophisticated towers were bombed. I wasn't involved in the redesign. In fact, I had nothing to do with the project again until late August 1968, when the railhead was almost linked. Suddenly, the authorities informed us that my original red-flag design would be used for the bridge towers. We had one month, until 26 September, to complete the construction of the towers to guarantee trial opening of the railway on 1 October, the nineteenth anniversary of the founding of the PRC!

It sounded impossible—to construct such large buildings, over 70 metres high, in so short a time, and with only a rough design. But the order put us in no position to argue. For twelve days, I led students drawing up basic blueprints based on my original plan. Then we moved to the bridge site and worked and lived right there. Many detailed designs had to be drawn up while construction was underway, something I normally avoid at all costs, since it leaves no time for careful consideration or correcting mistakes. Luckily, I don't think we made any major ones, but the quality was pretty bad. I was amazed the towers were completed in time at all. For example, it usually takes twenty-eight days for the concrete to dry completely. To solve the problem, a powerful train engine hooked up by a pipe was used to supply constant steam that helped dry the concrete faster than nature. In the end, our construction speed was a remarkable one floor per day! Work continued throughout the night by workers on different shifts.

The entire bridge project was conducted under military supervision. Our leader, Commander Ge, was neither architect nor engineer. I appreciated his efficient military style but not his unscientific approach. As a matter of fact, he made our work difficult and our lives miserable. At the beginning, the steps leading to the ground floor were paved with marble. Commander Ge ordered a stop. 'China is not a capitalist country where we can afford to waste such fine material!' When the higher authority repeated that only the finest materials be used, he suddenly changed his tone: 'Why don't you use marble? The bridge will be a great feat of socialist China; are you trying to undermine it?'

Due to pressure of time, some trial methods were used without prior experimentation. For example, the flags were made of steel 3 millimetres thick, covered by red glass 6 millimetres thick. The sample pieces of plastic, produced by Nanjing Glass Factory for the first time, were red, shiny, and attractive, and looked perfect material for the flag. But the 60,000 pieces, made by workers day and night without stopping, were all different colours. Some were dark red, others light, some even orange or yellowish. These were then stuck to the steel flags by volunteers, not skilled workers, in a chaotic and hasty fashion. In the end, the flags, dirty and multi-coloured, looked torn and broken. Commander Ge decided to paint the glass red, but the paint simply wouldn't stay on the smooth surface, and the glass soon fell off and injured people. As a result, the plastic cover had to be removed, leaving hard-looking steel covered by red paint.

Zhong Xunzheng on the Nanjing Yangtze Bridge, 1999

There are actually four towers, a pair each north and south, topped by the 8 metre by 8 metre red flags, shaped as if flying in the air and decorated with golden tassles. Once the bridge was opened, the towers won enthusiastic praise. 'The eyes on a dragon', some suggested. Of course, one could only say good things about such a political project. Those who didn't like it or had doubts about it had to remain silent. Actually, it was only a small decoration compared to the bridge itself. Like lipstick on a pretty young woman's face, the tower might brighten it up a little. The three-flags image grew so hot it almost became the symbol of Nanjing for a while and was adopted in many contemporary architectural works.

Chinese people can indeed take pride in this double-decker bridge, the longest in China, designed and built all by ourselves at that early time. The earlier completion of the Wuhan bridge, another double-decker, broke a lot of ground, and the Chinese engineers who worked there with Russian experts must have learned a fair amount from their communist brothers. These experienced engineers also worked on the Nanjing bridge. The project's importance meant the Nanjing bridge had the best people and materials and enjoyed maximum government support and unlimited financial backing. Thousands of professionals, and countless volunteers, laboured away.

Yet judging by today's standards, there were major miscalculations in the bridge construction. The rail bridge was set so low that ships over 10,000 tonnes can't pass underneath, while the highway is so narrow that nowadays the bridge is blocked with daily traffic jams. Both mistakes were made due to lack of long-term planning, but then who could have guessed China would develop so quickly in recent years?

After its completion, streams of delegations from China and overseas came to visit. Sometimes, I was dragged along to receive them. Premier Zhou once brought a French delegation in the early seventies. In his introduction, Commander Ge lied, 'The bridge was built solely by ourselves without any foreign help or foreign materials.' But one of the delegation noticed a railway track marked, 'Made in France'. Commander Ge also told them the whole bridge was built by Chinese workers without any blueprints. Such ridiculous lies! I know he wanted to stress the role of 'workers, peasants, and soldiers' at a time when intellectuals were disgraced as the 'stinking ninth grade'. But as designer of the tower, I did feel insulted. Later, Premier Zhou sharply criticized Commander Ge.

I am pleased to see China does not repeat such mistakes these days—the new Nanjing airport was designed by Americans—but in some ways, there is little change, like the tight deadline pressure on particular projects to devote them to Party or government. China plans to build a national theatre near Tiananmen Square. A satisfactory design had not been agreed when they asked for my comments on it, yet they still hoped to complete it before 1 October 1999, as a gift to greet the fiftieth anniversary of the founding of the PRC. I said forget the unrealistic deadline. We've made enough such mistakes in the past, resulting in high costs and poor quality. The Nanjing bridge tower is a typical example.

I have not gone back to the bridge for a long, long time. I take little pride in it, as it was not my favourite work. I did my best at the time, but there is little to draw me back. In its defence, it does at least stand as a reminder of that era. My red-flag design suited government requirements. Now politics have been transformed. The worker, peasant, and soldier statues look completely out of date. Let us consider them artistic works bequeathed by history. Young people going on the bridge today look not for symbolism but a backdrop for tourist photographs. They didn't go through that era. They don't understand it, nor are they interested in it.

Li Sha

Goodbye, Elder Brother

From 1958, the ever-more public Sino-Soviet dispute became the focus of Chinese foreign policy. As Mao became disillusioned with the Soviet model, Krushchev openly condemned the Great Leap Forward and the people's communes. The split finally came in July 1960, with the sudden withdrawal of Soviet aid, technicians, blueprints, and all economic assistance. The Cuban missile crisis in 1962—'adventurism followed by capitulationism'—and the US–USSR Test Ban Treaty further convinced the Chinese that the communist alliance offered no security. The Soviet Union had betrayed Lenin's dream of world revolution.

The history of relations between the Soviet and Chinese Communist parties offered many clues to their troubled partnership. Paying lip-service to the importance of China's peasantry, the Comintern in the 1920s nurtured young Chinese firebrands like Li Lisan to export its brand of urban insurrection. A student in France and the Soviet Union, Li was Stalin's choice as propaganda head and effective party leader in China in 1928. The costly 1930 assaults on Changsha, Nanchang, and Wuhan cost Li his post, yet Mao Zedong faced another five years, and the trials of the Long March, before he could wrest control from the returned Chinese students and discredit their preference for positional warfare over guerrilla tactics.

The 'Li Lisan line' was roundly condemned and its author dispatched to Moscow's Lenin University to correct his mistakes. It was in Moscow that he met and married Li Sha, born Elizaveta Pavlovna Kishkina, the daughter of an aristocrat and his servant, whom he married after his first wife died. Stalin's purges were not the only danger in late 1930s Moscow: Li was framed by Mao's future henchman Kang Sheng and jailed for two years as a Trotskyite. Then, on New Year's Eve 1945, Li was informed of his re-election to the Communist central committee. He could return to China.

Chairman Mao's visit to Moscow in 1949 was the first time he had left China, yet behind the socialist rhetoric Stalin remained begrudging of Mao's success in adapting Marxism to convert a rural nation. Mao was obliged to swallow his grievances and negotiate what support he could. The Soviet elder brothers sent over 10,000 experts to guide China's reconstruction. Mao seemed to have forgiven Li, appointing him labour minister and trade union chief, though in a major 1956 speech, Mao still offered Li as an example of an 'intellectual turned bad element'.

During the Cultural Revolution, both Li Lisan and Li Sha were persecuted as Soviet spies. On 22 June 1967, the day after his arrest, Li Lisan took his own life with sleeping pills, though rumours of poisoning persist. Mao's criticism still hurt: Li left a note to Mao, denying to the last the charge of 'selling China'. Li Sha was arrested that day and held in solitary confinement for eight years, plus three under house arrest. Her daughters were jailed at the same prison for two years. In 1978, she was allowed to return to Beijing and resumed teaching until a few years ago. As she and her husband were both rehabilitated, Deng Xiaoping attended a memorial service for Li Lisan in March 1980. Li Sha's lifetime of Russian teaching was honoured with Moscow's 'Pushkin' silver medal in 1997.

WHEN WE MARRIED IN 1936, my mother-in-law was none too pleased. I was born in the year of the tiger and Li Lisan was a pig. According to Chinese superstition, tigers and pigs are not supposed to get along. She predicted I would bring her son bad luck. In a way, she was right. I brought trouble because I was from the Soviet Union. All the ups and downs in both our lives were closely linked with Sino-Soviet relations.

I had volunteered to work in the Far East in 1931. I was 17 years old and my fate was sealed. Just like in China, young people willingly went to poor and border areas to build the Soviet Union. I was assigned to a publisher in Khabarovsk, on the Chinese border. I knew hardly anything about China, but there I met many Chinese editors, wonderful communists who greatly impressed me. Once, I saw a picture in a magazine of a tall, good-looking Chinese man. The caption gave his name as Li Lisan, though he had changed it when I met him later in Moscow. I took a year to realize his true identity. He worked in the Comintern's international workers' publishing house. I was attracted not only by his appearance but because he was a determined revolutionary. I myself was only a youth league member.

In the beginning of 1946, Li was recalled by the Chinese Communist Party to work in Harbin, ending a fifteen-year exile. I barely wondered whether I was emigrating to China forever, or if I would like the country or not. I just wanted to follow my beloved husband. There were many Russians in Harbin, who had fled the October Revolution [that had brought the Soviets to power in 1917]. Nobody stared at me as I walked in the street, and shop assistants spoke basic Russian. There were still enough differences for culture shock—how strange that women all wore trousers instead of dresses or skirts! We moved south to Beijing after Liberation. I watched the founding of the PRC in the company of a Soviet writers' delegation, and it was arranged that I would teach at the new Russian Language Institute.

There was a popular saying then: 'Today's Soviet Union is tomorrow's China.' Relations were at their height and Russian was far and away the hottest foreign language. My students were keen to learn everything Soviet. All longed to visit in person, and some were indeed sent to study or work. Our institute held Russian evenings, when students recited poems by Pushkin and performed Russian fairy tales or Soviet stories. The cinemas were always packed when Soviet films, dubbed into Chinese, were shown. People loved Russian and Soviet literature. The most popular books were about the Great Patriotic War (World War II), like *The Young Guards* and *How Steel Is Refined*, whose hero, Pavel Korchaguin, became an inspiring model for Chinese youth.

A Chinese colleague asked how I engaged the interest of even the worst students. My style was more relaxed and lively than the Chinese teachers, but the students really liked me because I was Soviet. I enjoyed warm relations with my colleagues too, but sadly they hardly ever visited me at home. China was a strict class society, so they felt it inappropriate to turn up at a high-ranking leader's home. I missed my own home, particularly when my Chinese wasn't good enough, but my husband did his best to create a familiar environment. Like any international family, we compromised: if we had Russian breakfast and lunch, we would have Chinese for dinner. He had some difficulties with his job but, overall, the fifties were a good and stable time for us all.

Many Soviet engineers and other experts were sent to help Chinese industries that were often so backward they basically had to start from scratch. Others worked in scientific research, national defence, culture,

Li Sha (right), Li Lisan, and daughter Inna, Moscow, 1946

and education. There were celebrities among them, like the film director Leslie, and the ballet dancers Gusev and Tsaplin. China copied everything from the Soviet Union. In the cities, there was industrialization following the Soviet Five Year Plan; in the countryside, there was transformation of agricultural cooperation, though I must say, the Chinese communes outdid even our collective farms. In education, Soviet influence was everywhere, in textbooks and administration, even the way we conducted oral exams, with a vase of flowers and a tablecloth on the exam table. Sometimes Soviet teachers brought fresh flowers to replace the plastic imitations. It was all such a novelty for the Chinese; for me it was just the way oral exams were held. This imitation of the Soviet Union made me feel at home, but in some areas, even I believed they went too far. Just like the Soviet Union, China encouraged women to produce more children by rewarding them as 'hero mothers'. We needed more people after the Great Patriotic War, but China already had 600 million! Both my husband and I agreed with Ma Yinchu's policy on exercising birth-control, but after Ma was criticized, no one dared say anything.

Soviet experts were treated so well, enjoying the best China could offer. I myself was privileged to be driven to the institute every day.

The garden-style Friendship Hotel was specially built in 1953 for Soviet experts and their families. It housed an excellent Russian school, where top teachers from the Soviet Union earned up to 500 yuan per month, even more than Chairman Mao's 450 yuan, which was the highest among the Chinese leaders. Every summer, they took their families for seaside holidays. They were respected and well-treated by their Chinese colleagues. The experts enjoyed their lives here in China. They had their rules too, and mostly ate within their hotels. You wouldn't see them going to restaurants and getting drunk on vodka like people nowadays.

At first, I thought the relationship between the two communist brothers was so warm and close, like a blue sky without a touch of cloud. That simply wasn't true. Although my husband never said anything to me, I sensed both sides were constantly on guard. When I tried to invite a Russian friend for dinner, she revealed strict rules against visiting Chinese families. Not long after my arrival in China, the so-called Yugoslavia Incident occurred, after which the Soviet leadership regarded [the Yugoslav leader Josip Broz] Tito as a traitor, withdrew their experts, and stepped up vigilance towards Yugoslavia. Such vigilance began to be turned towards China. When Khrushchev turned against Stalin, the Russians were informed internally about his speech at the twentieth congress. A Russian colleague quietly told me the shocking news. Like many Chinese, and quite a few others around the world, I viewed Stalin as a God. I am no historian, but from what I can see, the Sino-Soviet relationship took a turn for the worse after that speech.

The tensions were obvious on 1 October 1959, when I was invited onto Tiananmen to watch the national parade, on the tenth anniversary of the founding of the PRC. The Chinese leaders and their wives lined up to welcome Khrushchev, but when he passed by, I noticed he looked gloomy and uneasy. [The Soviet ideologue] Mikhail Suslov beside him also appeared unhappy and nervous, his hair in a mess. His nickname back home was the Grey Bishop, as he was a very powerful figure but was rarely see in public. I guessed talks with the Chinese had not gone well. They left hastily the very next day, after the shortest stay of any Soviet delegation. It was a distressing signal.

The Guo Shaotang Case that summer was another. It started innocently enough, when Chinese scholar and Soviet passport-holder Guo Shaotang visited China in 1957 at Zhou Enlai's invitation. Guo, an early Chinese Communist, went to Moscow in the 1920s, where he worked for the Comintern and was friendly with Li Lisan. When he came with his Russian wife, many, except Mao, invited him for dinner, as did we, together with Yang Shangkun and Li Weihan [both of whom had studied in Moscow]. After his return, he sent gifts to his hosts—we received a television set. At the Lushan Conference, which began in July 1959, Kang Sheng called together all members of the central committee who had invited Guo, and asked what dealings each had had with Guo and what gifts we had received. Then he declared Guo Shaotang was a Soviet spy and demanded we sever all ties.

The Sino-Soviet split was finally marked by the withdrawal of Soviet experts in July 1960. I was on holiday with my family in Lushan, where we took a villa. A Russian family took the adjacent villa. The husband was a geologist and the son a classmate of our younger daughter. One day, we agreed to go swimming together, but they did not show up. Normally, I would not dare go to the home of a Soviet expert, but when I did I found the villa in a mess and the wife on the verge of tears. She had to pack for immediate return to Beijing. Her husband had been called back. 'I don't know why. It's not just my family; all the Soviet experts are being pulled out. I have loved living in China. There must be some misunderstanding; we will come back soon.' My heart sank, as I instinctively thought back to Yugoslavia in 1948. The same thing was happening to China. I sensed the problem between the two countries would influence our lives, but I could not expect to what degree.

In just one month, over 10,000 Soviet experts were called back, breaking contracts and leaving projects unfinished. Many left reluctantly, bidding farewell to Chinese colleagues in tearful scenes at railway stations. When I visited Russia in 1961, relatives and friends all asked why Chairman Mao had driven the experts home! I tried to explain there were ideological differences and both sides might have made mistakes. Both the PRC and the Soviet Union wanted the leading role in the communist world, and the characters of their two leaders played an important part. Mao must take some of the blame, but Khrushchev deserves more. His Ukrainian blood made him reckless and explosive, acting on impulse without considering the consequences. Even as leader of a large nation, he did not know how to compromise.

The Sino-Soviet split turned our lives upside down. Kang Sheng spread rumours that since Li Lisan's wife was a Soviet citizen, he most likely had secret Soviet connections. Taking the cue, someone we liked and trusted reported to the central government that I had close relations with the Soviet embassy, engaged in revisionist talk, and could well be a Soviet spy. It was all unreal—given my husband was a Chinese minister, I was the last person with whom the embassy would be friendly! Yet in 1962, a group was established to investigate me, without my knowledge, and my husband was questioned many times. What I did know was that people began to isolate us. My colleagues shunned me and my husband's friends no longer called.

He came under enormous pressure. Later that year, Premier Zhou formally demanded he divorce me, or face serious consequences. He refused. 'Deprive me of my Party membership if you wish. But I guarantee with my head she is not a Soviet spy!' He wrote long letters to Zhou defending me, until the Premier suggested a compromise: I surrender Soviet citizenship. I hesitated for two years. I was taught to believe giving up one's citizenship meant betraying one's country. Then I thought of my family. If this could save them, I would do it. Most Soviet citizens who married Chinese had left China with their children. But I didn't want to leave China, or my husband of twenty-six years. I became a Chinese citizen in 1964.

Yet that didn't save him. He was accused as a Soviet spy during the Cultural Revolution, brutally persecuted, and died. I didn't even know about his death until my daughters visited me in jail during Spring Festival in 1976. I was imprisoned in Qincheng without charge for eight years and exiled to Shanxi for another three. When I was rehabilitated in 1979, my certificate said I too was held under suspicion of being a 'Soviet spy'. Despite the troubles, I grew to love my adopted country. It may sound strange, but my affection towards China grew stronger during my exile in Shanxi, where I experienced so much kindness from the ordinary people.

The era of chaos is over and I live a peaceful and comfortable life. My greatest concern is the situation in Russia. Not 'the collapse of

Communism', as [Boris] Yeltsin termed it—communism will never collapse since it reflects the human pursuit of an ideal situation. What collapsed was a system that had been there for too long. My worry is that the country's wealth has been swallowed by a few powerful and corrupt individuals, while many ordinary people go hungry. I am confident China will not fall into that trap. Its top leaders did not just sit and watch what happened to the Soviet Union. They have drawn lessons from it and will not loosen the reins all at once. I approve of pushing grass-roots democracy step by step, but the so-called freedom a few dissidents demand is only fantasy and not suited to the reality of large countries like China and the Soviet Union. I am happy Sino-Russian relations have normalized; there are many good reasons to be friendly, as the two great nations and great peoples need each other. For the future, who knows? Look how we called each other brothers one day and traded insults the next.

Qiao Anshan

Rustless Screw

While fellow leaders argued for more time to recover from the Great Leap Forward, by early 1962 Mao was impatient to resume rigorous pursuit of socialist goals. As party and state were clearly obstructing his plans, Mao turned increasingly to the army for moral and factional support. Since the decline of Marshal Peng Dehuai, the sycophantic Lin Biao had turned the PLA into a 'great school of Mao Zedong thought'. In 1963, as the prototype Little Red Book of Mao's sayings circulated through the ranks, Lin found the perfect vehicle for reasserting Mao's authority: a model of the New Socialist Man, and, better still, a martyred soldier, whose memory could be shaped to serve any end.

'I will be a screw that never rusts and will glitter anywhere I am placed': Lei Feng was born in 1940 outside Changsha, in Mao's home province of Hunan. His future comrade-in-arms Qiao Anshan was born a year later in Liaoning province, where Lei was sent in 1958 to join the battle for steel. Soon after they enlisted in 1960, Lei's socialist work ethic and devotion to fellow comrades attracted military spin doctors. While he had hoped for a classic martyr's death in combat, Lei's demise exemplified a life of quiet self-sacrifice. In 1962, Qiao drove their PLA truck into a pole, which felled his best friend. Lei would forever retain his boyish smile as he polished the bonnet of his truck, darned his comrades' socks, or absorbed the Chairman's writings. The truck takes pride of place in the Lei Feng museum.

On 5 March 1963, all the papers in China ran Mao's inscription, 'Learn from Comrade Lei Feng'. His calligraphy also adorned Lei's posthumously discovered diary, a suspiciously well-crafted volume brimming with Maoist sound bites. The diary became a school textbook, as Mao extended the campaign by calling on the nation to 'learn from the PLA'. As the diary stressed, 'Honour should always go the collective. . . . If a small stream does not join a big river, it can never flow majestically for hundreds of miles.' After this first 'high tide' of learning from Lei, he became a weather-vane for socialist values, dusted down whenever China's moral fibre was perceived to be sagging: 1977, 1983, 1987, 1990, and again in 1993, when President Jiang Zemin became the third generation of the Chinese leadership, after Mao and Deng, to offer calligraphic tribute.

For many years, Qiao hid his guilt in the remote north-east, until a military writer co-opted his story into the most recent Lei Feng revival, *The Day I Left Lei Feng*, the top box office film of 1997. Cynics noted that attendance was mandatory (and free) for many work units, but Qiao's life struck a chord in depicting the difficulty of aping Lei in a modern, individualist China. Chairman Mao's good fighter was already anachronistic in the reformist 1980s, yet Chinese children still grow up singing his praises. On 5 March, 'Learn from Lei Feng Day', work units dispatch volunteers to cut hair and mend bicycles for free, while the Party machine offers latter-day saints, such as martyred cadre Kong Fansen and angelic bus conductress Li Suli. When not lecturing throughout China on his old comrade-in-arms, Qiao contemplates retirement from his driving job in Tieling, Liaoning. His other career is a lifelong task. 'Other people can stop believing in Lei Feng spirit; only I can never stop.'

IN 1959, WHEN I MET Lei Feng at Gongchangling mine, how could I know we shared a 'life and death destiny'? We had both been transferred from Angang Steel Factory. I worked at the iron mill, and Lei was assigned to the coking plant. As the plant lacked sufficient dormitories, he was arranged to stay with me. We were similar in age and soon became good friends. Since I was illiterate, Lei Feng wrote letters to my family and read theirs to me.

One day, we went to the cinema to see *Taking Huashan By Strategy*, an exciting film about the PLA soldiers who bravely seized a bandit-held mountain. Afterwards, Lei Feng solemnly said to me, 'Let's join the army.' On 8 January 1960, we formally enrolled, though Lei almost failed the physical, since he was too short at only 1.54 metres. But his eagerness moved people. Then Party Secretary Li from the coking plant refused to let Lei Feng go. Lei had frequently been praised as an 'advanced worker'. Li pretended Lei Feng's file was lost during his transfer from Hunan. But the army was determined and enlisted him anyway. Li finally gave up the file.

He distinguished himself on his very first day in the army. At a welcoming ceremony, Lei Feng gave a passionate speech on behalf of us new recruits. When a strong gust blew away his script, he continued without it, describing how he, a poor orphan, had been saved and raised by the Party. Now he was becoming an honourable soldier of the People's Liberation Army. He promised that we would listen to the Party and work hard to master military skills to defend our country and people. The local Party secretary was so impressed he decided to foster him as an activist.

After training, we were assigned to different platoons of the 7343rd Engineering Unit, based in Fushun. Once Lei became a squad leader in 1961, we worked together again as engineer–soldiers. Both Lei Feng and I were drivers, transporting supplies like coal, vegetables, and rice.

Not too long after we enlisted, a 'socialist education campaign' began in the army. At the time some people began to talk as if the Great Leap Forward had been disastrous, while others even questioned the country's achievements. Chairman Mao wanted the Chinese people to consider the positive achievements that the Great Leap and socialism had brought China. So he launched the new movement, calling for people to recall the bitterness of the old society and the sweetness of the new.

Lei Feng's poor background left him plenty of bitter stories to tell. When he was 5, his father died after a savage beating by the Japanese. To support the family, his 12-year-old brother worked twelve-hour days at a small workshop. One night, the boy dozed off and mangled his arm in a machine. The hard-hearted capitalist boss not only didn't treat him but drove him away. He begged his way home but without money for treatment he soon died. The family became desperate. Lei's 3-year-old brother died of sickness and hunger in his mother's arms. She was forced to become a landlord's servant, but on the night of the Mid-Autumn Festival, she was raped by the landlord's son. She hung herself, leaving behind 7-year-old Lei Feng. The village head, Peng Demao, an underground Party member, kindly took him in. New China gave Lei Feng a new life. From 1950, the Party and local government sent Lei Feng to primary school for six years' free education. After graduation, he was hired by a county farm and trained as a tractor driver. Later, he worked as an errand boy for the county government until he was recruited by Angang in 1958.

Lei Feng told his story so well. When he talked about his mother's death, he would sob uncontrollably. There were no dry eyes in the audience either. He became a model in the socialist education campaign. Military units, schools, and factories invited him to give talks. He travelled by train from place to place, performing various good deeds along the way, such as helping children to board, sweeping the floor, and bringing water to passengers.

In August 1960, Lei Feng made his name again. As bad floods hit the region, we were ordered to strengthen a nearby reservoir. Despite a bad cold, and the reluctance of the platoon head to take him, Lei Feng insisted on coming. We were digging tunnels, but the soil grew slippery in the rain. Combined with his short stature, Lei felt he worked too slowly with a spade. He began to dig the mud with his bare hands, working tirelessly until his fingers began to bleed. An old farmer urged him to bandage his fingers, but he said he was fine. His mouth was as busy as his hands, yelling, 'Come on, comrades, let's work harder! Protecting Fushun is our honourable task!' Encouraged by him, people's spirits were uplifted. He was awarded a Class Two Merit Citation for his role.

As he wrote in his diary, 'Treat one's comrades with the warmth of spring, do one's work with the zeal of summer.' He was so kind to people. Liaoyang county suffered heavily from the floods, so he donated 200 yuan from his small savings. Lei Feng knew from the letters he read for me that my family was also affected. Three times he sent them 20 yuan, pretending it was from me. This was no small sum, as our monthly allowance was only 6. It was meant to buy toothpaste, stamps, cigarettes, or cinema tickets, but he gave away his hard-earned money to the needy. One hot summer day, watching a sports game, everyone but Lei Feng bought 3-cent ice lollies. He quenched his thirst with tap water.

Lei Feng was such a friendly person, always with a smile on his boyish face, I don't remember him ever being cross with anyone. Every year, we were given four pairs of socks, two thick and two thin, though Lei took only one of each, to save the country's money. He was always darning them. In summer, his one pair of thin socks smelled strongly. There were strict rules about where we kept things in the army—socks had to go under one's pillow. One hot day, the soldier in the top bunk could stand the stench no longer. He threw the socks to the ground, whereupon Lei Feng picked them up and placed them under his pillow. Again they were thrown to the ground. Lei Feng once more picked them up with a smile. This infuriated the soldier. He threw them out of the window. 'Get out, stinking socks!' We all thought he had gone too far. Lei Feng must get angry this time. He went outside and came back with socks in hand, laughing, 'I know how to deal with them. Look, I'll wrap them in my shirt!' He placed it under the pillow and the other soldier gave up.

Lei Feng never showed off his good deeds. Sometimes, people only found out when thank-you letters arrived at the platoon. At the first Youth League Representatives Conference of Shenyang Military Region in 1961, Lei was elected a Model Youth League Member and a model of learning Chairman Mao's works. He was soon invited to give more talks. How did he learn from Mao's works? He applied his 'rustless screw spirit', studying them in great depth. After we finished our tiring work I would fall asleep once my head hit the pillow. But Lei Feng would sit down, read Mao's works, and write down what he learned. I often told him, 'Come on, it's late. Go to bed.' He replied, 'I cannot sleep without reading Chairman Mao's works.' He carried them everywhere in a green

army bag, reading them whenever there was time. By the time he passed away, he had read all four volumes more than four times!

The tragedy I will regret all my life took place on 15 August 1962. It was about ten in the morning when we decided to wash the truck at Company No. 9. We needed to turn the truck 90 degrees. My driving was not as good as Lei Feng's, so he encouraged me to practise. He stood outside as I turned the steering-wheel three times. 'Good, go ahead!' None of us noticed the left rear wheel had flattened a wooden laundry pole. When I drove off, the pole sprang back and hit Lei Feng on the head. I parked the truck 30 metres away and turned to see Lei Feng lying on the ground. I rushed over in a panic, shouting his name, and held him in my arms. To my horror, his head, nose, and mouth were bleeding and he was unconscious. We took him to the hospital for emergency treatment, begging the doctors, 'He is a good soldier of Chairman Mao. Please save him!' They failed. He was only 22.

Those were the darkest days of my life. I lost my best friend, my comrade-in-arms, and it was all because of me. I came under enormous pressure, though the investigation concluded it was an accident. The Party secretary told me it was not my fault, but I ought to keep it quiet. If anyone asked, I would say vaguely, 'Lei Feng died when he was on duty.' When the film director of *Lei Feng's Story* asked how to portray his death, the company leaders said, 'Any way you like, only don't damage the hero's image.' The film showed Lei being struck by an electric pole when he was on duty on a stormy night.

I was grateful the leaders treated me kindly. I was even a member of Lei Feng's funeral committee. After his death, our squad was renamed the Lei Feng Squad, where I stayed until 1965. I worked at another engineering regiment until it was demobilized and I became a driver in a construction team. During the Cultural Revolution, some began to question my past. I had to guard the secret despite my terrible guilt. When people joked, 'Hey, Old Qiao, how could you kill your comrade-in-arms?', I felt a dagger in my heart. In 1973, I took my wife to Tieling city, in the farthest corner of Liaoning, where I drove trucks and public buses. Apart from the old Party secretary who saw my file, nobody else knew my connection with Lei Feng.

In public, I had nothing to do with Lei Feng. But he lived in my heart. My motto is simply, 'To live like Lei Feng'. All these years, I have hung his picture above my bed. Each time I see it, I feel upset; yet I must look at his picture, to remind myself to follow in his footsteps and perform good deeds for other people, even if they do not understand. During one train ride, everyone stared at me like a madman when I began to sweep the floor.

Sometimes, doing good deeds can get you into trouble. One day in the mid-eighties, as I drove a truckload of shoes to Dalian, I noticed an elderly man lying on the ground near Shenyang. I rushed him to hospital, where I had to leave 1,000 yuan as deposit. When I went to retrieve the money, I met the old man's daughter, who asked for my driving licence. I thought she wanted my address for a thank-you letter, but as I replied, 'It was just something one ought to do,' she snatched the licence and put into her pocket. Only then did I realize they were going to blame me for the accident. They might never find the person responsible, so they would have to bear the medical costs themselves.

During the four months before the police caught the real culprit, I nearly collapsed myself. The old man's medical care totalled 40,000 yuan, but my monthly salary was only 55 yuan. My boss said that because of my 'heroic behaviour' the company would have to pay half the amount, even though it was not profitable. But as for the rest, my colleagues laughed, 'How foolish you are and what a nice reward you have won!' At home, my two children complained we couldn't even afford good shoes. I could bear it no longer. I travelled to Lei Feng's tomb in Fushun, where I sat up all night. I asked him how could I get into such trouble merely by wanting to save an old man? I then decided I would not take my own life. I swore I would 'take up Lei Feng's gun' and continue the path he did not finish. I knew he would do the same. My wife found me the next day and we went home together. The incident was resolved in the end.

Despite such difficulties, I don't regret what I've done. Lei Feng, my old squad leader, was my great benefactor, and, accidental or not, it was still my action that led his death. Every single good deed eases my sense of guilt a little. Unfortunately, there are less Lei Fengs in the reform era. Before, everyone's life was more or less the same. Now some are rich and others poor. People are more interested in money and more selfish than before. There has been a moral decline and Lei Feng has become alien to many. Some even consider Lei Feng and those like him as fools. But like Lei Feng I say we need such fools. The more of them the better! And it's not only the Chinese who can learn from Lei Feng, but people from capitalist countries too.

In recent years, there has been all sorts of unkind talk about Lei Feng. They say he wouldn't have become such a big hero if he hadn't died. Yet he was already a much-photographed model in the Shenyang military area, and became a Party member only ten months after joining the army. I heard the regiment had decided to invite him to Beijing to attend the National Day celebration. Lei Feng's dream of seeing Chairman Mao in person would have been realized. Some question if Lei Feng's diary was fictional. Of course it wasn't! I saw him write it with my own eyes and can swear not a single addition was made after his death. Others even asked if Lei Feng was a real person. Of course he was real! I lived and worked with him, and accidentally caused his death. All these years, he never had a relationship with a girl, though some people claimed he had. It was totally untrue because I was there with him.

Some vicious people try to deny Lei Feng: they say, 'Lei Feng comes in March and goes away in April.' What is Lei Feng spirit? It's not just sweeping the street for free, though that is one aspect. To me, Lei Feng spirit means selflessly contributing to one's country and people. Whatever you do, put the interests of your country and people first without thinking of yourself. Lei Feng spirit also means listening to the Party and the leadership. Of course, the leaders have to be honest and righteous—you must refuse to engage in any bad practice.

As long as humans live, we will need Lei Feng spirit. People must learn from him to love and care for each other. Some new Lei Feng have emerged, like Li Xiangqun, the son of a Hainan millionaire, who joined the army and died of exhaustion fighting floods in 1998. It's impossible to ask everyone to be like him, but at least we should all try to be good and responsible citizens. Recently, some students from Wuhan set up a Lei Feng website on the Internet. They wish to spread his spirit through modern technology. It's just another example proving that the Lei Feng spirit will never die. We need it now more than ever.

Making Revolution

1966–1976

By late 1965, as Chinese politics polarized into ever-more hostile factions, Chairman Mao left Beijing for Shanghai, where his third wife, former movie starlet Jiang Qing, was gathering strength for an assault on Chinese art and literature. The publication in November of a literary critique by one of her allies fired the first salvo of a power struggle that pushed the country to the brink of collapse. Far more than a purge of traditional culture, the Great Proletarian Cultural Revolution (1966–76) was an attempt to remake Chinese society. Mao saw his People's Republic straying from its proletarian goals down the slippery slope of revisionism. Like Lenin, he resented the privileged bureaucratic élite, who were growing ever more remote from the people who had sponsored the Party's rise to power. Where Lenin tried and failed to co-opt peasants and workers to supervise Soviet government, Mao chose class struggle to purge the party apparatus.

China was so highly charged in the mid-1960s that an imperial drama could spark it into chaos. The play *Dismissal of Hai Rui*, written by a vice-mayor of Beijing, ostensibly lauded the upright Ming official who fell foul of a wayward emperor, though few educated Chinese missed the inference of Mao's disgrace of Marshal Peng. To the coalition grouped around Mao, the playwright and his mentor, Beijing's mayor Peng Zhen, were prime targets for their insolence and resistance to cultural reform. They were dismissed in April 1966, and Jiang Qing was appointed to a radical Cultural Revolution Group that would challenge the Politburo in authority and later emerge as the Gang of Four.

When in the spring of 1966 the Beijing University administration tried to stifle wall posters attacking its president, Mao defended the right of protest with reference to his 1939 slogan: 'To rebel is justified.' In early June, Liu Shaoqi sent work teams into universities to contain the worsening anti-Party disturbances. The teams' withdrawal after fifty days signalled Liu's fading star. By contrast, on 16 July, at the age of 72, Mao swam the Yangtze River in a dramatic display of physical and political vigour. Two days later, after many months away from the capital, he returned to Beijing with a vengeance. During a meeting of the Party's central committee in early August, Mao demoted Liu down the hierarchy and displayed his own poster manifesto, 'Bombard the Headquarters', aimed squarely at Liu and Deng Xiaoping.

The Sixteen Points made public on 11 August set the course of the Cultural Revolution: 'Mobilize the masses without restraint... they will educate themselves in the course of the movement'. If this exercise of popular power later proved a bitter education for all urban Chinese, it was at first an exhilarating release for the students who donned the armbands and paramilitary style of the Red Guards, the vanguard of Mao's revolution. They received his blessing at a series of messianic reviews in Tiananmen Square, where the 'Great Teacher, Great Leader, Great Supreme Commander, and Great Helmsman' greeted over 11 million Red Guards. 'One single sentence of his surpasses 10,000 of ours', Lin Biao told ecstatic throngs chanting Mao's name and waving aloft his Little Red Book.

Stirring up trouble like the Monkey King, Mao's favourite folk hero, teenaged Red Guards smashed the Four Olds—old customs, old habits, old culture, and old thinking—in an orgy of vandalism and rebellion against every authority figure bar Mao himself. Their activities ranged from harmless absurdities like proposing the reversal of traffic lights—revolutionary red must signify 'go'—to a wave of vindictive brutality that savaged every aspect of Chinese society. Red Guard violence against their teachers, and the denouncing of their parents, represented the triumph of class struggle over traditional Confucian respect for elders and relatives. Intellectuals were derided as the 'stinking ninth grade' in a crowded rogue's gallery of class enemies. Since 'more knowledge means more reactionism', culture was pared down to Jiang's eight model operas, while true artists like the novelist Lao She, a patriotic returnee in 1949, were driven to suicide by Red Guard abuse, one of an estimated 1 million victims of the violence.

Class tensions fuelled bitter rivalries among different Red Guard groups. Students boasting 'five red' backgrounds—workers, peasants, soldiers, cadres, or revolutionary martyrs—joined conservative factions to preserve their gains under Communism, whereas students from 'bourgeois' families tried to prove their revolutionary credentials through radical attacks on their superiors. In January 1967, with the tacit support of Mao and his allies, radical groups seized the reins of local government. With its legacy of colonial exploitation, Shanghai seemed an ideal location to emulate the Paris Commune of 1871. However, after musing on the possibility of a People's Commune of China, even Mao pulled back from anarchy by reaffirming the need for the Communist Party: 'We must have a hard core.' Jiang's allies were ordered to transform the Shanghai People's Commune into a revolutionary committee, a three-way alliance of the PLA, Party cadres, and the 'revolutionary masses'.

In 1967, as military authority was asserted nationwide, China suffered a bloody summer of factional fighting. Over 1,000 died in the Wuhan Incident between April and July; Chongqing in Sichuan province was another flashpoint. The violence continued into 1968, notably in provinces where revolutionary committees were yet to assume control. In April, several thousand people were killed in Guangxi province, after weapons bound for Vietnam were stolen by opposing factions. Their trussed corpses floated down to Hong Kong, itself racked by unrest exported from the Mainland. By July even Mao felt obliged to condemn the 'mad fratricidal combat'. The Red Guards were forced to accept worker–peasant Mao Zedong Thought Propaganda Teams during the 'cleansing of class ranks' that took place from 1968 to 1969.

The first direct exposure to the Cultural Revolution for many peasants followed Mao's December 1968 order that China's educated youth go down to the countryside to be re-educated. These scapegoats for an urban insurrection even Mao could not condone became a 'lost generation'. While many were disillusioned by their fall from grace, others did their utmost to contribute to local communities by educating illiterate peasants and their children, offering badly needed medical care, and promoting better agricultural technology.

The Ninth Party Congress in April 1969, the first in thirteen years, concluded the most turbulent phase of the Cultural Revolution with the recognition of Lin Biao as Mao's 'close comrade-in-arms and successor'. Seven months later, Mao's original heir, Liu Shaoqi, condemned as China's Number-One Capitalist Roader and beaten repeatedly at mass struggle sessions, died in a Henan prison, deprived of medical care. A single word from Mao could have saved the former president of the PRC and chief drafter of the state constitution, but it never came. Zhou Enlai's attempts at mediation were often frustrated. He was unable to save either his cabinet—the minister for coal was beaten to death—or even his own adopted daughter, a victim of Red Guard torture. The Number-Two Capitalist Roader Deng Xiaoping, perhaps saved by his loyal support of Mao in the fifties, survived in exile at a provincial tractor plant.

Despite the decline in public hostilities, further campaigns maintained an atmosphere of terror and turmoil for another seven years. Thousands were executed in the 1970–1 witch-hunt for members of the May Sixteen Group, a counter-revolutionary faction that may never have existed. Up to 3 million of China's bureaucrats followed the students down to the countryside to toil with the peasants by day, and with Maoist texts by night, at May Seventh cadre schools, named after a utopian Maoist speech from 1966. Rural China was embroiled in crack-downs on sideline production, such as raising chickens, and continuous searches for hidden class enemies.

In the early 1970s, China began efforts to end its isolation from the West. Fear of US aggression had spurred massive investment—almost 50 per cent of China's capital budget from 1963 to 1975—in the Third Front, military and industrial facilities moved to the relative safety of the hinterland provinces. By the time the transfer was underway, the Soviet Union appeared the greater threat, particularly after the Sino-Soviet split escalated into border clashes in 1969. In February 1972, a year after the 'ping-pong diplomacy' breakthrough of the visiting American table-tennis team, Mao had the satisfaction of receiving President Richard Nixon in Beijing. The head of the world's leading power had come to his door. China finally entered the United Nations and Western technology imports began.

Rapprochement with the United States was a crowning triumph in the long career of Premier Zhou Enlai, who was now battling both cancer and the radicals who sought to derail foreign policy. Warmer relations may also have been hastened by the dramatic demise in September 1971 of Marshal Lin Biao, Mao's 'lifetime disciple', in a plane crash en route to Moscow after the apparent failure of a plot to assassinate the Chairman. Lin's downfall shocked the nation and speeded the restoration of Party supremacy over the military. Zhou enlisted Deng Xiaoping, returned from internal exile in March 1973, to strengthen the administration and the side of the moderates. Arrayed against them were radical elements centred on Mao's wife, who in 1973 and 1974 attacked the ailing premier through campaigns to 'criticize Lin Biao and Confucius'.

As universities reopened in the early 1970s, priority went to people with work experience among the workers, peasants, and soldiers. The hopes of many young people exiled to the countryside were scuppered by Zhang Tiesheng, an educated youth sent to Liaoning, who in 1973 returned a blank exam paper with a note explaining that his eighteen-hour days as a production-team head left no time for studying, unlike the 'bookworms' who did nothing for the country. He was admitted amid a blaze of publicity that exacerbated corruption in the enrollment process and confirmed the primacy of 'revolutionary purity' in a highly politicized society. It was still better to be 'red' than 'expert'.

With Zhou on his sickbed, and Mao suffering from Parkinson's disease, the key issue became succession. Jiang's faction maintained the 'politics in command' line of the Great Leap Forward—'a socialist train which runs late is better than a capitalist train which runs on time'—but for all their manoeuvring, Deng emerged as first vice-premier at the National People's Congress of January 1975. Soon after, he seconded Zhou's call for the Four Modernizations—in industry, agriculture, science and technology, and defence—to lift China out of poverty. Basic improvements in agriculture and public health, such as the 1 million 'barefoot doctors' nationwide, had improved life expectancy at birth from forty-one years in 1960 to sixty-seven in 1975. Yet the population explosion, from 586 million in 1954 to 880 million in 1974, served only to negate China's economic gains and condemn most Chinese to the same standard of living for two decades.

'Class struggle is the key!' maintained a New Year's editorial in Mao's name in January 1976, but most Chinese were moved more deeply by the death on 8 January of Zhou. Banned from mourning by Jiang and her allies, the people of Beijing chose the Qingming Festival in April, a traditional time for remembering the dead, to mourn their beloved premier at Tiananmen Square and protest against the Party. After the leftists blamed Deng for this spontaneous outburst, Mao's last political act was to dismiss him from all posts. On 28 July, the Tangshan earthquake took over a quarter of a million lives. Chinese tradition suggested a celestial portent of profound, dynastic change. On 9 September, just after midnight, Mao went, in his own words, 'to meet Marx'.

Mao's twenty-seven-year reign proved above all his unsuitability to rule the country he had conquered. Time and again, impatience at China's transformation returned Mao to the kind of life-or-death struggles that characterized his rise and the tempering of the Communist movement. Hidden from the consequences by a terrified court, he believed to the end his policies of permanent revolution were building a socialist system that would long survive him. The arrest of the Gang of Four on 6 October 1976 capped a stormy year. Mao's wife was now declared as evil as the traitorous Lin. A loss of faith in Party and ideology was inevitable. To engage the people productively would require an appeal to baser values than Mao had ever wished to admit.

An Wenjiang

Shanghai Rebel

As Shanghai's turmoil typified the Cultural Revolution in much of urban China, so An Wenjiang exemplifies the exhilaration and opportunity of life as a Red Guard. Born in 1944 into a seaman's family in Dinghai, Zhejiang, he moved to Shanghai as a youth, and first slept on a proper bed only on entering prestigious Fudan University. In 1966, An's final year of Chinese literature studies, the university became a hotbed of protest and internecine struggle. Seizing on his quotations—'Learn to swim by swimming; learn revolution by making revolution'—the student Red Guards became Mao's furies, out of their depth and revelling in the lack of restraints.

Amid chaotic competition to claim the Maoist line, Shanghai was held hostage to clashes between the Workers Headquarters, Scarlet Guards, and several hundred splinter groups rejoicing in names like the 'Red Hearts and Iron Bones Combat Regiment of the Spark that Sets the Prairie Grass on Fire Revolutionary Rebel Headquarters'. An and his young colleagues were emasculated in January 1967 by factions under Zhang Chunqiao and Yao Wenyuan, Jiang Qing allies and fellow Cultural Revolution Group members, and workers' leader Wang Hongwen. Yet their ascendancy did not signal defeat for the ultra-leftist policies An had espoused. Together with Madame Mao, Zhang, Yao, and Wang would soon comprise the Gang of Four, under whose radical influence the Cultural Revolution had several more years to run.

In the very next month, the municipal government and local Party organization were overthrown and briefly replaced by the Shanghai People's Commune, until the army was called in to restore order. From August 1968, An laboured at a copper mine in a backward county in Jiangxi province, though the factional fallout from his rebel experience was far from over. In 1973, he was accused as a 'May Sixteen element', extreme leftists reportedly opposed to Zhou Enlai and named after the 1966 order abolishing the first Cultural Revolution team. Following rehabilitation in 1979, An worked at a local school before transferring to Guangdong's

Fushan University in 1988 to teach Chinese literature. In southern China, where people tolerate politics but are interested in business, he has found a more relaxed atmosphere for his writing and reminiscence.

WHEN I WAS TEACHING at middle school, one of my students wrote in an essay 'the Red Guards were evil thugs'. She thought I was joking when I told her I was not only a Red Guard, but 'commander' of a rebel group. It made me realize the importance of portraying a truthful picture of the Red Guards in history. There were over 100 million of us. If we are accused of causing the Cultural Revolution, of being hooligans and criminals, such verdicts ignore the chief instigator of it all. Who turned innocent youth into monsters? Perhaps my story will help people understand us better.

On 18 August 1966, Chairman Mao went onto Tiananmen to review the Red Guards. It signalled China's entry into a crazy age. In Shanghai, the municipal government was obliged to declare support for establishing Red Guards there. Mayor Cao Diqiu organized the first city-wide group, the General Headquarters of Red Guards from Shanghai Schools and Colleges, later known as the First Headquarters. This was the conservative group always supporting the municipal government and Party, and made up of children of high-ranking officials, student leaders, and party members. Therefore, there was a strange phenomenon in Shanghai: official Red Guards were responsible for all the vicious behaviour like beating up 'cow's demons and snake spirits', throwing paint on people, and forcing them to wear 'high hats'.

Someone with my low background was naturally excluded from the official Red Guards, so I became more eager to participate. We formed our own combat teams, which later developed into various sections of rebel groups. I joined one called the Scarlet Third Headquarters, also known as the Revolutionary Rebel General Headquarters, to show we were in line with the Third Headquarters in Beijing, which was more radical than the First or Second Headquarters.

Before the movement, I had been quiet, obedient, and almost shy in class, but only because my free and reckless nature had been suppressed. Given the opportunity, I grew radical, daring, and enthusiastic. My

natural talents were an asset: I was a good writer and could talk for hours without written notes. I became leader of a Red Guards group. I can't deny there was a selfish element, a desire to show off, in my becoming a rebel leader, but it was mostly a conviction that the son of a working-class man should be allowed to participate in revolution. I rose to be the commander of our Scarlet Third Headquarters.

Interestingly, at Fudan University, most of the violence was conducted by the conservative Red Guards. It was growing more obvious that Mao supported the rebel groups—as he said, 'To rebel is justified!' The conservatives felt lost and depressed, but to prove they could also rebel they launched a 'beat the devils' campaign on campus. I'll never forget how they struggled against well-known professor Su Buqing. The Party secretary of the youth league, normally a gentle and kind girl, accused him at the top of her voice, then dashed a bottle of red ink on his head. Having pushing him down from the platform, she ordered him to crawl like a dog on the burning hot bituminous road.

On 24 August, Chairman Mao's first poster, 'Bombard the Headquarters!', appeared on campus. It had not been publicized before, and we were excited by its harsh criticism of 'certain' leaders for suppressing revolution. It happened that on the same day our section's representative returned from being reviewed by Chairman Mao. She had even shaken hands with him! We regarded it as a victory for our rebel groups. In a state of exhilaration, we organized a mass gathering to celebrate and invited radical students from other major colleges to share our joy. Near midnight, 1,400 of us marched off in high spirits to invade Shanghai's drama academy at the invitation of its rebel minority. Along the way, we held aloft Mao's poster, 'Bombard the Headquarters!', and sang the 'song of the rebels'. After our invasion, I chaired a heated debate that continued all night. Interestingly, some Tibetan students who came to Shanghai to learn opera were among the most outspoken and swore to defend the honour of the Party with their lives. A couple of them fainted from fatigue and overexcitement.

The next day, *Liberation Daily* ran an article praising drama academy moderates for their 'correct handling' of the dispute. It left no doubt we radicals were not in favour. On the twenty-sixth, conservatives from Fudan organized a 40,000-strong rally, attended by representatives from all Shanghai colleges, where Mayor Cao condemned the 'Twenty-fifth of August Incident' and criticized me by name. I was anxious but put on a brave face. As it was a low time for us rebels, I decided to make a pilgrimage to the capital to see Chairman Mao and understand the real situation. I boarded a northbound train, without my parents' knowledge. At the same time, millions of Red Guards from all over the country were also making their way to Beijing. It was called *da chuanlian*, exchanging experiences. I made contact with rebel Red Guards from Beijing and Qinghua universities, where the very first Red Guards started. Nie Yuanzi and Kuai Dafu, who were already famous, assured me that Chairman Mao was on the rebels' side. I felt overjoyed with relief, as I knew they received instruction 'straight from Mao'. Through some well-connected Red Guards, I was arranged to be on top of Tiananmen for the 15 September review.

What a privilege! I was not one of tens of thousands of faceless Red Guards down in the square, but among thirty lucky ones up top. We rose very early and arrived at Tiananmen before sunrise. We waited for several hours until, all of a sudden, Chairman Mao appeared to the music of 'The East is Red'. Wearing a green army uniform and a Red Guard armband, he walked slowly towards us, accompanied by Lin Biao and Zhou Enlai. I was breathless with excitement, as my heart raced and tears poured down. A girl behind me fainted from happiness. My own joy was beyond words. Back home, I had been criticized, but here on top of Tiananmen, the heart of China, I was reviewed by our great leader Chairman Mao, and at such close range (so close I couldn't help noticing he wasn't quite as 'radiant' as the papers claimed). The whole square seethed with young people crying and chanting. He was our God and we worshipped him absolutely: 'Chairman Mao! Chairman Mao! Long live Chairman Mao!'

Afterwards, I ran to the post office to send a telegram. A notice explained all telegrams about Chairman Mao's review were free, so I sent four long messages to family and friends. I wanted them to share my happiness. My trip to Beijing convinced me more than ever that Mao was on our side.

On returning to Shanghai I threw myself into the movement with doubled zeal and organized a number of friends to buy pictures of Liu Shaoqi from the large Xinhua bookstore on Nanjing Lu, Shanghai's busiest road. Then we burnt them in broad daylight. People were stunned. Liu was chairman of the PRC—how daring we were! More and more people surrounded us, some with condemnation, most with curiosity. We burnt Liu's picture because we heard Mao accuse him as a capitalist roader. I didn't know Liu personally, of course, but if Mao said he was bad, he must be bad. Even if no one else had yet dared to speak out in Shanghai, we certainly did!

Burning Liu's picture was not the craziest thing I did. The 'January storm' struck Shanghai in 1967. It was triggered by the *Red Flag* editorial for New Year's Day, which encouraged the revolutionary people to overthrow power held by the capitalist roaders in the Party. After Mao's approval of the rebel takeover of the *Wenhuibao* newspaper, the Party mouthpiece in Shanghai, as well as the ouster of city leaders, many government organizations, ports, and railway authorities were seized by radicals. I chose a hard nut to crack: the city's Public Security Bureau [the police force].

On the morning of 11 January, I directed over 3,000 Scarlet Third Headquarters Red Guards on a march from People's Square. The Public Security Bureau was the tool of the proletariat dictatorship and we were the proletariat revolutionary people. We had contact with rebels within the bureau, and did not meet strong resistance, as if the leaders knew what was coming. At the time, all party and political organizations in Shanghai were paralyzed or semi-operational. We called all high-ranking cadres to a meeting to declare our take-over. They were hardly happy about it, but few raised opposition. We established a take-over committee and seized the ten district and county security bureaus, though we kept administrators at their posts and didn't release any criminals.

There were obvious conflicts among the rebel workers and students in Shanghai. We talked about working together, but in reality neither kept the other side informed. I believe most Red Guards taking part in the January storm were convinced they were making revolution, while some worker rebels were more interested in power and material interests. On behalf of the Workers Headquarters, Wang Hongwen said our take-over was illegal, because it was not a collective rebel act. He sided with Zhang Chunqiao, Jiang Qing's closest ally and deputy director of the central Cultural Revolution Group, who was sent to Shanghai at that time. Zhang should have supported our rebellious action, but for some reason got cold feet. For two days we came under enormous pressure until a *People's Daily* article expressed continued support for the rebels' power seizure in Shanghai. Only then did Zhang change his tone.

As if I hadn't been reckless enough, I helped organize the 'Bombard Zhang Chunqiao Incident' that was praised over ten years later: 'Some students already saw clearly the evil face of the Gang of Four.' That wasn't really the case; rather I had an instinctive dislike of Zhang, and we were guided by the theory of 'suspecting everything'. After the old Shanghai government leaders were overthrown, the Red Guard radicals looked for new authorities and targets to attack. A few days after our victory at the security bureau, we attacked Zhang and his followers with wall posters entitled, 'Beware the Two-Faced Counter-Revolutionary', and 'Long Live the Spirit of Suspecting Everything'.

On 26 January, the attack on Zhang came into the open. More posters like 'Beware China's Khrushchev' attracted many people to Fudan. That afternoon, he was invited to the Friendship cinema to meet 600 Red Guards from the radical Red Revolutionary Committee. He and Yao Wenyuan were verbally attacked and abused for nearly six hours. Meanwhile, Fudan Red Guards from the same group kidnapped Xu Jingxian and Guo Renjie, Zhang's closest allies, and detained them inside the foreign languages building. On the evening of the twenty-eighth, Zhang sent armed vehicles to Fudan, threatening to rescue the pair by force and crack down on troublemaking students.

Under such pressure, the three different radical groups stopped their in-fighting to form an 'anti-Zhang sacred union'. Even moderate students were outraged by the military presence and

An Wenjiang struggling against Shanghai Mayor, Cao Diqiu, 1967

responded to the call, 'Protect Fudan!' During a massive emergency assembly, some friends urged caution, but instead I sharply attacked Zhang: 'Pointing guns at us Red Guards means pointing them at our great leader Chairman Mao!' It was agreed a city-wide meeting would be held on the thirtieth at People's Square, followed by a mass demonstration. Our slogan was '10,000 Cannons Bombarding Zhang Chunqiao'. Everyone was so excited; the powerful yelling of slogans seemed to have shaken the sky. At this point, I really thought we could bring him down. I was totally mistaken.

The next day, propaganda teams drove into Fudan spreading an emergency telegraph from the central government. It was a strong warning against those who tried to oppose Zhang. On the same day, Xu and Guo left by car from Fudan, which fell into the hands of Zhang's protectors. In disbelief, a few of us even went to Beijing to confirm the authenticity of the telegraph. How naïve I was. Shanghai had become the example of power seizure in China, and Zhang was the hero of the January storm. How could we possibly overthrow him? I was struggled against after returning to Shanghai. A Red Guard friend despaired: 'It's all finished! We destroyed too much, including ourselves!' I became disheartened with the whole movement.

In January 1967, the Red Guard movement had reached its height, and it rapidly went downhill. One no longer read about 'revolutionary salutes to the Red Guards' in the newspapers. We had caused enough trouble; our historical mission was complete. In his own words, we served as Mao's 'monkey king', someone with revolutionary fever who was willing to fight in the forefront, yet lacked cool and sensible judgement. He made use of the ignorant, irrational, and enthusiastic nature of the Red Guards to bring down Liu Shaoqi and other leaders. But once the fire was lit, we were no longer his darlings. It was time for us to calm down and for the workers, peasants, and soldiers to take over the movement. Mao's heart could not be at ease with these kids taking control of power. Before long, most of us were sent to the countryside.

Why did we become monsters? It was the system! Mao himself must certainly shoulder part of the blame; he can never avoid that, nor many of the older leaders, even Premier Zhou, who said and did things against his conscience to please Mao. If every official was like Peng Dehuai, how could teenage Red Guards stage a drama that turned China upside down?! On top of 1,000 years of feudal dictatorship were seventeen years of Communist education designed to serve the political system. University students were taught revolutionary education, dialectical and historical materialism. Middle school students were more naïve and irrational. With even less exposure to Western literature and its humanitarian themes, they were the most radical and destructive Red Guards.

Almost all our heroes were from wartime. We admired the red uprisings by the Communists. Violence and brutality were not negative words, if used against class enemies. The more violent and brutal the better! We were made to believe enemies were all around us. There had been the anti-rightist movement, there was talk of Chiang Kaishek retaking the Mainland, the anti-revisionist struggle was raging . . . now Chairman Mao called on us to rebel, to bombard, to destroy, and we did so without hesitation. Just like a bunch of mad dogs, once angered each tries to be madder than the rest. If you dared to kick the bottom of the person we are struggling against, I would strike him on the head with a stick.

We were told to learn from Lei Feng, a soulless tool. People from such a nation have no independent thinking and inevitably end up slaves of trends or ideology. Political movements followed one after another, but this wasn't socialism. We called the Soviet Union 'social imperialism', yet ours was 'social feudalism'. Only such a nation could be the breeding ground for a red dictator like Mao Zedong. We sang 'The East is Red', praising Mao as our great saviour, and that's how China worshipped him: '800 million people, one mind!' Yet the Internationale states, 'There has never been a god or emperor.'

The Red Guard movement was a historical tragedy. As executors of the movement, we caused irreparable damage, suffering and misery beyond words. We must reflect on the past and our wrongdoings. After I reported a classmate who criticized Lin Biao, he served fifteen years' imprisonment. I still feel terrible guilt and would apologize if I could find him. But if only the Red Guards are made to repent, we don't learn the real lesson from the Cultural Revolution. The whole Chinese nation must repent.

As time goes by, most people will gradually forget the Red Guards' past. Those who suffered at their hands may forever regard them as evil. A friend who did suffer recently saw a tomb for a group of Red Guards aged from 13 to 19 in a Chongqing park. Did they die for fame or for personal interest? No. They died shouting 'Long live Chairman Mao!' They died defending their 'revolutionary cause'. My friend began to sense the Red Guards were victims too. Many lost their lives in the movement, yet history regards them not as martyrs but mere sacrificial offerings. No matter how you view them, do not doubt their sincerity and loyalty. And may China never forget the simple lesson we need to draw: let people live like human beings; don't treat them like machines who know only to obey.

Wu Xiaoping

Down to the Countryside

For many Chinese, the phrase *laosanjie*, Old Three Grades, evokes some of the most poignant memories not only of the Cultural Revolution, but the entire, bitter-sweet experiment of the past fifty years. By the spring of 1969, almost all the 10 million students who had graduated from China's middle schools in 1966, 1967, and 1968 had been dispatched to learn from the peasant masses and contribute to rural production. *Laosanjie*, those lost three student years, became a byword for all 14 million 'educated youth', some 10 per cent of China's urban population, who were forced to 'go up the mountains and down to the countryside'.

Mao had long advocated the benefits of urbanites sharing experiences with China's peasants (the Maoist Pol Pot would later take this philosophy to even further extremes), yet it was the failure of the Cultural Revolution that turned his policy into a mass movement. Wu Xiaoping had always been a reluctant Red Guard. Not only did she repel from struggling against her teachers or smashing the Four Olds; often she was simply not invited. Born in 1951 in Zhangjiakou, Hebei, to soldiers-turned-teachers, Wu later moved with her family to Xi'an. When her parents' college assumed civilian status in 1965, Wu's background became neither too 'red' nor too 'black'. She may have been ignored when her peers were raising hell, but neither was she attacked.

By July 1968, the Red Guards were a spent force. They had failed in their mission, Mao said, but how to handle the hordes of young activists clogging China's cities? No colleges (shut) or factories (barely functioning) could take them. It was time to institutionalize their thirst for new experiences. Like her classmates, the 18-year-old Wu was torn from her home and sent into remote, rural exile. The country paid a high price for Mao's dream, both the city families striving to support distant dependants and the communes forced to receive these additional burdens on already scarce resources. Besides the lost opportunities for education and advancement, some students were persecuted, women were raped, and many chose suicide, while accidents, heavy workloads, malnutrition, and lack of medical care killed thousands.

Admittance in 1973 to an agricultural college 200 kilometres from Xi'an served as Wu's stepping-stone back to a 'normal' life. Her family found a husband in the hope she could come home, but residence restrictions kept them apart until 1981, when Wu returned with their young daughter. Wu blames her subsequent divorce on the special circumstances that underlay many marriages, and the difficulty of resettling in a society poorly equipped to deal with *laosanjie*. Working for a trading company, Wu now lives alone in Xi'an, while her daughter studies in Beijing. The wider introspection of the nineties has seen former students gather to recall the camaraderie of harsh but more simple times. Many suffered and were toughened by their experience. Former *laosanjie* include some of China's foremost writers, film directors, enterpreneurs, and government officials.

WHEN CHAIRMAN MAO called on China's youth to go down to the villages to be re-educated by peasants, all my classmates responded enthusiastically . . . except me. Some might have truly believed they could achieve great things in the 'vast new world of the Chinese countryside'. I didn't want to go for one important reason: I was not that active during the movement. I thought life in the countryside was hard and I was too young. My parents didn't want me to go either.

Naturally, I was very keen when the Cultural Revolution first started. I joined millions of other students to go to Beijing to see Chairman Mao in October 1966; one of the most unforgettable experiences of my life. But after that, when the situation turned chaotic, I hardly participated in the rebellious activities—in any case, my weak background did not permit me. Soon, pressure mounted for me to go to the countryside. People came to our home to persuade or threaten. In the street, neighbours would ask, 'Everybody else has gone, why are you still here? Anything wrong with you?' It was awkward for my mother that her daughter remained at home, for she was a teacher assigned to persuade reluctant students to go down to the countryside. Delay provided no real escape.

As all my classmates had gone, my family began to search for companions for me. Somehow, we felt the move to the country was permanent. Many parents matched their children with potential partners in the hope they would look after each other in the countryside, and possibly marry in future. The guy my family found lived in the same compound; he was fine (though I never took a fancy to him!). It was January 1969 when we left, with his younger sister and another girl and boy from his school. When the first few batches of students had left, they were accompanied by lively farewell ceremonies, beating drums and gifts of flowers at railway stations. We departed quietly, to a remote village in the Qinling Mountains of south-west Shaanxi.

Naturally, the place was chosen for us. The people who came to persuade us described its beauty: lovely mountains, clear water, birdsong all day long . . . you know, we urban people often harbour romantic notions about country life. Reality was quite another picture: desperately poor, isolated and backward, not even that pretty, Qinyangou couldn't be reached by bus or any other form of transport. When we arrived, some of the older men still kept their hair in long pigtails like Qing-dynasty queues, while the younger men had long, loose hair down to their shoulders. I found them rather frightening. Most never went beyond their commune and few saw rice coupons. Only after a rocket factory was moved nearby from the outskirts of Beijing was the total isolation of the village broken: in the late 1960s, fearful of Soviet nuclear attack, Mao ordered some important factories to be re-located to the Third Front in the remote hinterland.

Wu Xiaoping on a home visit, Xian, 1969

In the very beginning, I didn't mind the tough farm work too much, as everything was new to me. I was young and took whatever life gave. We five comprised the eighteenth family in the village production team. Each house was built far from another, wherever the hilly loess land was flat enough. They arranged for us three girls to stay at the headquarters of the production team, while the two lads occupied the kitchen of an old couple. After a few months, they put us together in a mud barn deeper in the mountains. It was actually a cow shed, simply built, with no window and a bamboo fence separating male and female halves, though, of course, one could easily see through. When we cooked, the whole room filled with smoke, for the wood and leaves we foraged outside were often wet. It took us a long time to master how to light the fire and keep it going: we had to blow it with a pipe, but after each blow, our faces would be covered by ash. How funny we looked! It was part of the excitement of our new environment.

We felt so free with no teacher or family to control us. The production team did not meddle much in our business, either. We were given some food to start with, before we could earn our own; then we were very much left alone. It was the first time the commune had ever received any 'educated youth', so no one knew exactly how to deal with us. While peasants in the Shaanxi plains were so attentive to their land, the local peasants merely scattered seeds and harvested whatever happened, purely depending on nature. With scarce rainfall and water sources, it was quite impossible to water everything. They paid most attention to the maize they grew on flatter fields or riverbanks.

Unlike students in some areas, we did not have to labour till we dropped. In a typical morning, we would till one row and reach the end near noon when people stopped to chat, smoke pipes, do needlework, and gossip. After lunch, we tilled back to where we had started! At the end of the day, the peasant team leaders would judge each person's work points. The top mark for a day's work was 10: an able-bodied man could usually achieve 9 or 10, and a local woman 7 or 8. I normally got only 4 to 6, but I didn't care one mark more or less. I earned just about enough for my basic food; for the rest I had to rely on my family. Without our families' support, none of us would have survived.

Another twist was that we had been sent down to learn from the 'poor and low peasants', but the local peasants were either former bandits or remnants from Nationalist troops who fled into the mountains after the Communist victory. Our Party secretary, a former beggar from Gansu province, was made village head principally because he had not been a bandit or enemy soldier! These discoveries did not boost our already low morale. In any case, the relationship between the educated youth and the local peasants was universally bad. I never felt part of them, even when I later lived with a local family. They called us *zhiqing ye* or *zhiqing nai* (lord or lady of educated youth), meaning we were stuck-up urbanites who looked down on dirty farming work.

Fierce fighting with the local peasants broke out at a neighbouring production team where more educated youth were stationed. The students kept a nasty dog, who was friendly to them but often bit the locals. This snobbish dog started the trouble, though the urban lads made it worse by stealing chickens and killing other dogs. We stole too. One boy became an expert chicken rustler. In the winter, he would go out at night when our craving for chicken was too strong to resist. He wore a large People's Liberation Army coat with a string tied around his waist. He used a torch to mesmerize and silence the chicken. Snap! He quickly broke the chicken's neck, tied it around his waist and ran home. We would all help to clean and prepare it for stew. When the poor chicken was being cooked, we would gather round the huge cooking pot to watch with watery mouths. Even before it was ready, most of the chicken would have been eaten! The taste was heavenly. We also used a rope to strangle dogs—the meat was equally tasty and nourishing.

After the initial excitement was over, life grew hard and dull. What drove us to kill chickens and dogs? Not only did we labour in the fields, but the food was awful and always the same: sweetcorn, noodles made from cornflour, cornflour buns, porridge with sweetcorn, or cornflour paste. The locals did not grow vegetables—all they had were edible tree leaves picked in the spring to dry or pickle. On 29 September 1969, I wrote in my diary: 'Today, the brigade distributed some crops to us. Can you imagine that we have now begun to live the life of "Peasant's Happiness"? Yes, it is a fact. In the coming winter months, we'll grind the wheat and corn and collect firewood for cooking—everything we do is for our mouths! I've not been happy for several days under this grey rainy sky. Time continues to disappear on my bed, in my room, at the cooking stove. In future, when I recall these days, won't my face be red, won't I feel ashamed? Yet I can't do anything.'

Life repeated itself day after day. We rose at about eight, but were usually woken earlier by the noise of the nearby assembly of the village's 'five bad elements'. Every morning, these poor people had to gather to admit their errors and ask for punishment from Chairman Mao. After breakfast, we marched off to work at a place assigned the previous day by the production-team leader. This could be anything from half an hour to two hours' walk. If the site was close enough, we would return home to cook lunch (the same as breakfast); otherwise, we took corn buns for lunch. After supper (the same as lunch), we were often called to meetings at the production-team headquarters, to struggle against the bad elements or listen to somebody reading the latest government circular or party newspaper.

On evenings without meetings, time didn't pass any quicker. We had no books, magazines, newspapers, or television. We sometimes sang in our little room, accompanied by a miserable oil lamp. Our favourites were the bitter 'songs of educated youth', like this one:

Having said goodbye to mother, we left our hometown.
The golden age as a student has become history and will never return.
The future path is so hard and long.
The footsteps of life are marked in the remote countryside.
Rising together with the sun and returning with the company of the
    moon.
The heavy work of tilling land is my sacred task, as well as my fate.
Ah! We are embroidering the globe, making it red throughout,
Looking forward to tomorrow.
With faith, it will certainly come.

Yet I was fortunate to spend each Spring Festival, the most important festival in China, with my family in Xi'an—it helped keep me sane, especially in the later stages, though I didn't dare stay too long, for food was rationed and I thought good behaviour in the village might win me the chance to study or work in the city. One by one, my four companions exploited their parents' good connections to become 'honourable' soldiers; my family tried too, but without success. The last two years on my own was the hardest time. I felt deserted not only by my four mates, but also by the whole world. The loneliness almost drove me crazy. There were other educated youth in other production teams, but all too far away. We educated youth were discriminated against by the workers at the rocket factory. At that time, workers were respectfully called 'big brothers' and the peasants 'second brothers', a rather insulting term. We were kind of 'neo-second brothers'. Once, the daughter of the factory head lost her shirt at the public showers. Convinced I had stolen it, she ordered people to overturn my room. That night, I cried to myself for a long, long time.

Some workers took a fancy to me, while others hassled me, but I was adamant. No way! I'd rather die in the city than marry there and be stuck in that damn corner of the earth all my life! Many girls were sexually abused by local peasants, particularly village heads. We had no toilets, just open pits that were emptied for use as fertilizer, and one girl sent to a neighbouring production team had to fight off a rapist when she went out at night for relief. My mother decided it was too dangerous for me to live alone—the village accountant even tried to break down my door. The family I moved to were so kind to me; I had one of the two bedrooms all to myself. In return, I gave all my food to them and bought them goods unavailable in the country. The family's son was engaged to a girl from a neighbouring village; each year they were obliged to provide her with gifts. One year, I gave her some green woolen thread. In 1993, when I returned for a visit, I noticed the daughter-in-law was still wearing the tattered jumper knitted from the thread I bought in Xi'an over twenty-two years earlier! After all these years, their lives were still so poor.

My country experience showed me an ugly side of rural life I had never known before. My landlady was a strange-looking woman without a nose—a result of severe gonorrhea. Sexually transmitted diseases, supposedly wiped out after the founding of New China, were rife in this remote mountain village, for the locals' sexual behaviour was rather animal-like. At first, when I visited a local family, I didn't even dare sit down for fear of contagion. Some feudal marital customs, such as child marriage, were still practiced: young girls were married off to the future husband's house to work as labourers long before formal marriage. That usually took place when the couple were well under 20, the legal age. Surprisingly, without any family-planning policy, the population was quite low—one or two children per family, and sometimes none at all. The lack of medical facilities maintained a high child-mortality rate.

Hope arose when the universities re-opened in 1971, at first accepting only students with worker, farmer, soldier backgrounds, and not through entrance exams, but on political recommendations. Yet rumours

Wu Xiaoping visiting her former landlady, 1993

suggested 'ordinary' young people too could compete for places. Towards the end of my rural exile, I made better use of my time by studying. I reviewed courses learnt at school and others like chemistry which I had missed.

During 1973, my last year there, I could not spend so much time studying. I was busier than ever with farming work, since the 'Learn from Dazhai' Movement inevitably reached us. We had to create terraced fields like the model rural commune Dazhai. If the terraces had worked for Dazhai, they certainly didn't here, yet it was a central government order, so everywhere and everyone had to follow. I heard that terraces were even built in the plains! It was disastrous for us: before, there was at least a thin layer of soil on the steep slope; after carving the terraces, the barren, rocky earth yielded no harvest at all. Working there was dangerous too— shortly after I left, a young woman was buried alive in a landslide.

That year's university entry exam was open to 'society'—to my amazement, I obtained excellent marks in chemistry, and my overall marks were number two in the area. With these marks, I could easily have chosen a good university but for Zhang Tiesheng and his blank exam paper! It seemed destined that my life would not be easy. I was finally taken by Baoji Agriculture College, though at first I was reluctant.

Over four years stuck in the countryside had made me sick of farming—I never wanted to be connected with it again. My parents argued the key issue was getting out; as an ordinary family, their means of doing so were very limited. I grabbed the chance, even to study tractors for three years! It was not quite the same as my hometown Xi'an, but already another world from the backward mountain village I hated so much.

Now, I can talk about my country experiences calmly, even with a smile. But there were moments when I was tempted to jump off the cliff and take my own life. True, the experience toughened me, but the price was too high. Over four years of my youth, the finest time in one's life, were a complete waste for me. I learned nothing useful. Without being sent down to the countryside, my life could have been very different. I was too young to have definite plans for the future, but I had always wanted to attend Beijing University, where my father studied. I was confident I could achieve that goal; I had a good academic record, at the best school in Xi'an. Yet I was lucky compared to many others. I was very young when I went, and stayed for 'only' four years, while others endured up to ten. When many older students eventually returned to the cities, it was simply too late. No wonder people call us the 'lost generation'.

Only six months after meeting him, one of my girlfriends married the peasant accountant of the production team. I still don't understand why, whether she was pregnant or drawn by the practical benefits of his position. In any case, a 19-year-old girl, away from home for the first time in a thoroughly strange environment, was highly vulnerable. They quickly had two children. Once married, with rural residency, it was complicated for her to leave. Only in 1979, when almost all educated youth had left the countryside, did she manage to find a job, selling rice coupons at a dining hall in a nearby county, not even Baoji city. When she recently visited her family in Xi'an, I hardly recognized her; only two years older than me, she looked some twenty years older. A face full of wrinkles told of all her hardships.

Looking back at myself, I used to pray so hard: please, please let me go back to the city. I'd be happy even if I were a street sweeper. Now I am back in my hometown, working in a decent job. My 20-year-old daughter studies English at university in Beijing, something I dreamed of in my own youth.

Feng Jicai

Voices of Madness

If it remains difficult to quantify the physical suffering of the Cultural Revolution—among 100 million Chinese adversely affected, at least half a million died from execution, torture, or suicide—then what of the psychological damage to a people turned so savagely on one another? The Communist Party declared it a disaster, but banned further debate. Writer Feng Jicai was one of the first to insist on addressing the 'decade that seemed to last a hundred years', lest future generations forget and past suffering be in vain. His quest to collect and publish oral histories drew thousands for the catharsis of release and confession.

Feng is well-qualified to understand his confessors and the pain of recall. Born in Tianjin in 1942 to a prominent banker's family, Feng was destined for trouble. Innocent praise for a US-made nail-cutter made him a target of mass criticism at school in 1957: he should not have appreciated something from a capitalist country. When he offered financial help to poor rural students, they reported him. Under his mother's influence, Feng became a talented painter and candidate for the Central Academy of Fine Arts. His capitalist background cast a long shadow and he was rejected, though he still got to use his hands after his height attracted the Tianjin basketball team.

As the Cultural Revolution began, Feng was reproducing classical portraits and landscapes at a small painting institute. When the Four Olds Campaign banned such works, the institute switched to printing Mao quotes onto plastic bags. So too did Feng switch from art to literature, as the movement inspired him to risk his life recording the stories of those around him. He wrote perhaps 1 million secret words, using foreign names, dates, and places, then hiding the scraps of paper in wall cracks or flowerpots, before the terror of discovery forced him to hide anew, even inside bicycle tubes. To protect his wife, he would write, memorize, and destroy. After the Tangshan earthquake reduced his house to rubble, Feng's chief concern was gathering his reactionary scraps.

Such covert operations are thankfully no longer necessary. With almost fifty books to his name, from novels like *The Miraculous Pigtail* to his 1998 diary of World Cup fever, Feng is one of China's best-known writers. Back in 1949, over a thousand publishing houses were closed, as the Party established ideological control of the presses. In the reformist 1980s, after the Cultural Revolution had been rejected, and 'Scar' literature by Feng and others explored its terror through fiction, strict censorship still dogged works about political movements. In recent years, the ban on political writing has been somewhat relaxed, permitting eyewitness accounts of the Cultural Revolution and earlier campaigns. Feng Jicai was a key catalyst in the thaw.

MANY OF THE NOTES I recorded secretly during the Cultural Revolution served as excellent raw material for later fiction. Then I realized fiction wasn't powerful enough to reveal the ten years' history. No fiction, no matter how skillful the writer, can summarize the extraordinary, complicated, and unprecedented movement that swept across the whole nation and changed everyone's life. In the face of a major disaster, fabrication is pale and superficial.

Yet I still don't have the nerve to write up my own experience. I hardly talk about it to others. In late July 1966, my family was among the first to be ransacked in Tianjin. Like many formerly rich families, we lived in the old foreign concession. Streams of student Red Guards came raiding from the schools that surrounded our home. Each member of the fierce 'beating dogs team' from Middle School No. 99 carried a stick or hammer to destroy, smash, and pillage. The boys raided in a roughshod manner, leaving girls to ensure no item was left intact, such as knocking spouts off antique tea pots. The broken possessions were piled up in the yard. They burned everything they could and confiscated the rest.

Then the interrogations began. The young Red Guards were as naïve as they were brutal, convinced we had guns, radio transmitters, and blacklists for overthrowing the government. One minute they demanded we hand in guns, the next they would hysterically search for transmitters. They forced us to stay awake at night and inflicted vicious, short haircuts on my parents, myself, and a disabled younger sister. My younger brother, absent during the raid, later wrote a statement rejecting his 'reactionary family'. Once, when I was about to collapse under the pressure, I asked him to return home and show support. As soon as I left, he reported our conversation to his work unit, who came to accuse me. I am proud I never said anything against anybody. I always believe the Cultural Revolution was a test of an individual's integrity.

Throughout the ten years of chaos, I was like a 'bird startled by the mere twang of a bowstring', convinced disaster was imminent. My position in charge of production couldn't save me from frequent struggle sessions. One leader would order me to drink with him and tell jokes or stories. When he got drunk, I would become his toy; when I tried to go home, he would threaten, 'If you dare go now, I'll make you a counter-

revolutionary tomorrow by your reactionary talk to-night.' I couldn't escape. Once, he drew a burning hot rod from the fire and stabbed my army coat, just for fun. He ordered me not to move, I could easily be hurt. When I eventually got home, my wife burst into tears, then sewed up all the holes so I could wear the coat again the next day. It was my only warm clothing for the winter.

I am not going to go into details. Let my wedding suffice. We married during the darkest days, on 1 January 1967, after dating for six years, so we could go through the difficult time together. The head of my wife's neighbourhood committee kindly gave us a tiny room in a run-down building. When you marry in China, you need new clothes, but all my mother could find were a pair of long johns and a singlet. She only had 40 yuan, but gave 20 yuan to my wife, who bought a blue-coloured padded jacket. 'Why didn't you buy red,' asked my mother, 'the traditional colour for weddings?' She replied, 'How could I, accused as the "offspring of stinking dogs", dare to wear "revolutionary" red?' My mother handed her the last 20 yuan. 'Wear the blue jacket during the day, but buy yourself a red one for the night.'

That evening, my father-in-law took us to a small restaurant. We didn't dare make much noise but raised our cups and said good wishes in our hearts. My long johns were stolen from the back of my bike, so I went to our new home completely empty-handed. As we were about to settle down, on the bricks I piled up for a bed, flashlights shone in on our ceiling. The Red Guards downstairs were making trouble for the two 'offspring of stinking dogs' getting married that night. People under attack were not allowed to have curtains, lest they conceal reactionary activity like radioing the enemy. Ridiculous! They blew trumpets and beat drums every fifteen minutes, and threw pebbles at our window. My poor new bride, wearing her red jacket, trembled the whole night in my arms.

So many years have passed away, but some interviews remain vivid. 'The story I am going to tell you has no plot, you might find it very boring,' warned one man. 'Even the character is boring, without a story.' A botany major from a poor peasant family, his goal was to develop herbicides; at that time, only developed countries had them. Under attack since the 1950s, though not formally labelled a 'rightist', he concluded that serious achievement in China depended on catching nobody's attention. Acting like a nobody became the principle of his life. He did his utmost to stay in the countryside for fieldwork, to avoid political troubles in the city. Since foreign languages were highly suspicious, he practiced with English editions of Chairman Mao's selected works, plus all the Marx and Lenin he could find. When forced to attend meetings, he always sat in the far corner; he lowered his head when he walked in the street, never spoke to people or expressed personal views, never grew angry even when bullied. He learned not to look into people's eyes: 'Only when you have eye contact with others can they remember you.'

Feng Jicai at home, 1971

In ten years, he researched hundreds of weeds and developed many herbicides that freed China's farmers from manual weeding. As the top expert in the field, he became head of his institute, attending conferences worldwide. It looked like a 'success story', but he complained no one knew the price he paid. 'I have become a person without a story, colour, and personality. I have never lost my temper. Do you understand the pain I experienced in order to "lose" myself for nearly twenty years? I had to pretend to be stupid, make others look down at me. In order to make some contribution to my country, I had to make myself "vanish" and twist my character. Wasn't this a tragedy?'

The greatest tragedy of the Cultural Revolution was its torture of people's souls. The scars on one's heart and soul take much longer to heal. If the calamity of the fascist regime was its damage to human bodies, the calamity of the Cultural Revolution was its damage to human souls. My father suffered badly, under attack during the Four Clean-Ups Campaign in 1963, then again during the Cultural Revolution. In the seventies, after countless struggle sessions, he developed a strange problem. At night, he would wake from his nightmares and begin to scream. It was a small place. When he screamed, no one could sleep. But he dragged on until 1989.

Another story that struck me was of a female doctor who killed her father. She sought me out, but when we met began to cry uncontrollably. Apart from 'I am guilty. I killed my father,' she couldn't say anything else. She grabbed me on my way out, 'No, I must talk today.' After ransacking her home, the Red Guards began to torture the whole family. They cut off their hair and forced them to kneel in the street as public humiliation. On the third night, the woman and her parents could take no more and decided on suicide. They searched the broken house for a knife. The couple asked their daughter to kill them first, for she was a medical student and knew the quickest way. At the last moment, she hesitated. The father begged her: sparing him from the endless physical and mental suffering was the greatest favour he could ask from his daughter. She found the blood vein near his throat and sensed its strong pulse. 'I'm sorry, Dad.' As soon as the sharp knife cut in, warm blood shot everywhere, even onto her. At just that moment, noise from downstairs suggested the Red Guards had returned. She jumped from the third floor balcony.

Sentenced to life for the 'murder', the daughter tried many times to commit suicide in jail. Then she learned her mother too had survived the fall from the third floor, though badly injured. The strong desire to see her again kept the daughter going. On her eventual release, she discovered her mother, denied all medical treatment, had died a week after the incident. If she had not slit her father's throat, perhaps he might have endured the suffering and lived to this day. 'Many others suffered and survived, why not *my* dad? Even though he asked me, he died by my hands after all.' The courts ultimately found her not guilty, but the poor woman was unsure her conscience would allow her to think so. When she finished her story, she sobbed violently. The next day, her blood pressure reached 180; she was so emotional she couldn't sleep. When her health recovered, she wrote thanking me for hearing her. As commentary, I wrote, 'In a time when humanity was destroyed, suicide is the highest form of humanity.' Her husband reported she enjoyed peace of mind ever since.

In 1996, the thirtieth anniversary of the launch of the Cultural Revolution, I met Chen Yingzheng, the left-wing Taiwanese writer, who still believed the movement promoted social progress in China. 'What was the greatest damage done to China by the Cultural Revolution?' he asked. The economic damage was huge, but it can be made up, I answered. Look at China now, the economy has boomed under the reform policy. More serious was the incalculable loss to China's traditional cultural heritage. Still the greatest damage was to the Chinese people's simple and honest nature. The Cultural Revolution made us more calculating, shrewd, brutal, practical, hypocritical, and vain. Simplicity used to be the loveliest virtue in China's national character. It is no longer so. This change may not be reversed in one or two

generations; the damage may be permanent. On the other hand, today's young people are not so easily cheated or misled, nor do they follow things blindly. Perhaps for this reason, the Cultural Revolution will not take place again. It awoke the Chinese people.

I don't believe the Chinese government and people are treating the Cultural Revolution properly. There is still not one real film about it, nor proper education at school. Sadly, our nation tends to forget the past too easily, perhaps because we lived for so long in a suppressed, feudal society. The ordinary people used to cope with suffering by wiping out bad memories. Officially, the government considers the nature of Cultural Revolution to have been decided in 1978: it was a disaster, and that's that. They worry that re-opening old scars would discredit the ruling Chinese Communist Party, arousing distrust and suspicion. My view is completely the opposite: to see history clearly, you must face it bravely. Only in this way can we draw lessons from the past and prevent the tragedy from happening again.

The thirtieth anniversary barely won a mention in the Chinese press. My article 'To End the Cultural Revolution' argued that the only way is to remember it thoroughly and truthfully. At concentration camps I visited in Poland, everything has been preserved to remind people of the horror of the fascist regime. The calamities of the Cultural Revolution are no less than the fascists, yet we don't have a single museum. When I say it will not recur, I only mean not in the same form. Interviews I conducted with young people who never experienced it send a warning signal: most know little or nothing about the Cultural Revolution; some said their impression was of great fun—you didn't have to go to school, you could do whatever you liked—while other youngsters suggested China needed the movement all over again.

As for its causes, I am no historian. In my understanding, thousands of years of feudal culture and emperor worship served as a rich breeding ground for the Cultural Revolution. Politically, the movement was the inevitable product of a dictatorial political system, a general explosion of disease in politics, culture, and national character. To understand it completely needs major effort, courage, and time. My literary project had no intention of providing a wise answer to readers. My only hope is by reading the victims' stories and spiritual journeys, people might be inspired to think.

David Crook
Foreign Prisoner of Mao

In the long and complex interaction between East and West, many foreigners have come 'to change China' and left disheartened and unsuccessful. Edgar Snow's 1937 classic *Red Star Over China* encouraged many more, but this time they were backing the winners. These sympathetic 'Old China Hands' offered lifetime contribution to their adopted homeland, yet the Cultural Revolution made little distinction. Everyone's past was suspect, as activists swapped charges and counter-charges, old scores were settled, and competing factions strove to outdo one another in public devotion to Mao. The resident 'foreign experts' were no exception, forming their own Red Guard units, with junior sections for their children.

David Crook's conversion to communism greatly distressed his family, London Jews who had watched him leave for the United States in the 1930s with dreams of becoming a millionaire. He was fighting the fascists in Spain when he happened upon Snow's eyewitness account of the new society being forged in northern Shaanxi. Inspired, he sailed for Shanghai to teach and spy, as the KGB sought his help to identify Trotskyites among the expatriate community, a paradise of adventurers from many lands. He was fortunate to lose touch with his mentors, and turned his attention to Isabel, the attractive Canadian girl he met while teaching in Chengdu.

David and Isabel's total commitment to education in China ensured their total immersion in its political upheavals. Just as there were foreign Red Guards, so there were foreign activists—an American from an opposing faction may have masterminded David's arrest. Suspected for wartime intelligence work in the Royal Air Force (against mutual enemies the Japanese), David spent over five years in solitary confinement in Beijing's Qincheng prison, home to many of China's top political prisoners. Allowed no visitors, nor even a pen, he kept himself sane by reading Mao's works, pinpricking his Chinese dictionary with toothpicks made from broom twigs to remind him of characters already looked up. Discrimination as 'children of foreign spies' finally became too much for his three sons labouring in local factories. In 1971, the boys were permitted to leave China to study in England.

In the Crooks' Beijing home, opposite the poster of Mao liberating Beijing, hangs another of Zhou Enlai, the man responsible for ending David's imprisonment. On 8 March 1973, Zhou left his sickbed to make a public apology to 'Comrade Crook' and other wronged friends of China. After his speech, several deportees returned; more remarkably, David and many other foreign jailbirds chose to remain, unswerving in their devotion to duty. The Crooks' sons retain close emotional and professional links with China. While they address their parents in English, they chat to each other in Chinese.

WHEN WE RETURNED TO CHINA in 1947, we intended to study land reform in the liberated areas for just eighteen months. More than half a century later, we are still here! There was never a time when we *decided* we would settle here permanently. We just stayed on and on. Honestly, we feel life is meaningful and purposeful here; even political troubles didn't change us.

We had rather naïve faith in the various movements every few years. When the Cultural Revolution began, we didn't know what to expect, but hoped for the best and participated as enthusiastically as any. The Beijing Foreign Languages University was split into opposing factions, both of which claimed to support Chairman Mao. I was teaching abroad until spring 1967, by which time Isabel had decided which group to support. We put up big-character posters, went on demonstrations, and attended mass meetings. There was even a special Red Guard group for foreigners called the Bethune–Yan'an Regiment. Our three sons belonged to its junior section, but, as far as I know, were never involved in horrible acts such as beating and killing people. One day, one son reported he had given a speech to a public meeting. 'How many people attended?' 'Oh, about 7,000.' We were amazed! In Britain, a meeting of 7,000 people is a fair size! But it was nothing unusual in China of those days.

I am sorry to say some students from our university played a leading role in the demonstration against the British chargé d'affaires. We

opposed the demonstra-
tion, but it went ahead
nevertheless. They
burned down part of the
chancery, seized confi-
dential documents, and
manhandled staff.
Eventually, this operation
was denounced as
counter-revolutionary by
Chairman Mao and
Premier Zhou. But the
damage was done.

As I was collecting mail
on 17 October 1967, I
heard people fighting with
bricks at the playing fields,
and the opposition group
shouting from a nearby
building. I decided to take a look, purely out of curiosity, and *naïveté*.
For a moment, I looked at them and they looked at me. Then they
seized me and took me inside for interrogation. They unscrewed my
pen to search for a hidden camera (then asked me where I had put it).
As I was being driven to a commune in the outskirts of Beijing, squeezed
between some burly chaps, I had wild ideas of plunging out of the car,
or upsetting it into a ditch. Fortunately, I didn't carry them out. That
evening, they informed me my briefcase contained documents I was
not supposed to have. 'We must detain you for the time being.'

I was kept for months without explanation. I spoke the truth at each
interrogation, and each time I was disbelieved. When asked to describe
myself, I was supposed to reply, 'imperialist spy', not 'I am a
communist!' But I still see myself as a communist with a small c (I had
a capital when a member of the British Communist Party, and I still
believe in the principles of communism). Around 1 May 1968, I was
transferred to Qincheng, where I signed some paper, still without formal
charge, and was put in a cell by myself for five years. During my
imprisonment, I reconciled to myself that civil rights would not be

observed during revolutionary activity. At other times, I even thought I was being held for my own good, as it kept harm away—so many people were injured or killed. Apart from three-quarters of an hour exercise each month, we were kept in our cells, never allowed to see, or be seen by, another prisoner.

Interrogation became my only social life. They told me there were two ways I could get out of there: 'One is to walk out vertically, on your own two feet, *if* you confess all your misdeeds; the other, if you do *not* confess, is to be carried out horizontally, as a corpse.' I don't understand why they thought me an 'imperialist agent'. I had always worked conscientiously, researching language-teaching as well as I could. All in all, I was a good and faithful servant of a regime I believed in. My interrogators might have truly believed what they were told about me, or maybe were just doing their jobs. I often wished I could get together with them over a glass of beer and discuss the whole procedure.

Every interrogation began: 'Your family is well. They are not worried about you as they know you are properly treated.' Then I read out two Mao quotations that hung on the wall. 'Those who admit their misdeeds honestly will be leniently treated; those who do not will be severely treated.' 'Severely treated' meant God knows what. Once, after Nixon had come to China, I was offered a chair, luxury compared to the usual drum I squatted on. 'What do you think of Nixon's visit?' I had read *The People's Daily*, so answered, 'Nixon is a bastard who is always anti-communist, but it was good he came to China to improve relations.' We spoke in Chinese, which was mostly fine, bar the idiomatic phrases they delighted in using. Sometimes there were Chinese students on the interrogation board. One day I puzzled hard over such a phrase and finally stumbled upon it: 'Oh, it means you think I'm like a mangy dog!' The student and I burst into laughter. He was criticized for laughing with a class enemy and never appeared again.

Conditions improved slightly over the years, with more frequent trips for fresh air to an area like a typical cell, minus a roof. When I did my jumping exercises, I could glimpse the distant hills. Once I picked some wild flowers to remind me of my three sons. But I was spotted and they took them away. Even during these outings, I remained in isolation from other prisoners. I heard the chap who designed this high-security prison was jailed in the very same place. When he got out, he confessed: 'If I had known what it was like, I would have designed it differently!'

Life dragged on in this way. I did my exercises, read Mao's works in Chinese during the day and in English at night. I couldn't write a diary, since pen and ink were only for reports after each interrogation. I tried to analyse why I was arrested—I thought it was a genuine error, during a widespread hunt for spies—and believed I reached a reasonable understanding. Not that it did me any good, until my eventual release in January 1973, after five years and one hundred days! I went back to work in three or four days, just like that, to brief some scholars about to study in Britain. I was rather out of touch, but did my best—Premier Zhou's influence meant I was considered trustworthy again. Later, Isabel and I were made advisers to the university. We accepted as graciously as we could.

One day, we sat at home discussing my experience. During my imprisonment I had reviewed my whole life, what I had done, mistakes I had made, matters that influenced my thinking, and my decision to settle in China. There probably *was* a good side to my incarceration. It was the critical analysis of my life. Of course, when I talked like this, my boys said, 'Oh dear, the old man's gone nuts.' Anyway, that was what I thought, and, to a certain extent, still do. My only regret was the

waste of five years not teaching, but I was still ready to play my part. We stayed on in China. 'Why?!' everyone asked. Well, I was not mistreated by the Chinese, but by a small number of people who are the enemies of the Chinese people. To leave China was tantamount to accusing them of hostility towards me. The truth is I've spent over half of my life in China, doing work which interests me. My best friends were Chinese and still are. China changed my life, overall for the better. There was no reason to leave, and, honestly, if you look around the troubled world, China is not a bad place to be. Yet, after all these years, I still feel I am British. My culture is English and I love to listen to Shakespeare.

Looking back, I believe the Cultural Revolution was a potentially positive movement that went badly wrong. Certain aspects were commendable: trying to avoid the polarization of different classes of people, bridging the gap between intellectuals and non-intellectuals, and demolishing privilege. Condemnation as entirely negative is incorrect, an over-simplification, yet the most terrible acts— imprisonment, torture, and killing—occurred during that time. I have no illusions about that. Fortunately, it is all over and China is heading more or less in the right direction. I am very optimistic about its future. A country with over 1 billion people with such great qualities does carry some weight. Whatever happens, China will become a great power.

Ma Jingjun

The Red Sun in Our Hearts

No corner of China's great expanse went untouched during the Cultural Revolution. Kazak nomads in the far north-west marched across grasslands carrying Mao's portrait. In 1968, Chinese mountaineers drew Mao's poetry in the snow atop Mount Everest. In every school, children sang, 'Father is dear, mother is dear, but Chairman Mao is dearest of all,' while around the world China's diplomats chanted his slogans in the streets. Thousands of factories were commandeered to supply revolutionary essentials: some 2.2 billion Mao portraits, or three each for every mainland Chinese, and 40 billion copies of Mao's works, notably the Little Red Book, *de rigeur* Red Guard accessory, to be waived aloft at mass meetings and fiery denunciations.

If the Maoist bible impressed with circulation, the Mao badge offered astonishing variety, almost a million types in a total of 2.5 to 4 billion. The innocent hobby of collectors like Ma Jingjun, proud owner of 60,000 badges, hides an obsession that gripped the nation. Worn to show love and loyalty to an increasingly sacred leader, Mao badges grew with the Cultural Revolution, from 1/4-inch pins to 6-inch medallions. To leave home without one shining proudly on one's chest was asking for trouble. Badge designers were inspired by events and places central to Mao's, and therefore the country's, story, for he personified Communist China. 'Chairman Mao is the red sun in our hearts' ran a song line from the revolutionary pageant *The East is Red*, inspiring countless sunflower motifs, loyally turning towards the light.

Ma was not even a teenager when the badge craze took hold in 1966. His parents worked at a Beijing military college, an excellent hunting-ground for a budding collector. Enrollment in both the army and the Party in the early 1970s sustained Ma's affection for the Chairman despite nationwide de-Maofication later that decade. From the late 1980s, Mao badges began to acquire nostalgic and even artistic value, while the centenary of Mao's birth in December 1993 inspired a mini-Maoist revival, fuelled by a commercialization he would have abhorred. The icons of the past competed with new Mao-morabilia, kitsch like Mao lighters and diamond watches. Revolutionary karaoke sold millions, while artists experimented with his once sacrosanct image. Deep in the Shaanxi, Henan, and Hunan countryside literal deification emerged in the form of Mao temples, with the usual pantheon of deities replaced by statues of Mao, flanked by Zhou Enlai and Marshal Zhu De.

China's 100,000 Mao-badge collectors enjoy a distinguished patron: Zhou had a large collection and was a badge-wearer to his deathbed. The influence of China's revolution and personality cult is still evident in the Orwellian–Maoist time warp that is North Korea, where every citizen to this day bears Kim Il Sung on his breast. The Mao-badge phenomenon raises intriguing questions about Chinese popular culture, and Mao's place as demon or demigod. The current leadership is well aware of the delicate legitimacy it claims through him. His portrait still dominates Tiananmen, and his mausoleum Tiananmen Square; these will remain the barometers of his legacy. For now he remains EveryMao, all things to all men, from hero of the Revolution to villain of the century.

I WAS ONLY 11 when I got my first Mao badge in August 1966. The Cultural Revolution had just started and Beijing produced the classic Mao head on a small, simple red base. It was the only type available in town and I treasured it. Many Red Guards stayed at the meeting hall of my parents' college. They came from all over China to see Chairman Mao. How I envied them! One lad, just four years older than me, wore a badge from Shaoshan, Mao's birthplace. The Red Guards loved to pay pilgrimage trips to sacred revolutionary places such as Shaoshan, Jinggangshan, and Yan'an. I made friends with him and we swapped badges. Later, I exchanged more with the Red Guards who came and went. My collection had begun.

My parents were my main source, mostly free from their work units. I was really thick-skinned, asking their friends, colleagues, and neighbours. 'Little man, why do you want Mao badges?' they asked. 'I love them and collect them.' Yet I myself didn't understand quite why I was so fascinated. They were shiny, interesting, and fun, and despite my youth, I did have deep affection for Chairman Mao, through education at school and at home. Each new gain delighted me. I pinned them to large handkerchiefs and proudly showed them off to my friends, none of whom had so many. The badges produced by the army were generally better than civilian efforts. At first, I enjoyed wearing interesting badges that guaranteed attention in the street. Once, a nasty older boy snatched a new badge from my chest, which left me wailing for some time. Since then, I carefully kept my dear badges at home. Stealing happened from time to time, but it was not for money in those days. Mao badges were simply the most desirable item. In December 1970, at the age of 15, I joined the army and had to leave my fine collection of eighty badges at home.

I resumed my hobby in 1991, almost by accident, after a colleague showed off a large Mao badge. 'You collect all sorts of things, why not Mao badges?' I had been collecting matchbox covers and key-rings for a while. From a collector's point of view, Mao badges were produced in great volume and variety during the Cultural Revolution. As this was recent history, there would be many materials to aid my research. Inspired by his words, childhood memories flooded my mind. Excitedly, I went straight to my parents' house to look for my old collection. To my amazement, my father produced 600 badges, including my own,

carefully wrapped in foam. Holding my new-found wealth, I was almost dizzy with happiness! Only then did I realize my parents were collectors too. 'During all these years, why didn't you throw them away?' 'How could I?' my father replied. 'I even took them into exile at a May Seventh cadre school in the countryside. These badges reflected my feelings towards Mao. Without him, a poor peasant boy like me might have died a long time ago. These badges are works of art too.' Although my father was attacked during the Cultural Revolution, that didn't change his love for Mao. He accepted the official verdict on Mao: 70 per cent right and 30 per cent wrong. That sums up my attitude too.

Encouraged by my success, I launched a collecting campaign. I jumped when my mother-in-law said, 'Oh, I just sold 20 kilograms of badges for scrap metal!' I had high expectations, as my father-in-law was once director of the Chairman Mao badge office under the army's railway division. Luckily, they kept the most attractive 100 badges. I was just as thick-skinned as a child, asking everyone for badges. I am a sociable sort of chap with many friends, and within two years amassed over 11,000 badges. Was I busy in those days! An exhibition is the best way to show your credentials, so in June 1993 I joined hands with Yan Xinlong, Beijing's top collector, who boasted 120,000 badges. The exhibition was held at the Haidian district library. As the first large-scale Mao-badge exhibition in Beijing, it roused a great stir, for Mao was popular once again. Many taxi drivers hung his picture in their cars, hoping Mao would protect them. Still, we didn't expect the thousands of people queuing up on the first day. The visitor's book showed all sorts, from old people nostalgic about the past to a younger generation vague and curious about the cult and Cultural Revolution. Most came for a bit of fun.

We felt greatly rewarded. It took three hard months to prepare: our fingers were torn and bleeding from pinning up 40,000 badges. They were arranged into three sections according to historical development. The first stage was the pre-Cultural Revolution badges. The first-known Mao badges were handmade from aluminium toothpaste tubes back in Yan'an in 1945 for the Seventh Party Congress. Only the one for Chen Yi, later foreign minister, survives in China's Revolutionary Museum. Most early badges were commemorative: National Day, the liberation of Tibet, 'Resist America, Aid Korea!' Others rewarded model workers or were given as souvenirs to foreign friends. All were limited editions and finely made in good materials like copper, silver, and gold.

The second stage was the Cultural Revolution, particularly from mid-1966 to mid-1970, during which the overwhelming majority of badges were made. We Chinese went crazy about them. Aluminum was the first and main material, but over thirty were tried: copper, iron, enamel, metal mixture, silver, gold or gold plate, bamboo, wood, plastic, china, pottery, bones, glass, ivory, cloth. Badge production grew out of control, from the largest government organizations—the ministries and armed forces—to the smallest, schools, communes, or Red Guard sections. Individuals created their own handmade designs. Sizes grew bigger and bigger, until people hung them as medallions in front of their chests to show their dedication to Mao. Talk about dedication and devotion, people even pinned Mao badges onto their bare chests! One Chongqing collector has a huge iron badge for public display, 1.2 metres in diameter and weighing 19 kilograms. I once made a special trip to be photographed beside it.

The result was massive quantities of aluminium consumed, even that allocated for military use. The craze came to an end only after Mao angrily remarked, 'Return my airplane!' in the summer of 1969. Mao himself was probably fed up with the personality cult. After his death came a silver-coloured pair we call the 'closing door badge'. The 'opening door badge' was the little red one I had swapped with the Red Guard. The final stage were post-Cultural Revolution badges, starting from 1977 to commemorate the opening of the Mao's mausoleum and again in 1993 for his centenary. But badges were only a small part of the memorabilia produced that year and quality had really gone downhill.

I tell you there is great knowledge hidden in these badges. Of course they are highly political. They record the history of the Cultural Revolution through Mao's personality cult: Mao swimming the Yangtze, Mao and the Red Guards, Mao and revolutionary opera; red suns, sunbeams, red flags, plum blossom and, overwhelmingly, sunflowers—three symbolized the three devotions (to the great leader Chairman Mao, to Mao Zedong thought, and to Chairman Mao's proletarian revolutionary line); seven meant 700 million people's devotion to Mao; nine commemorated the Ninth Party Congress, and so on. When the last revolutionary committee was established in Tibet in late 1968, countless badges proclaimed, 'All China's mountains and rivers are red!'

My favourite set features thirty-four of Mao's poems from the 1920s to the 1960s. Look, each bears an extract written in Mao's grass calligraphy beside a Mao image from the time the poem was written. On the back is the printed poem. Beautifully produced, the set is a true work of art, worth at least 30,000 yuan today. In the years after the Cultural Revolution, badge values crashed: a few kilograms sold for 1 yuan at recycling stations. Some people threw them away, while others deliberately destroyed them, particularly those who had suffered badly. The government then demanded badges be returned for melting down. About half disappeared this way, while the rest still circulate among the ordinary people. Over the past decade, Mao badges entered the market as 'revolutionary antiques', and have become the third favourite collectable after stamps and coins. Some people, who merely happen to have many badges at home, I wouldn't call real collectors, and I look down on those who collect for commercial reasons; some collect to remember that special period of history and others purely out of love for Mao.

As for myself, my love for Mao is the sole motive for collecting and researching his badges. I wouldn't have been a collector for so long without loving the man. He founded a new China which was a much, much better place than the old, fedual China. Without him, the victory for the Chinese Revolution might have come much later. All Chinese have reason to be grateful to him, though, as a human being, he made mistakes too. Since he was a great man with great influence, his mistakes were also great, like the Cultural Revolution. Yet we should not totally deny Chairman Mao because of those mistakes. The search for hidden knowledge sustains my fascination for collecting. The creation of Mao badges during the Cultural Revolution took place in such a spontaneous and chaotic fashion that there is no proper record of these badges at all. One day I dearly hope to publish a comprehensive book with pictures of the badges and sound knowledge about them.

I am obsessed with Mao badges. Every day, after helping my wife with housework, I'd sit down to play with my badges. My son grew up hearing metal badges clinking together. Once I sat down to watch TV instead, but he couldn't sleep without the sound, until I pretended to play with the badges as usual. I clean them, polish them, sort and study different designs and back inscriptions, year of production, by whom, for what purpose and belonging to which set. My eyes become fixed on them, and apart from the badges in front of me, the whole world does not exist for me anymore.

Zhang Hanzhi

The Nixon Shock

By 1968, Red Guard assaults on the Foreign Ministry meant Chinese foreign policy appeared one long tirade against the world. Besides symbolizing the capitalist West, the USA was targeted for its war against Vietnam. The fiercely anti-communist Richard Nixon presided in the White House by 1969. How could the two ever be reconciled? Many American visitors had sympathized with the Communist experiment in Yan'an in the late 1930s and early 1940s. President Franklin Delano Roosevelt even considered arming the Communists to fight the Japanese in 1944. But American support stayed firmly with the Christian Chiang Kaishek. His defeat in 1949 sparked accusations that America had 'lost China', while the Korean War hardened the American attitude, symbolized by the cold shoulder Secretary of State John Foster Dulles showed Zhou Enlai at the Geneva Conference in 1954.

For years, official Sino-US relations were conducted through occasional harangues between their resident diplomats in Geneva and Warsaw. By 1970 the two sides remained ideologically opposed, yet common ground lay in their distrust of the Soviet Union, and perhaps too in their rulers' concern for their place in history. Mao's shock at Lin Biao's betrayal may also have pushed him towards *détente*. Yet the fierce rhetoric of the political scene concealed this policy shift even from those close to the inner circle, such as Zhang Hanzhi. Suddenly, in February 1972, Zhang was doing the unthinkable—interpreting for the visiting United States president.

She was well-qualified for the task. Father Zhang Shizhao, celebrity scholar and political activist, had befriended and helped a young radical called Mao Zedong in Hunan in the 1920s. At Chairman Mao Zedong's birthday in December 1963, Zhang introduced the Chairman to his daughter, a foreign languages teacher. She initially thought Mao was joking when he asked her to teach him English, but for over a year she cycled to Zhongnanhai each weekend to teach from the political texts Mao chose. He took particular interest in English grammar, delighting in examples like revisionism and revisionist. In June 1970, Mao recalled Zhang from labouring at a textile factory for a poolside chat and appeared keen to let students return to classes. In view of impending developments, Mao also recognized the need for diplomatic talent and in spring 1971, Zhang was transferred on his recommendation to the Foreign Ministry. There she met her future husband Qiao Guanhua, future foreign minister and the first Chinese representative to the United Nations.

Parkinson's disease, bronchitis, and heart failure almost prevented Mao from meeting Nixon, but on 21 February 1972, he roused himself to hear Nixon flatter him by quoting 'seize the day, seize the hour'. Zhang took the First Couple sightseeing ('It truly is a Great Wall,' said President Nixon), while the final wording of the Shanghai Communiqué was hammered out. A document of great compromise was inevitable, yet it forced a reconsideration of world politics. After twenty-two years of hostility, China rejoined the family of nations, and global tension subsided.

Although the visit could not keep Nixon in power—Mao was baffled a president should resign merely for taping conversations in his own office—he succeeded in opening trade and a new era of dialogue with his wish to 'start a long march together'. The Sino-US relationship has had almost as many twists and turns as the Communist epic. It went downhill after Nixon's fall and has been a roller-coaster ride of mutual accusation ever since. China's modern leaders desire a multi-polar world in which China is a major player, and Europe acts as a counter-balance to US hegemony. Living in a beautiful Beijing courtyard passed down by her father, Zhang is still engaged in international cooperation, through a research centre under the State Council.

THE EARLY 1970S saw the most dramatic scene in China's diplomatic history: China's top leaders decided to break the thick ice with America. When the announcement was made public about Nixon's upcoming visit, many Chinese, diplomats among them, were startled. It was an adventurous step for both sides to take, considering they had been hostile for decades. I had been transferred to the Foreign Ministry in spring 1971, but like my colleagues I had no hint of the impending drama. In July that year, [Henry] Kissinger made his secret visit, so confidential that only the few people involved knew it was happening. Why such secrecy? At that early stage, neither side was sure anything positive would come of the visit.

My Foreign Ministry friends Wang Hairong and Nancy Tang, who enjoyed the privilege of frequent entry to Mao's residence, suddenly disappeared for a week. When they came back, they looked hugely excited. One noon at the dining hall, they were surrounded by a crowd curious to learn what was afoot. They briefly replied there would soon be an announcement, but Wang took me aside. 'Let me tell you. Tang and I went to meet Kissinger!' I was shocked. 'Do you mean that American Kissinger?' I thought it was incredible, but she explained this was Mao's wise and decisive strategy: to open up the relationship with America in order to contain the Soviet Union. And Mao had decided to invite President Nixon to visit China.

Apart from being surprised, people in the diplomatic service generally welcomed the move. China was isolated in the international arena. The Cultural Revolution had spurred many ultra-leftist actions, such as burning down the office of the British chargé d'affaires. On the one hand, China was in a cold war with the Western world; on the other, the relationship with the Soviet Union had entered a tense period. After the border clash on Zhenbao Island in March 1969, they sent more troops to the border. It was like the Chinese phrase, 'being attacked from the front and rear simultaneously'. Breaking the ice with the United

Zhang Hanzhi and Nixon at the Great Wall, February 1972

States would mean a breakthrough for China on one front, so we could better deal with the Soviet Union.

Maybe I shouldn't have been surprised. When I taught him English back in the sixties, I knew Mao was very interested in international affairs, contrary to the impression of many Westerners. He was greatly excited by the establishment of diplomatic relations with France, and had a high opinion of General [Charles] de Gaulle. He was keen to open up relations with Europe, though it was still impossible to discuss Sino-US ties.

The move became obvious when Mao invited the American table-tennis team to visit China in the spring of 1971 after the world championship in Japan. This became known as 'ping-pong diplomacy'—the small ball that started the big ball rolling. Before that, Mao invited Edgar Snow and his wife to stand beside him on top of Tiananmen for the 1970 National Day review, though few at the time realized the significance behind the scene. People regarded Snow as a friendly Westerner who had long been friends with Mao and the Communist Party. Actually, Chairman Mao hoped Snow could pass a message to the American administration.

From Kissinger's second visit in October 1971 [to prepare for the presidential visit, and discuss the joint communiqué], I became directly involved in the negotiations. The talks were tough: at that early stage, the Chinese and Americans didn't know each other, so both were on guard about the other's motives. There was a unique atmosphere, but friendly, since both sides wanted to improve the relationship and make Nixon's visit a success. There were so many differences that it was hard to come up with an agreement. But without one, the visit would be considered a failure. It was a very daring move for Nixon, and was expected to create a major impact. The Americans had to guarantee its success.

My late husband Qiao Guanhua, then vice-minister of foreign affairs, was Kissinger's counterpart. I think both sides chose the right men for the job, as both were tough negotiators. I noticed Qiao grew excited several times, even a little angry, because they couldn't reach any agreement. He would say, 'We probably should stop discussions right now!' Kissinger was a very capable diplomat, knowledgeable and firm, yet flexible enough to attain his goal.

From the very beginning, the Taiwan issue proved the most challenging. The Americans had always insisted on Chinese commitment that the Taiwan issue would be resolved by peaceful means. Of course, our government refused. The United States still wanted to protect Taiwan as their old friend. We would not allow this either, as we insisted Taiwan was an internal issue in which no foreign country should interfere. The disagreement over Taiwan was finally settled just before the signing of the joint communiqué, when Nixon himself was visiting.

During Kissinger's second visit, China was accepted into the United Nations to replace Taiwan. China's victory came as a surprise not only to the Americans, but also to us. After China and America started to work for a *détente*, our admission was inevitable, but the American timetable had China admitted *after* Nixon's visit, so confident were they about their influence at the UN. Quite frankly the Chinese agreed admission naturally followed the visit, so we didn't push it at all. When the resolution was adopted, Kissinger was about to leave China. Convinced nothing exciting would happen at the general assembly, he went to sleep at Villa No. 5 at the state guest house without checking the news. China knew immediately, around midnight our time, as the secretary general sent a congratulatory telegram. Early the next morning, Zhou Enlai called in to say goodbye. 'So, Dr Kissinger, you have heard the news?' 'What news?' 'China was admitted to the UN!' You can imagine the surprise that gave Kissinger!

I interpreted for General Alexander Haig, who led the advance party in January 1972 to prepare for the presidential visit in February. I remember one incident very clearly. On 6 January, Zhou Enlai held a meeting with Haig. On the personal front, it was a heavy day for Zhou, as Marshal Chen Yi, a close colleague, was critically ill (he passed away that night). But Zhou was such a professional that he didn't let this influence his mood. On the whole, it was a good meeting. When Haig touched upon the draft joint communiqué, and the threat posed by the Soviet Union, he said the United States was concerned about China's viability. Zhou did not argue on hearing that, only frowned a little, and afterwards told us, 'Get me all the dictionaries to find out exactly what viability means.' I guess it was natural for Haig to use that term, but he didn't realize that as a revolutionary country China would not accept *any* patronizing terms from *any* Western country. Zhou called Haig in the next day and made it clear to him: 'We do not like the way you use that kind of language to Chinese. China and the United States should be on an equal footing, not one under the nuclear umbrella of the other.'

At three o'clock that night, I was called into Zhongnanhai to see Chairman Mao. He had the strange habit of staying up very late and calling people in to see him at small hours in the morning. Mao wanted a direct report about the progress of Haig's visit, as he was very concerned about the matter and looking forward to Nixon's visit. I mentioned Haig's 'viability' and why Zhou Enlai thought it wrong. Mao agreed with Zhou.

When the presidential trip began, I accompanied Mrs Nixon to the Beijing Zoo and a Beijing hotel kitchen to show her Chinese cuisine. I only interpreted for President Nixon as a result of his humorous suggestion. Since Zhou had a young lady as his interpreter, Nixon said it was unfair he had a big man, Ji Chaozhu—one of the best interpreters in China. Ji was a good friend, who didn't mind swapping, but I lacked the nerve to face the big crowds in Beijing. Once out of town, I interpreted for Nixon and witnessed various behind-the-scenes dramas. We were about to leave for Hangzhou when I found Secretary of State William Rogers and his people in an uproar at their hotel. I guess Kissinger gave them the draft of the joint communiqué, which had just been agreed by the two sides and approved by Mao and Nixon. They were very angry about certain words and phrases, and felt left out of the final decision.

Evidently, during the Nixon administration, all the major diplomatic issues were decided by the White House. The State Department was very much kept outside the decision-making process. Though Rogers came to China as secretary of state, he was not in the intimate circle with Nixon. Everything was determined by Nixon and Kissinger, who was lower-ranking than Rogers. I know this was their internal problem, but I mentioned it to Zhou Enlai nevertheless. It was natural for me to do so—we interpreters enjoyed close relations with Zhou, as he was so pleasant to everyone. Zhou took it up from there. That was something very special about him; though it was not his problem, he always tried to smooth things out. In Shanghai, Zhou visited Rogers to thank him for his support of the friendly move between the two countries. He added that the draft had to be settled urgently, as it would soon be signed, meaning maybe you should put your minor differences aside to achieve the major goal of this trip. The simple fact that Zhou came to his room was so touching to Rogers that he accepted Zhou's point.

I enjoyed interpreting for Nixon. It was a challenge, as it included many large banquets. But everyone relishes a challenge. Nixon, as a public character, was charming and flattering to me. At the last banquet, he praised my interpreting skills. Of course, I couldn't translate that. Someone else jumped onto the stage and did so. Like everyone else on that occasion, he was so relieved the Shanghai Communiqué was finally signed that the whole atmosphere was joyous.

Looking back, it really was 'a week that changed the world', as Nixon said. I must say Chairman Mao Zedong was the architect of the strategic move to break the ice with the United States. Nobody else would dare take such a decision. Considering China's political situation at the time, if anybody else *had* made such a move, including even Premier Zhou Enlai, that person would have been condemned. As for the Americans, maybe only a Republican president like Nixon had the courage to take such a daring step as opening the door to Communist China. I was happy and proud to play a part in this eventful period in China's history and diplomatic life. It remains a very memorable part of my life too.

Gobro Runqi

Imperial Cowherd

While the events of the twentieth century have inflicted great turmoil on all Chinese families, few upheavals rival that experienced by the imperial Aisingioro family from Manchuria. At the turn of the century, the Qing dynasty established by their forebears still laid claim to a vast land empire, the second largest of twenty-five successive dynasties stretching back over two millennia. The foundations had badly weakened since the glorious rules of the Kangxi and Qianlong emperors, but the Qing court still presided over China from the Forbidden City, lavish symbol of the Son of Heaven's terrestrial prominence.

The Nationalist Revolution in 1911 forced the abdication of the boy emperor, Pu Yi, but his life of luxury, sequestered within the palace's vermilion walls, ended only with his eviction in 1924 by a local warlord. Pu Yi's delusions of recovering long-lost grandeur implicated many of his family, including 'double' brother-in-law Duke Gobro Runqi: his sister Wan Rong was Pu Yi's empress and his wife Yunying was Pu Yi's sister. Runqi loyally obeyed when dispatched to Japan in 1928 for military training. In 1944 he joined Pu Yi in the Japanese puppet state Manchukuo, a ranking lieutenant but, crucially, a non-combatant teacher. After the Japanese surrender, Pu Yi, Runqi, and other Manchu refugees were captured by the Soviet Red Army and detained in Russia for five years before extradition to the newly founded PRC and a war-criminal detention centre. Runqi's positive nature pulled him through the darkest days of re-education. Once he even raised the roof of the male-only prison, colourfully dressed as the heroine of a Mongolian morality musical.

After a dozen years' separation, Runqi was finally reunited with his family in 1957. He was permitted only manual work until Zhou Enlai, who like Mao retained his fascination for China's imperial heritage, secured a more fitting post. While Pu Yi's death from cancer in 1967 ended his persecution during the Cultural Revolution, Runqi's feudal background and Japanese connection ensured further loss of liberty. Three years in a Party school-cum-labour camp, where cadres and intellectuals toiled in fields and classrooms to deepen 'proletarian political consciousness' and study Mao Zedong Thought, were followed by six in the countryside.

Runqi's skills and personality enabled him to make the best of the experience, which led to his octogenarian medical career, administering 'Gobro-Style Cupping Therapy'. From 1983 to 1993, Runqi was even co-opted by the government that once vilified his family: as a CPPCC member from 1983 to 1993, he tried to assist his native Daur minority in northeast China. Runqi makes only occasional return visits to the Forbidden City, his former playground and now China's largest museum. He remembers introducing the bicycle, which soon became Pu Yi's favourite pastime. In order to bike around freely, the Emperor had removed all the wooden thresholds from his quarters at Yangxindian through to the imperial garden. The childhood passion remains, only today Runqi prefers the motorbike he rides daily for recreation, armed with a special licence—at the age of 87 he is the only Chinese above 70 years old who is officially allowed to drive.

I WAS THE VERY FIRST at my work unit, the Beijing Translation Company, to be attacked after the Cultural Revolution started. Almost overnight, dozens of big-character posters went up criticizing me as a counter-revolutionary and a 'major member of the Three Family Village'—a so-called anti-government organization. Some people were obliged to put up such posters. Even my own brother-in-law Wan Jiaxu wrote one, saying I was dissatisfied with socialism because I once said a female newsreader did not look like a real woman. All the posters were untruthful and empty. It was unpleasant, but I wasn't panic-stricken, as I knew I had done nothing wrong—the National People's Congress had long before cleared me of the charge of 'war criminal'.

Pu Yi once apologized to me: 'I nearly ruined your life because of my silly dream of restoring the Qing.' Looking back, I feel embarrassed and ashamed that I followed his dream. It was wrong and the goal simply impossible, but we were taught only to be loyal to him, not to question him. However, there is no point moaning about the past. My motto is always to live each day and make the most out of it.

After I was attacked, no one dared be close to me. As soon as I went to sit down in the dining hall, anyone nearby would immediately run away. Well, at least I had no trouble finding a seat. In just one month I 'received' over 1,000 posters, before others were targeted and criticism against me quieted down. Maybe they were under instruction from the authorities, I have no way of knowing, but I remained a 'target of the dictatorship'. When the translation company was disbanded in the autumn of 1968, I was one of thousands including disgraced cadres, intellectuals, and artists sent to study, on half our normal salaries, at the Beijing Government Party School. Apart from attending study sessions, we also took part in manual labour.

In spring 1971, my 'problem' was eventually cleared, I graduated from the school, and was sent down to the countryside, as part of the campaign to 'send down cadres to be re-educated by peasants'. Huangta commune, my destination of exile, was only 60 kilometres west of Beijing, but deeply set into Hundred Flowers Mountain. I stayed in a small spare room of the production leader and was treated like any ordinary commune member, tilling the fields and looking after the animals. Though in my early fifties, I was still in good health and tried hard to be a good farmer. I wanted to carry as much as the young lads did. After some practice, I could carry over 50 kilograms of human waste in a basket on my back up to the terraced land along the mountain road. I reported this proudly to my family back in Beijing.

Also exiled to Huangta commune was a Mr Xiao from the Beijing government, who commanded a fair amount of medical knowledge as his father was a doctor of traditional medicine. I had studied acupuncture in Japan, purely out of interest, and had treated people around me, so the two of us began to treat villagers with acupuncture, cupping, and herbal medicine. There was a clinic in the village and one or two barefoot doctors, but their facilities were appalling and the barefoot doctors, with only limited medical training, were not really up to their jobs. All the villagers preferred us. Indeed, we 'served the people wholeheartedly'. We would go whenever we were needed, no matter daytime or evening, rain or shine, and cured many people. Our principle was 'neither grow arrogant from success, nor embarrassed by failure'. Once, when I treated an old granny suffering from stomach-ache, my acupuncture needle went right through her deformed, bound foot. She 'sacked' me the next day.

Puyi, Gobro Runqi, Pujie, and Reginald Johnston (from right to left) at the Imperial Garden in the Forbidden City

After two years, I was moved to a small farm further into the mountain, with cows, goats, and horses. I was charged with looking after two cows used for ploughing. Spotty was the hostile one and impossible to control, preferring to forage on the crops instead. When I pretended to sleep, Spotty saw his chance and began to retreat. I startled him by striking his snout with a stick. Two failed escapes later, and he gave up the idea altogether. I love animals and gave Spotty the best care, offering fresh grass and keeping him clean, until gradually Spotty let me stroke him and we became close friends. Spotty obeyed and looked after me, pulling me up slopes with his tail and even visiting my dormitory, though I doubt my room-mates appreciated such visits! Once, a shepherd spotted Spotty kneeling down before me. The cow was higher up the terraced slope than me and just wanted its neck scratched. But the shepherd had previously seen me play tricks for the local children; now he was convinced I possessed some magic power!

After the shepherd spread his story, my reputation grew far and wide. Country fellows are simply and poorly educated. They adore you if you can do something beyond their comprehension, like the time a middle-aged woman fainted but regained consciousness right after my acupuncture. Anyway, I did my best, hoping not to abuse their trust. Apart from practising as a doctor, and repairing lights, radios, and tractors, I was also put in charge of propaganda! On the little farm blackboard, I wrote out the latest instructions from the central government, and composed poems to praise Mao and the Party.

As I said, country fellows are simple and honest, with their own way of judging people. Any sensible urban person would be reluctant to befriend someone like me, a 'leftover from the old society', as I was often described. But the villagers treated me very well. If a family had something good to eat, they always offered it to me first. In 1975, I suffered intestinal obstruction and was stretchered in great pain to the county town, Zhaitang. Everyone came out to say goodbye. Someone began to cry and everyone else followed. I was touched and waved back at them: 'Don't cry, I'm not dead yet!' At the hospital, when they discovered my 'black' background, they didn't treat me properly, but gave me some painkillers and sent me away. A few days later, my situation worsened and I had to be carried back.

At the kind suggestion of the farm leader, I spent a long time recuperating at home. After the downfall of the Gang of Four, I remained at the farm, apart from four days a month at home. I would rise at 2 or 3am and walk a few hours along the winding mountain road to board the only bus to the nearest train station. The daily slow train would take me to the west corner of Beijing by early afternoon. I would be ravenous by then and always tucked into a hearty meal at the station, washed down nicely with beer. I would buy bags of sweets too, all those little luxuries unavailable in the mountain village. After four days' happy reunion with my family, I had to return, until in 1978 I was taken by the legal research department of the Chinese Academy of Social Sciences (CASS).

I didn't choose to go there, but I can't say I suffered badly down in the countryside. Both the peasants and Spotty the Cow treated me kindly. I was busy all the time and found my life meaningful, as I made myself useful to the locals. My experience there stimulated my interest in medicine, enriched my clinical practice, and to a large degree led to my new career. After I retired from CASS aged 75, I learned medicine properly and now practise as a licensed doctor, specializing in treating gynaecological diseases, such as menstrual problems and menopause depression, and problems caused by nervous system disorders. In the countryside, women's diseases were among the most common problems, due to ignorance and poor hygiene. For example, in the Hundred Flower Mountain region, new mothers must avoid wind and water for a month, and remain in bed behind shut doors and windows, even in the hottest summer. As a result, there is a high death rate among such women. I tried to explain that these women died from infection, not because they were exposed to wind!

On the other hand, my country experience was a waste in many ways. I was in my prime then, and could have done good translation work. During seven years of exile, I forgot almost all my German and English. I deeply hate the Cultural Revolution for its damage to our country and myself. In November 1980, I was invited to attend the trial of the Gang of Four. Many witnesses revealed bitter stories of persecution. Among them was Wang Guangmei, wife of the late chairman Liu Shaoqi. She calmly and clearly told how she was struggled against and humiliated in mass meetings, wearing a string of table-

Exiled to a rural commune, 1970

tennis balls around her neck—
Jiang Qing had accused her of
wearing a pearl necklace on state
visits. I remember too Liao
Mosha, a famous writer and key
member of the so-called Three
Family Village. He was hit so hard
in the face all his teeth fell out.
He burst into tears and cried
uncontrollably on the witness
stand. Compared to these people,
I was luckier. When the guilty
verdict and death sentence was
announced, Jiang Qing, who had remained cool till this moment, began
to jump up and down excitedly; she obviously missed the part about
the suspension of the death sentence. When she was helped out of the
courtroom, I noticed she collapsed. Watching her from far away, I
couldn't help but laugh to myself. Justice had been done to this evil
woman.

Fortunately, the nightmare is over. I don't believe it will ever return
because China is now open to the world. It's interesting that there are
always people in the West who want to know if China will restore its
system of monarchy. Since Pu Yi, the last emperor, had no children of
his own and his younger brother Pu Jie has died, I am among the closest
to the former royal family. People sometimes ask if I want to be an
emperor. Of course not! I don't really want to be called 'duke' either.
When I gave lectures at the Oriental Medicine College of Oregon
University recently, a colleague put up a sign: 'Welcome Duke Gobro
Runqi'. I told them there are no dukes in socialist China, only ducks.
They told me the duck is their college mascot! Modern China does not
need an emperor, but if you elect me as president, I'd be more than
happy to go for it. I'll concentrate on China's economy to make it strong,
not on political movements. I'll try to make China free and democratic,
where there is no place for massive tragedies like the Cultural Revolution
to occur.

Becoming president is wild talk. I'm very happy where I am now.
After all these years of ups and downs, I am enjoying my peaceful

time. More importantly, I still earn a living with my own hands and feel I am doing something useful for society. As an old man, I have no more to ask from life. No, there is one thing: give me a clinic at an affordable rent so I don't have to work at home!

Opening the Doors

1977–1989

When the Gang of Four's downfall was announced in mid-October 1976, celebration was the first concern of many Chinese—liquor sales broke all records, and crab stocks were exhausted in feasting that made joyful word-play on the wicked quartet. If a new era had dawned, its ideology sounded remarkably familiar: 'Whatever Mao did and whatever Mao said was right.' Chief 'whateverist' Hua Guofeng, the Mao look-alike anointed successor in the Chairman's last days, faithfully followed his leftist line. In agriculture, Hua lauded the Dazhai model commune, and in industry the Daqing model oilfield. The latter, however, could never fuel Hua's fantastic Ten Year Plan, a Maoist vision with little concession to Chinese reality.

It would take bolder leadership than Hua to satisfy a people weary of slogans and disillusioned with authority. In July 1977, Deng Xiaoping emerged from disgrace, for the third time in his career, to reclaim his vice-chairmanship. The ever-pragmatic Sichuanese, a Party man since the 1920s, soon recognized the demand for material incentives and a return to normality. Wage hikes, after a freeze of fifteen years, were typical of measures to assuage popular discontent. Beginning in April 1978, Deng began salvaging Party legitimacy through the rehabilitation of millions of Chinese citizens wronged in the myriad campaigns since Liberation.

In May 1978, Deng challenged the 'whateverist' line with the Maoist motto 'Seek truth from facts', to which he added, 'Practice is the sole criterion for testing truth'—implicitly rejecting the formulaic application of political theory. Deng may have failed to win Mao's blessing as leader, but the Democracy Wall protests later that year revealed where public support lay. As countless wall posters and magazines debated China's future, Deng's ascendancy was confirmed at a Party conference in December. Economic construction replaced class struggle as the 'key link' and national priority. Ignoring Hua's grandiose plan, the Party urged moderation in industry and opposed egalitarianism in agriculture: peasants should be paid according to work, not need, and private plots could co-exist with people's communes.

Following the establishment of Sino-US diplomatic relations on 1 January 1979, Deng paid a high-profile and highly successful visit to America. On his return he ordered the predictable crack-down on the Democracy Wall activists. The first liberal outburst in two decades had served its purpose. Deng moved to pre-empt further calls for political reform by issuing the Four Cardinal Principles: China must uphold the socialist road, the dictatorship of the proletariat, the leadership of the Party, and Marxism-Leninism and Mao Zedong Thought. While the principles ensured no one would challenge the Party, they also disguised the economic revolution the new leader was unleashing.

Deng faced a bureaucratic command structure which hoarded national income, refused to stimulate consumption, and stifled initiative. In 1979, up to 30 per cent of industrial enterprises were operating at a loss. Meeting the annual plan outweighed any notion of product value and quality. Eating and shopping required endless coupons, and one might wait years for a bicycle. In response, decision-making was slowly decentralized to encourage better management, while bonuses were offered to encourage the workforce. As rigid pricing controls were eased on certain goods between 1979 and 1982, people complained that inflation, a capitalist curse banished in the early 1950s, outpaced wage rises. The Four Modernizations were China's blueprint for development, opening the door to foreign technology and capital. In July 1979, four 'special economic zones' were established on China's south coast to attract foreign investors. The joint-venture law was issued in 1979, and the first joint venture followed the next year.

The rehabilitation process climaxed in May 1980 with a memorial service for former president Liu Shaoqi. *The People's Daily* admitted that vindication of Liu, vilified as a 'renegade, traitor, and scab' ever since his death in 1969, was 'bound to cause a certain amount of shock and misinterpretation'. The paper had a lot of explaining to do that year, from exposing the lies behind Dazhai to admitting the 'great mistakes' of Mao's later years. At the November trial of the Gang of Four, Jiang Qing spat invective at the court and maintained: 'I was Chairman Mao's dog; whomever he told me to bite, I bit.' Many Chinese knew it was a 'gang of five' but Mao, as China's Lenin and Stalin, remained fundamental to Party credibility. After the four were committed to jail, scapegoats for the Cultural Revolution, the verdict on Mao's legacy in June 1981 mirrored his own judgement on Stalin: 70 per cent correct, 30 per cent incorrect. Across China, most Mao portraits and statues slowly came down.

While the Party was laying its misdeeds to rest, a revolution was underway in China's villages. Like Mao, Deng's revolution began in the countryside, home to 80 per cent of his citizens. Yet where Mao corralled them into people's communes, Deng chose to set them free. Following the brave lead of an Anhui village, where desperate peasants secretly divided up the land in 1978, Deng disbanded the communes. By 1983, when over 90 per cent of rural households were managing individual plots, agricultural output had soared.Under Party Secretary Zhao Ziyang, Sichuan was another pioneer of reform. His successful rejuvenation of agriculture and industry earned him the premiership at Hua Guofeng's expense. With another protégé, Hu Yaobang, installed by mid-1981 as Party chairman (later general secretary), Deng had his team in place.

The 1982 state census revealed the enormity of their task. China was home to a billion people for the first time in its long history, an administrative burden without precedent worldwide. The one child per family policy, instituted in 1980, was given renewed urgency. Enforcement was unpopular, but without birth control no amount of economic growth could make China rich. And that remained Deng's goal, to be reached by 'socialism with Chinese characteristics', the ideological gymnastics that shaped Marxism to Chinese conditions. The patriotic appeal of this policy served to allay conservative fears about the effects of the open door. After decades of self-imposed incarceration, when foreign things were branded counter-revolutionary, Chinese were hungry for new ideas. Artists and journalists responded with a new openness and daring. The Party replied in late 1983 with the Anti-Spiritual Pollution Campaign, opposing the corrosion of Chinese culture and Marxist philosophy.

The success of rural reforms saw their extension to the urban sector in 1984. Market mechanisms threatened the 'iron rice-bowl' of lifetime employment as enterprises won greater managerial autonomy from the state. 'Pauperism is not socialism', Zhao Ziyang explained. Deng put it more memorably: 'To get rich is glorious.' *Getihu*, private businessmen, entered everyday life bringing snacks, services, and bustling markets back to China's long-deserted streets. The new phenomenon of '10,000-yuan households' enjoyed lavish press attention. The year 1984 was to prove a watershed: the greatest harvest in Chinese history was complemented by the nation's first-ever Olympic gold medal and the Sino-British agreement that would return Hong Kong to China in 1997. At the thirty-fifth anniversary of the PRC in October, people displayed their pride in Deng. Yet trouble lay ahead.

As the economy overheated in 1985, numerous corruption scandals exposed the temptations that accompanied new economic opportunity. Hu Yaobang was quoted complaining that Marx and Lenin couldn't solve China's current problems. *The People's Daily* rushed out a correction, but many Chinese were frustrated by raging inflation that shrank salaries and threatened life savings. In May, China experienced its first football riot; a year later, its first bankrupt enterprise, a milestone in a 'proletarian dictatorship'. In October 1986, Deng warmly greeted the Queen of England, while warning Chinese that 'we must not imitate the West'. But the open doors had attracted democratic values as well as expensive technology. Student protests in December in Hefei, Shanghai, and elsewhere shocked the old guard into dismissing Hu Yaobang as party chief. Railing against 'bourgeois liberalism', Deng warned: 'We cannot do without dictatorship. We must not only affirm the need for it, but exercise it when necessary.'

But the reforms continued. After Zhao Ziyang's progressive manifesto was adopted at the Thirteenth Party Congress in October 1987, *The People's Daily* commented on the new pragmatism: 'We have finally come back from heaven to earth.' China remained in the primary stage of socialism, Zhao declared, when the need to expand production permitted capitalist practices. The Open Door policy was reaffirmed and an ambitious coastal development plan launched in 1988. Zhao's theoretical agility capped a decade of economic restructuring that transformed China's Marxist experiment and achieved spectacular results. In the 1980s, China's GNP grew at almost 9 per cent per annum, three times the world average. When Deng rose to power in 1978, the 'three big buys' for Chinese consumers were bicycles, watches, and sewing-machines. By 1988, they were televisions, washing-machines, and refrigerators. China would become the world's leading producer of all three.

In 1980, Deng had hoped for ten peaceful years. He almost achieved it, but for one major shortfall in his reform programme: the lack of voice for those who believed in underpinning economic change with political relaxation. That shortfall would set a million people onto Tiananmen Square, the symbolic heart of the PRC, as the death of Hu

Yaobang in April 1989 escalated into the Beijing Spring protests for cleaner and more open government. Zhao Ziyang was sacrificed by nervous party elders, a lifetime of class struggle away from the young protestors who looked abroad for China's answers, not backwards to the battles and privations of the 1940s and 1950s. On 4 June 1989, the tanks of the PLA enforced a brutal reiteration of the political status quo. The party that had promised a new China had become the embodiment of self-interest and repression. The world watched in horror. Would China's doors stay open?

Wang Shan
The Writing on the Wall

T he Tiananmen Incident, during the celebration of the Qingming Festival in 1976, had allowed people a brief avenue of grief for the loss of Premier Zhou and a channel for dissent against the surviving leadership. It would be two years before its 'counter-revolutionary' tag was formally removed. That decision, and the rehabilitation of rightists begun by Deng Xiaoping in April 1978, encouraged writers into an outpouring of Cultural Revolution suffering known as Scar literature. On the ragtag posters of Beijing's Democracy Wall in the late autumn, the discussion deepened into political debate that would culminate in the unforgivable threat posed by a lone electrician, Wei Jingsheng, and his Fifth Modernization: democracy.

Wang Shan, one of China's best-known political analysts, belongs to a generation of young intellectuals whose careers were shaped by the heady events of the late 1970s. He was born in 1952 in a Zhejiang army camp, to a senior officer's family. Studies at a premier Beijing boarding-school ended in 1967 when Jiang Qing disbanded it in a campaign against leaders' privileges. Release from this isolated circle enabled Wang to form friendships with common children. He came even closer to 'real' China when he was sent to Shanxi in 1968 to be re-educated by the peasants and labour at the Datong coalmines. Enlisting in the army and Party in 1970 provided welcome escape. On his eventual return to Beijing, Wang Shan was assigned to the Party committee of Beijing Normal University.

In December 1978, the Democracy Wall protests coincided with Deng Xiaoping's own political manoeuvring. Deng told an American journalist at the time, 'The people want to speak. Let them!', while quietly warning that not all the ideas pasted up were correct. Once he had successfully concluded his trip to the United States in February 1979, he could condone the increasingly radical movement no longer. Wei Jingsheng was arrested in March and the magazines and discussion groups were steadily banned. The Maoist right to 'engage in great debate and put up big-character posters' was dropped from the Constitution the following year.

As the democracy movement was put on hold, Wang returned to university and the task of reversing the verdicts on those wronged in past campaigns. From 1988, he pursued literary writing as deputy director of the Beijing Opera Troupe until the 1994 publication, under a German pen-name, of his controversial best-seller *Viewing China Through a Third Eye*, a challenging look at reform-fuelled problems. The censors' efforts to ban it saw pirate sales exceed 1 million, yet even President Jiang Zemin sang the book's praises, until he discovered the author was Chinese. Democracy Wall still claims great resonance in certain circles, though today's visitor will look in vain for the wall itself, victim of Xidan's daily struggle with Wangfujing to emerge as the nation's premier shopping street.

THE DEMOCRACY WALL MOVEMENT began in autumn 1978 with the pasting up of some 'big-character posters' (*dazibao*) on a blank wall in Xidan, about 2 kilometres west of Tiananmen Square. The earliest posters described personal suffering and tragedies: their authors were mainly people who had been wronged during the Cultural Revolution. Many had come from outside Beijing; now they wanted rehabilitation for themselves or their families.

The Wall became so popular it attracted hundreds and thousands of people. Every day after work, people rushed to Xidan to see the new posters. There were quite a number of people like me, from fairly privileged backgrounds, who were drawn to the movement. During the Cultural Revolution, we all ended up at the bottom of the society, where we saw plenty of injustice, caused to a large degree by the undemocratic social system. We were interested in politics and hoped to change that system.

The posters soon progressed from telling personal stories to discussing wider political issues. Young intellectuals, who comprised most of the participants, began to ask what were the causes of these tragedies—some even dared to point fingers directly at Mao—and how to prevent them. Democracy Wall responded very sensitively to the struggle underway in the leadership. Posters went up demanding the masses have a say in politics and for Deng to assume a higher position. Poems were written to praise him; articles emerged introducing Western-style democracy.

It was a very primitive form of democracy, inherited from the Cultural Revolution era, for the big-character poster was Mao's creation. Yet it also showed people were seeking modern democracy—to express one's views freely and independently in public, without approval or censorship by any authority. It was unprecedented in the thirty-year history of the PRC.

As the movement unfolded, I was working for the Party committee at Beijing Normal University 'reversing verdicts' of people wrongly accused in the past. At our university, more than 300 cases needed review. Most were ridiculous: these people were wronged not because their cases were complicated, but because during political campaigns intellectuals were deliberately made the enemies of the government for crimes they didn't commit. The root of the cause was still in the system. That was another reason why I was attracted by the Democracy Wall movement.

As the movement developed, young activists formed groups based around publications. Most influential were four magazines: *Exploration*, run by Wei Jingsheng; *Beijing Spring*, with its chief editor Wang Juntao; *Today*, featuring modern poems; and *Fertile Land*, of which I was a founding member. Each had its own style: Wei's *Exploration* was purely political; our *Fertile Land* emphasized literary works and poems, as well as political essays and articles, which suited my interest.

Before Democracy Wall, Zhou Enlai's widow Deng Yingchao had called on writers to write for women. I created the feminine pen-name Bai Xue (White Snow), which I kept until the Wall fell, to describe a woman's fate during the Cultural Revolution, the true story of a beautiful soldier I had met. She was so eager to join the Party, but was rejected by jealous bosses and colleagues who accused her of 'bourgeois thoughts'. She was a dancer at the performing troupe and would sometimes confide her unfulfilled dreams to me, until tears choked her words. Later, the skin on her face fell off in black flakes, poisoned by lead. People said she deliberately left her make-up on after performances. She retired from the army and died of depression. It was naïve and not so-well written, but *Punishment of Beauty* let me express how the Cultural Revolution destroyed beauty, humanity, and individualism. It was how I began to write.

All the magazines were run by a few friends; we joked ours had five 'standing committee' members: Hu Ping, Jiang Hong, Peng Yidong,

Tie Zhu, and myself. Hu Ping, from Sichuan, seemed shy and quiet, not so aggressive and experienced as us locals, but actually very sharp and thoughtful. Both his parents died from persecution. He now runs *Beijing Spring* in the USA. Jiang Hong was chief editor. An economics graduate, he joined the People's Bank of China after Democracy Wall and for a time was one of China's key financial policy-makers. He seems to have lost all interest in politics.

During the movement, Peng Yidong (whose pen-name was Wang Jing) collaborated on a hit screenplay for the film *In Society's Archives*, where the corrupt behaviour of high-ranking officers, and their suppression of the people, would be recorded; in time, the crimes would be punished. For the first time after the Cultural Revolution, a work of literature pointed out that the ruling regime naturally suffers conflicts with the ordinary people. It predicted bureaucratic corruption would lead to the eventual overthrow of the Communists. The film made a big splash throughout the country.

Tie Zhu, son of the famous writer Xiao Qian, was a poet who wrote a series of political poems on the theme, 'Why has democracy not come to China?' He regarded both Sun Yatsen and Mao Zedong as democracy fighters—in fact, both tried and failed to realize democracy in China. Ulimately, apart from the obvious reason that China's feudal heritage was too strong, he could not find any satisfying answers. His poems were always sad, depressing, and puzzled, but we loved and could recite many of them.

We put our poems, essays, and short stories up on the wall, then compiled them for distribution. We printed forty copies for the first issue—it would be a good value now if you still possessed one!—and 200 copies for the second issue at the beginning of 1979. Later we printed about 400 copies for each issue. Altogether, we had seven issues before it came to an end. I guess nowadays only the five 'standing committee' members have all seven.

After the Party's Third Plenum in December 1978, Deng Xiaoping's political position was secured. As he gained more and more power, his popularity soared. Gradually, down at Democracy Wall, the restless youth began to ask questions about him. Firstly, how to prevent Deng from becoming the new Mao Zedong; secondly, though Deng is a wise leader with great political experience, if he does not give the people democracy,

is it not inevitable that he will
repeat Mao's mistakes?

At the very beginning, we
decided our magazine should
feature literature and advocate
liberal, but politically cautious,
ideas. So we never really
confronted the government
politically. At that time, China
was still barely 'open' and dealing
with foreigners was seen as
almost immoral. Unlike Wei, we
never associated with foreigners
at all; his magazine *Exploration*
was far more political and radical
than ours. Many of its members
were bold and daring, for they

*Wang Shan, at the time of Democracy Wall
(1978–9)*

were children of high-ranking officials. As a result of our caution, our
situation was not so bad after the crack-down.

By May or June 1979, Deng declared two of the publications illegal.
Back in March, Wei had been arrested, officially for leaking information
to foreigners about the border war with Vietnam. The war was supported
by the whole nation, but not Wei and a handful of other forward-thinking,
independently minded intellectuals. He believed that in an
undemocratic system, even important decisions like military action
largely depended on personal preference. That was why he raised a
new concept: the Fifth Modernization, democracy, without which, he
felt, the other four modernizations would be empty promises. Political
democracy is not only the purpose, but also the precondition for the
Four Modernizations. While some of the language Wei used then, and
the way he dealt with things, was far from pragmatic, the concept of
the 'Fifth Modernization' *was* a very new idea, raised by a young
intellectual who went through the Cultural Revolution and analysed it
independently. It is still not obsolete even today.

After the crack-down, all of those who took part in the movement
were asked to confess, then swear never to be involved in such events
ever again. As a Party member, I confessed to my Party committee and

was not treated too harshly. Everything I had published in *Fertile Land* was handed in to the literary and political professors, but they never reached a conclusion. At the time, a liberal tide was about to stir. Everyone could feel it, yet was nervous about it. The committee head moved to fire me from the 'reversing verdicts' task, but protective colleagues helped me remain until 1984. As for my friends at *Fertile Land*, after the movement, we began the painful search for our own future. Compared to Wei Jingsheng, we lacked his determination to confront the authorities directly; on the other hand, we all had ideas we wanted to pursue.

The spring of 1981 witnessed a remarkable political event: direct elections among university students for the people's representatives of Haidian district, in Beijing's north-west, home to the best universities in China. Hu Ping, studying for a master's degree, stood for election at Beijing University. We had not been in touch with him since the crack-down, as each of us had political investigations to hurdle. I remember a government spy was sent among us. He was very active, always finding meeting places for us. When we realized his true identity, we tried to spout things closer to the Party line to ease the political pressure on us. How funny it now seems.

Hu was one of the first students to stand for election. Wang Juntao [later imprisoned as one of the 'black hands' behind 4 June 1989] also ran, plus numerous others. It was an immature but brave democratic experiment. The most famous line at the hustings was 'I am *not* a Communist Party member'. Whenever someone uttered it, there was always huge applause from the audience. I believe Democracy Wall and that direct election bred the first batch of Chinese intellectuals with strong democratic ideas. They were outstanding, determined and brave. They remain the main force of the democracy movement right until today: Wei Jingsheng, Hu Ping, and Wang Juntao are typical examples.

In the end, Hu Ping was the only student elected, and he paid a high personal price. Viewed as a dangerous character by the government, he was not allocated a job after graduation. No job meant no salary, so life was terribly difficult for him. After two years, he found a job at a publishing company, from where he left for America. He still works and fights for the democracy cause in China.

Meanwhile, I concentrated on 'reversing the verdicts' at my university. The case of the teacher Li Jinkai sticks in my memory. He was expelled from the Party during the Four Clean-Ups Campaign in 1965. His crime? To marry the daughter of his 'bourgeois' professor, Li Jingxi, the foremost authority on Chinese grammar and language. Lu Dingyi, a senior official dispatched by the central government, accused Professor Li of using his daughter to corrupt proletarian teacher Li, who himself lost Party membership for being corrupted by 'capitalist poison seeds'. The verdict on Li Jinkai would have been reversed, if the marriage was his only 'crime', but, during the Cultural Revolution, he was a key adviser to Wang Hongwen as he rose from worker to PRC vice-chairman and member of the Gang of Four. When Li's rehabilitation was discussed, many were uncertain over his involvement with Wang. Li himself wrote many times to Lu Dingyi, demanding to resume his Party status. Lu faithfully carried out Mao's leftist line, but later suffered bitterly by the same line. Lu wrote to the university: 'As an old Party member, I beg you to correct my mistake!'

Under pressure from the central government, the university sent me to investigate Li Jinkai's involvement with Wang Hongwen. In mid-1984, I spent a few months in Shanghai's prisons, interviewing those who were in the same Worker Rebels group as Wang and Li. Later, I spoke to Wang Hongwen in a Beijing prison. But by the time I finished my investigation, the Beijing Party secretary who ordered the investigation had left. Li's case was dropped and he was never rehabilitated. His story reflects the complex relationship between the Communists and intellectuals. An orphan from Tianjin who made a living by selling cigarettes in the street, Li was brought up and trained by the Party. He was seen as a 'red' intellectual, our own intellectual, yet it was the Communists who dumped him. During the Cultural Revolution, he rebelled against them. In the 1980s, Li grasped the opportunities of the market economy to make a fortune in business and enjoy a lavish lifestyle until his death in a fishing accident.

As I continued 'reversing verdicts', I often compared Li with another teacher who also owed to the Communists his rise from poverty in Tianjin to a teacher's post at the same university. Unlike the opportunist Li, this one trusted the Communists almost religiously. Young, handsome, an inspiring teacher and Party member, he attracted many female students. The day before one pretty student left to join the air force, she finally revealed her diary, full of a year's expressions of love for him.

She wanted to go to bed with him. He tried to refuse at first, but became flattered, moved, and aroused. They kissed and hugged in his dormitory. Impulsively, they went so far as taking off their clothes. But, just in time, he remembered the Party's teachings, and put his clothes back on! Throughout a restless night, they took off their clothes and put them back on several times until daybreak, when she had to leave. He felt relieved he had refused the temptation of the devil, but mentally and sexually frustrated.

During the Four Clean-Ups Campaign, which encouraged people to 'search out the dirt hidden in the depth of one's soul', he confessed in detail about his encounter—at that crazy time, no one was permitted any privacy, even one's most intimate thoughts. He was expelled from the Party. When I later read his confession, I knew he believed in Communism as a religion and the Party as God. But God did not forgive him.

My sympathy was tainted with disdain. He was such a tame lamb that he lacked the courage to do what he wanted. Li Jinkai, boasting far stronger tendencies in liberalism and individualism, did what he wanted (in a public park before marriage) but while the cautious teacher was rehabilitated, Li was the only one of 300 cases not rehabilitated. The two different stories told me the same thing: at a certain historical stage, China's intellectuals and the Chinese Communists needed each other and liked to work together, but their different nature and path decided that the intellectuals would eventually part from Communist doctrine. My Democracy Wall experience lent me the same conclusion.

The central government's decision to 'reverse the verdicts' won back to a certain degree won back some people's support and trust. It demonstrated the unselfish, honest, and courageous side of the Party. It was also driven by a survival instinct, as the Communists wanted to remain the ruling party. But many people did not feel grateful even when they were rehabilitated. Why? Because the Communists did not change the political system; it was still the same undemocratic, totalitarian system under which they had suffered. Before, they were punished for their speeches; after rehabilitation, they had still not earned the freedom of speech.

After Democracy Wall, our journals were banned. Later, many other publications were banned due to the lack of freedom of speech. The *World Economic Herald* in Shanghai was a notable victim in 1989. Many wanted not only justice for themselves, but also a system that will guarantee justice for others. At the same time as the government was 'reversing' cases, they launched new campaigns to attack liberal bourgeois thought. In 1981, the well-known writer Bai Hua was under fire for writing the screenplay to *Bitter Love*—a patriotic intellectual returned from abroad to help the motherland he loved, only to find the motherland did not love him.

The first case I dealt with took place before the Third Plenum, when large-scale 'reversal of verdicts' work began across the whole country. I went to Tianjin to see a man accused as a counter-revolutionary during the Cultural Revolution. When I declared, right in front of him, that the Party had decided it was wrong to label him a counter-revolutionary, he burst into tears, sobbing, 'The Party is fair after all.' I was a young Party worker, only in my twenties. I also told him he had made some mistakes. He thanked me feverishly. I felt very proud of myself: representing our Party, I had corrected a mistake. I regarded mine a sacred mission.

The older man insisted on inviting me for a meal—actually, just steamed buns and porridge—over which he began to talk. He felt uncomfortable that he was still considered 'wrong in some ways', though no longer a counter-revolutionary. 'I did nothing wrong!' he protested. 'All I did was to follow the Party's instruction. I only said things in my own way, not exactly in newspaper language. What was wrong about that?' I was shocked. I realized the relationship between the Party and intellectuals is not after all like the relationship between a father and a son. A father beats up his son and then says, 'Sorry, son, I am wrong to beat you. But you have also made mistakes.' The son would not mind, as it is all within the family. But the intellectual *would* mind. There *is* conflict between the Party and intellectuals. The political system of the CCP does not allow people to have their own things, their own language, their own thoughts and space. But the intellectuals demand their freedom and independence. Years later, when the old man came to Beijing, I gave him another verdict—free of any 'mistakes' during the Cultural Revolution—which did not leave him any 'tail' of guilt. This time, he did not show me any gratitude.

Democracy Wall happened twenty years ago, but it had almost been quietly forgotten by me. I have never talked about it until now. Looking back, I see more clearly how important the period was for me. My participation in the movement and the work of 'reversing verdicts' taught me never to trust blindly in any line or ideology, but to analyse from a new and independent angle, like a third eye. I have been trying to do so, in books and novels, ever since.

Song Liying

The Red Flag of Dazhai

Rural reforms underway in Anhui and Sichuan at the end of the 1980s heralded a dramatic departure from twenty-five years of collectivized agriculture. The new household responsibility system returned land use and incentive to the peasants. After guaranteeing the state a certain level of tax and crops, they were free to grow more or pursue sideline business. While this new autonomy to manage their own land was seized upon by the majority of China's peasants, the retreat from the collective spirit was keenly felt in Maoist bastions like the model commune Dazhai.

'In agriculture, learn from Dazhai!' So screamed China's rural manifesto throughout the Cultural Revolution, a call for self-reliance, hard work, and political fervour. The drama began in 1963 when a fierce storm devastated the small village deep in the loess plateau of northern Shanxi. Inspired by their illiterate Party secretary Chen Yonggui, Dazhai's villagers drew strength from Mao's works, bare-handed determination compensated for lack of technology, and production increased fivefold. As the miracles piled up, Chen wore a peasant towel on his head all the way to a Politburo seat in 1973.

Too good to be true? Dazhai, the 'Great Stockade', is the Cultural Revolution in miniature. Ignoring local conditions, all China copied Dazhai's land reclamation by clearing forests, filling rivers, and carving terraces even on the plains. This model commune drew 7 million pilgrims by 1980, the year its falsified statistics and massive state support were exposed. Chen lost all his titles; his model was a sham. National disgrace and the break-up of the communes were hard blows for local cadres like Song Liying. A Dazhai native born to poor peasants in 1931, Song was only 12 when sold for a sack of sweetcorn to Jia Jingcai, Chen's predecessor and twenty years Song's senior. Song herself served as a deputy Party secretary throughout Dazhai's glory years until her retirement in 1975.

As a loyal Party member who accepts the current line, Song still defends the remarkable harvests of old, and denies Dazhai was helped by the state. Besides the ideological loss for Song and others, economic reforms did result in neglect of large projects in many communities, as expensive machinery went idle and basic services suffered. Enthusiasm for sideline businesses meant some peasants spent as little as sixty days per year in the fields, where once they toiled for as many as 300. Opportunities to escape the countryside entirely remained tightly controlled by village cadres in the mid-eighties. All four of Song's children managed to join the army and later to find jobs in Shanxi and other provinces.

By 1984, some 98 per cent of China's farming households had adopted the new system, and by 1987 rice and wheat output exceeded pre-reform levels by 50 per cent. Even Dazhai has become an unlikely champion of reform: non-agricultural activities now provide over 90 per cent of its income. Red rhetoric still covers village walls, but today the two great characters blazing 'Dazhai' from a hillside resemble advertising more than propaganda. The government is quick to point out that the responsibility system does *not* mean privatization, or capitalism, as ownership of land, the most basic means of production, remains in state hands. The peasants of Dazhai are too busy to argue.

THE 'HOUSEHOLD CONTRACT responsibility system' was introduced to Dazhai in 1983. We were summoned to a meeting hall where the news was announced. By that time, the system had been implemented in most parts of China. Of course we had heard about it, but it still met strong resentment. Almost everyone tried to refuse the new policy. For us, socialism meant the people's commune, where everyone worked together on land that was collectively owned. Since Dazhai was so famous, many communes in Xiyang county, even throughout Shanxi province, where the system had not been implemented, were watching us.

A work team from the county government was sent down to our village. They explained how the system worked—it did *not* mean capitalism, as was suspected by some farmers. The land still belonged to the government; a small piece of it would merely be contracted to us. They promised it would be good for us farmers, as we would have the freedom to run our own contracted land. Finally, they stressed how important it was to guarantee successful implementation in our village, since it might influence the work in other communes, in the county, and even the province. I didn't really like it at first, but I was an old Party member. If the Party wanted us to distribute the land, they must have their reasons. I should obey, and tried to persuade others to obey too. In fact, towards the end, it didn't really matter if you agreed or not.

The work team and village leaders did a good and thorough job, though it was very difficult to divide up the land. Some areas are more fertile than others; some are on terraced land, others more level; some areas are far away, others closer to the village. They spent a long time measuring and marking out the land, trying to give each family as fair an amount as possible. Families were organized into groups for the draw according to their size. Three of our four children were away in different cities, leaving my husband, myself, and our youngest son who was unmarried. I randomly picked a piece of paper, which showed our contracted land was on a terraced slope. We were lucky it wasn't hidden in the gullies, which would have been too difficult for an old couple like us to reach. On average, each person was given 1.4 *mu* of land. We grow wheat on the land, as most families do, though some also grow corn, potatoes, or other vegetables. In the days of the commune, we also tried to grow rice, but we just don't have enough water here.

Once the land was in their hands, the farmers worked hard. They deducted the amount they had to hand in to the government, and realized they would get more if they grew more. Production per *mu* increased, more or less. We did our best to look after our land, ploughing deep, weeding carefully. To make the land more fertile, we made our own fertilizer, mixing human waste with mud and straw. Before, no matter how one worked, each person was basically paid the same. In theory, each person's labour marks were frequently valued; in practice, they were always the same. An able-bodied man earned the full 10; an unmarried woman always got 7, and married women 6, as they often made trips home to look after their family. Our old Party secretary Chen Yonggui felt the labour-mark system was very fair and equal; we all accepted that.

Gradually, our lives improved, not only due to increases in grain production, but also in opportunities to make money. Before the reform, engaging in any sideline production was banned and criticized as 'the capitalist tail'. The policy was particularly strict in our Dazhai. We weren't allowed to grow anything on our backyard; we weren't allowed to produce anything for sale or engage in any kind of trade. In the early fifties, my husband, who was then Party secretary, tried to run a small coal-mining business. Of course, they gave up. As a village cadre, I would intervene myself if I knew anyone dared violate the rules. The only way to have extra cash was to sell a few eggs at the market. The locals called it the 'chicken bottom bank'.

Now, you can do anything you like, raise pigs to eat or sell, make cloth tigers, the local speciality, and sell them at market . . . . But I must say, in the eighties, even if some people made money, it wasn't much. Yet the overall living standard was better. In 1984, with the extra money we had, we bought a small black-and-white TV set. I still remember it was a Panda brand. We all thought the electric box was magic with its sounds and images. Many other families got theirs around the same time. In 1985, our son went to find work at Xiyang county, since he felt he couldn't make enough from the land. He was a senior high school graduate, fairly educated for a country lad, and eventually settled as a

Song Liying beside portraits of Mao, Zhou, and her husband, Dazhai, 1998

clerk at the railway bureau. After he left, we gave up two *mu* of contracted land.

Business really kicked off after 1991, when Guo Fenglian returned from ten years working elsewhere in Shanxi to work as our Party secretary. Guo is a very capable and talented woman. I know her very well; for several years, she lived in the cave house next door. The 'Iron Maiden' team of workers that she led no longer exists, but she remains a true iron maiden. The outside world opened up her eyes to the market economy. As soon as she came back, she led us villagers into business. There is plenty of coal in this region, so a couple of small mines started up. With experience learned from all over the country, Party Secretary Guo established township and village enterprises, including a sweater factory and a shirt factory, producing the 'Dazhai' brand name, as our name is still well-known in China. Later, Dazhai set up a cement factory (a joint venture with Hong Kong), and even took over a distillery to produce 'Dazhai Spring' white spirit. I hear it sells very well.

As there are only 530 people in our village, we have to hire a couple of hundred workers from elsewhere in our factories. Now, most of the field work is done by women. All the able-bodied men work at factories and enterprises, only helping out in their spare time. Of course, our living standards have leapt in the past several years. Before the reform, even if you were a full 10 marks, you only earned 15 cents a day. Our average annual income was under 300 yuan. By 1991, it rose to 730 yuan; by 1997, it jumped to 2,700 yuan! In 1997, we paid nearly 2 million yuan tax to the government, the biggest taxpayer among all the villages in Xiyang county. You might ask why an old granny like me cares about these things. I am still a Party member and a villager of Dazhai. I am proud of our village!

Many visitors wonder what we did before, and how we can now afford to be part-time farmers? Before, in the winter, when we didn't have to till the land, we worked on agriculture infrastructure, like reservoirs and irrigation tunnels, or terracing land that was often hard and rocky. In my memory, we were busy all the time. Of course, we studied Chairman Mao's works in the fields, during intervals of twenty minutes or so, and some evenings we had political meetings. But that didn't take too much time. I think we laid a good agricultural foundation in Mao's time. Now, with Deng Xiaoping's reform, we can be successful on top of that good base. Nowadays, people know how to make good use of time. Before, if you came to our village, you would see people standing around chatting, playing cards or mahjong. Now, you simply won't see anybody hanging around. They're all working!

I too enjoy a comfortable life now, together with my son's family, as my husband passed away in 1996. My son still works at the county town on a monthly income of 400 yuan. My daughter-in-law works at the village grain shop for 300 [yuan per month]. My granddaughter is at school. She's the luckiest one. When I was at her age, I worked as hard as a slave. Now, she has good clothes to wear, good food to eat, and all kinds of snacks I'll never be able to name. I'm still in good health, and look after our contract land, helped by the young couple. My three other children sometimes send money, though I tell them not to bother, as I have enough to spend. White flour has long replaced cornflour, our main staple for many, many years. And Spring Festival is no longer the only time we eat meat.

In 1998, the land was redistributed again under the same system [after the fifteen-year contracts signed in 1983 had expired]. This time, nobody resisted. If villagers have any concern, it is whether the policy might change back one day. Who does not want to be rich?

Don St Pierre

Same Bed, Different Dreams

In January 1979, within weeks of the resumption of diplomatic relations between China and the United States, four American businessmen stepped nervously off their flight to Beijing. A city of long, grey avenues awaited, where slow-motion cyclists faced little threat from mechanized transport. How the visitors wished to change all that! They came from American Motors Corporation (AMC), makers of the Jeep Cherokee. Their aim? To build and sell that brand name in the world's most populous nation.

At the end of the month, Deng Xiaoping's triumphant visit to America would formally kick-start a decade of remarkable US and world business interest in 'Red China'. The rationale for the open-door was stipulated in the Four Modernizations: technology transfer and the generation of foreign capital. Yet four years of hard negotiations were necessary for AMC to turn that initial visit into a joint venture with the state-run Beijing Automotive Works. After the fanfare that greeted the deal in 1983, the harsh realities of operation turned Beijing Jeep into a barometer of the Sino-foreign business relationship, highlighting the contradictions of capitalists in a communist system.

Just as Beijing Jeep became synonymous with foreign investment in China, so did Don St Pierre represent Beijing Jeep. The outspoken Canadian was drafted in as president and troubleshooter in 1985. The 44-year-old car man had no previous China experience (few Western executives did), but was battle-hardened in other Asian bureaucracies. Don proved his mettle in the 'Beijing Jeep Crisis' of 1986, as he broke all the rules to go public with his frustration at the debts and other problems crippling his company. Future Premier Zhu Rongji was authorized to broker a deal so sweet that by early 1987 Don was singing China's praises—'Jump in, the water's fine!'—and Beijing Jeep was acclaimed a 'model joint venture'.

The Americans' roller-coaster ride was chronicled in the 1989 book *Beijing Jeep: The Short Unhappy Romance of American Business in China*. The doom-laden subtitle reflected the feelings of many: after Tiananmen, could life (and business) ever be the same? The events of 4 June soured the Western appetite to invest. But not for too long. The return of high growth in the early 1990s spurred Don to start his own company, supplying Chateau St Pierre red wine to Beijing's growing class of affluent urban consumers. Fifteen years after his first visit, China has become home.

Beijing Jeep is another survivor, though its future is perhaps less rosé than Don's. The Cherokee that blazed a trail, driving the American dream through China's open door, has itself been outpaced by the market. Beijing Jeep sales dropped from 50,000 vehicles in 1997 to 30,000 in 1998. Yet the numbers add up for some—Germany's Volkswagen is China's most successful joint venture year on year—and the nation's irresistible scale still entices generous investors. In 1999, the first Buick sedan rolled off the assembly line of General Motors' US$1.5 billion joint venture in Shanghai.

SAME BED, DIFFERENT DREAMS? At Beijing Jeep, I would assemble all the department directors and turn that Chinese saying on its head: 'Same bed, same dreams! That's what we're gonna do!'

I didn't know how bad it really was until I arrived. A party for the mid-autumn mooncake festival in September 1985 was my first chance to walk around the factory. I had seen many plants worldwide, so it was not a total surprise—a new part to build the Cherokee, and the old part which hadn't changed in fifty years: old Russian design, machinery, and technology, heavily over-staffed (we estimated one of every five workers was needed). They were all dressed in Mao jackets, though the Chinese management soon took to wearing suits.

From the very outset, the Chinese had received me with great suspicion. They saw my name and concluded I was a Renault spy! They argued like hell to make the senior Chinese president, with me number two, but AMC held firm. Unlike my colleagues from Toledo, Ohio, and the like, I had worked in a Third World country, but here in China we faced a double whammy: a Third World country *plus* a communist system! Nobody had any experience with that second part. No one on our side knew what the Party leaders at Beijing Jeep were up to, though ultimately the political dimension was not a major problem. It is always so important to build relationships in China, to forge trust between two parties; then, anything can happen—they even invited me to their Saturday afternoon Party sessions.

One of the main frustrations was that no one was telling the truth. That probably included us too. The relationship had not yet developed, so neither side was truly straight about the real problems. We were telling our management back in Detroit something, and the Chinese would tell their bosses something else. If *we* were ignorant about how to do business in China, for the Chinese, this was *all* new: nobody knew what a joint venture was and how to work together. Teamwork was something the Chinese lacked—each department run as a separate little entity—and it remains a problem today. They thought we were crazy trying to coordinate the fenders with the hoods and so on.

Beijing Jeep was owed all kinds of money from various Chinese companies or government agencies, and I badly needed foreign exchange for machinery to produce the larger parts locally. That was an even greater requirement than the US$250 million needed to continue buying Cherokee kits from America to assemble in China. We had no money in Beijing, and in those days nor did AMC, yet none of the Chinese would bury their picture of AMC as a big, rich US company. As Chairman Wu said, 'If you can waste so much money on that lavish car-dealer show we saw in Las Vegas, then you must be able to find more funding!' But this was serious money: US$250 million is not a Las Vegas show, it's a hotel in Las Vegas.

When the 'crisis' became known to everybody, I told my Chinese colleagues: 'It's very difficult for you to go to your bosses, but let me play the foreigner and persuade them Beijing Jeep will only survive if the government injects cash.' I didn't understand Chinese politics then. I just asked who's the head guy, who do I write to? People suggested Hu Yaobang. 'Hu's he?!' I asked and learned his was more a Party role. Premier Zhao Ziyang was a better choice, more government than Party and well-disposed to business. The first time I met him he reminded me of a chairman of the board-type. He had a certain presence about him, well-groomed, in good suits, and very impressive. Pragmatic too—if you had a good point he would listen.

We were probably the first foreign company to complain publicly in China. VW in Shanghai and Peugeot in Guangzhou faced similar difficulties with partners and government, though the Germans enjoyed greater resources. Everyone warned me, 'Don't speak out!', but I had waited and no reply came, so I finally called Reuters and said I'm ready to talk. All the other reporters in town soon followed. I was in Detroit (probably getting fired) when the telex arrived from Zhu Rongji, saying, 'Zhao Ziyang sent me a copy of Mr St Pierre's letter. Send a delegation over. We will solve this problem.'

We scrambled five guys together and headed for China in pretty good spirits. At the old Beijing International Club, Zhu Rongji, then vice-minister of the State Economic Commission, had assembled the head of China's auto industry, a vice-mayor of Beijing, and many Beijing Jeep managers, though by this time Chairman Wu had bolted to the hospital—he didn't want any part of this. Zhu said, 'You Americans go first; tell us your view of the problems. You have twenty minutes.' My boss Todd Clare began talking—he's a wonderful talker, he could sell refrigerators to Eskimos; he had flip charts and a hand-out, but Zhu said forget them.

Right on twenty minutes (he was timing it to the second), Zhu interrupted Todd: 'Okay, your time's up; Chinese side—your turn.' Again, after twenty minutes, right in mid-sentence: 'Time's up; let's all go to lunch!' Fortunately I sat at his table, where he ignored my boss to query me in detail. I tried to answer as honestly as I could. Zhu appointed the vice-mayor and the auto chief to represent the Chinese side. We met for five days and nights at Beijing Jeep. Zhu's ingenious solution was to sell the old Russian jeeps at a higher price, and allow me to convert the Renminbi to dollars. Chinese companies were also ordered to pay foreign exchange for the Cherokee. I went from broke to having US$60 million in the bank in about five months.

As soon as the deal was done, the Chinese wanted me to go out

Don St Pierre with Zhu Rongji

and spread the good news, so all of a sudden the stories changed drastically. Me and the French guy at Peugeot joked he was the French panda and I the American—we were hauled out everywhere to show how problems could be solved, and to attract others to invest. Yet it really *was* a good model, not just propaganda—especially how the Americans and the Chinese were pulling together to get things done. The mood at the factory was good, cooperation was good, other than a couple of dissidents on both sides, and we enjoyed great directors' meetings every week.

Prior to 1989, the wider political currents didn't really affect us, as the whole Chinese management group was getting along well. I became involved in the social welfare side and tried to contribute to employee housing and other areas. The student movement of late 1986 and early 1987 didn't disrupt us at all, though I remember the Campaign against Bourgeois Liberalization, as Chairman Wu fell at that time. I went after him because of incompetence, not politics: he was preoccupied with where to park the bicycles when I felt there were bigger things to do.

Not only was I allowed into Party meetings, I also got to broadcast my own lunch-time propaganda over the factory loudspeakers! These usually carried terrible music and Party speeches, so one day I asked, 'Let me talk too!' With Bob Segar playing in the background, I would talk about Western ways of management, about capitalism, about whatever the hell I felt like saying. It was translated and played throughout the factory to almost 4,000 workers, with never an attempt at censure.

China has changed so much—wine is my business now, but no one drank it in the mid-eighties, nothing but white spirits like Maotai. The last I heard I still held the record at Beijing Jeep: at a banquet for our model workers, I had thirty-seven glasses of the stuff, made a speech, and walked home. I got in trouble that night with our Party and trade union chairman Mr Ji. In my speech I promised each model worker three months' bonus, as I had been arguing with Ji over the selection criteria, but it took a lot of Maotai courage to take him on in this way. The next day he stormed in: 'You can't do that. These people aren't even our best workers!' Exactly! I insisted we pay as promised, which encouraged everybody to take the whole charade much more seriously. I had great affection for our workers and was always trying to help them: during a match shortage in Beijing, I even brought them boxes taken from five-star hotels.

When the Chrysler take-over rumours began in 1987, I initially tried to convince the Chinese of the benefits. By that time I had become a real president of the joint venture, neither on the Americans' side, nor the Chinese. I simply hoped Chrysler's entry meant money to do things. I came to regret my cheer-leading. Chrysler had lost a car deal in Changchun to VW, so the company was negative about China and didn't like our joint venture. They reverted to AMC's failed approach of sending factory men over, not people with business ideas. They wanted to milk Beijing Jeep and lacked any long-term plan. In retrospect, this turned out to be one hell of a mistake. Every car company in the world would kill to make cars in China and Chrysler could have done it just like that.

Zhao Ziyang, by then general secretary, visited Beijing Jeep in February 1988, when I was in Hong Kong for a job interview! My poor colleagues were frantically trying to find me, but that was the one time I let nobody know my whereabouts. The first thing he said when he walked in the factory gate was, 'Where's St Pierre? I want to see this St Pierre.' He was very upbeat and supportive of joint-venture cooperation and Beijing Jeep in particular. Essentially, the Chinese were paying for the renovation of Beijing Jeep, and there's no doubt he wanted their money's worth. I was on their side on that.

During a round of farewell banquets that summer, I ate Peking duck eleven times in five days! I had built up many contacts and Beijing Jeep was the famous joint venture. Chinese people and leaders could tell that I liked them, and I believe they realized I always had the good of the company at heart. On 4 July 1988, the US ambassador Winston Lord presented me with a T-shirt, 'I survived China', at the Independence Day picnic. I left the next day, back to Detroit, full of regrets but resigned to the impossibility of working with my new Chrysler boss.

In late May 1989, a business trip brought me back to Beijing. I watched the build-up of marches and demonstrations snowballing in Tiananmen, then I travelled to Shanghai when [Soviet President Mikhail] Gorbachev was there. The movement grew so widespread that truckloads of our factory workers appeared on TV with Beijing Jeep banners. Remember the motorcycle gang that rode around delivering messages? The leader

Don St Pierre, Beijing, 1998

was a Jeep guy who subsequently disappeared. Nobody has heard of him again.

I hadn't worked for Jeep for a year and a half but I was still asked to decide when to evacuate the expatriate staff. On 9 June, I returned to Beijing on an empty flight to an empty hotel. Tiananmen marked the end of an era, and an end to illusion. When we all came back we had wider eyes and checked things a little more carefully. A lot of us who were close to China were bitter for a while. But we got over it. An important development after Tiananmen was Zhu Rongji's rise. Far from being tainted, he prevented disaster in Shanghai, where he was mayor, by putting workers, not soldiers, onto the streets.

China is definitely my home now. I have a house in California, but I feel a stranger when I'm there. My son and business partner is a fluent Mandarin speaker. What's the hold that China exerts? It's a fascinating place, *and* a great opportunity, if hard to realize. You can count the people really making a buck on the fingers on one hand: VW, Xerox, Motorola, Siemens, Proctor & Gamble, but not many others, I suspect. In the early days we wrote the rule book, yet that's still possible, that's why I'm still here. Everything seems impossible, but almost anything *can* be done. I'm not a wine guy. I just decided, 'I'm going to have a wine, on my own label, and we will produce it in China'—and here we are doing it! One difference with the old days was that I picked a date and we met it, right on schedule. I'm going to send Premier Zhu a bottle.

China seems so different now compared to 1985, but in so many ways it remains the same. I told a couple of General Motors guys to read *Beijing Jeep* after they arrived to finalize the huge sedan deal: 'It might tell you something about what goes on here.' When I ran into them a few months ago, they replied, 'We read the book, and things haven't changed one damned bit!'

Cui Jian

Nothing to My Name

After a decade of puritanical hysteria, when Beethoven and Schubert were banned as bourgeois and reactionary, getting China to let its hair down was never going to be easy. Back in Yan'an in 1942, Mao had set political parameters for art and literature that have been maintained with varying severity ever since. During the Cultural Revolution, his wife's model plays, opera, and ballet provided almost the only entertainment. Painters churned out socialist realism, while writers either toed the line or languished in jail, and often suffered both.

Only with Mao's death and the birth of the reform era could China slowly shed its cultural strait-jacket and experiment with new forms. In 1979, the 19-year-old Cui Jian joined the Beijing Song and Dance Troupe as a classical trumpet player. His father, a trumpeter with the air force band, encouraged his son to master an instrument to avoid political trouble. Yet by 1989, Cui Jian was China's foremost rock star, a reluctant rebel whose song 'Nothing to My Name' became the anthem of Tiananmen Square and a generation of disillusioned Chinese youth.

In the early 1980s, a flood of saccharine pop music from Hong Kong and Taiwan satisfied most listeners. But as the decade wore on, Cui's dissonant chords and ambiguous messages attracted a generation whose attitudes and aspirations were alien to their middle-aged parents, reared on little but class struggle. For the establishment, this gravel-voiced, long-haired singer embodied their worst fears of the 'spiritual pollution' leaking through China's open door. In January 1987, only seven months after his nationwide breakthrough, Cui was banned from live performance by conservatives railing against 'bourgeois liberalism'. In April, the Beijing Song and Dance Troupe expelled him. He has fallen in and out of favour ever since.

The expulsion obliged Cui to pursue the birth of Chinese rock 'n' roll full-time. A strong indigenous spirit, such as traditional instruments and peasant-like call-and-response shouts, underlies his debt to Western styles.

The influence of Shaanxi folk tunes led critics to herald a 'north-west wind' of Chinese artists, including 'fifth generation' film directors such as Chen Kaige and Zhang Yimou. Government censors continued to deny the audience's increasing sophistication, affording most Chinese only intermittent glimpses of their works. But in bars and galleries, karaoke lounges and student dorms, an urban undercurrent was spawning a grey or counter-culture championed by novelist Wang Shuo and his *liumang* (hooligan) anti-heroes.

Cui had just regained his right to play when the Beijing Spring of 1989 swept his music far beyond control. Though he gave an impromptu performance on the square, Cui was not arrested after the massacre—*The People's Daily* even called him the 'John Lennon of China' in late June. However, a clamp-down on popular culture was inevitable. Cui's pioneering efforts sparked a lively bar scene in the nineties, though official displeasure at the genre ensures he remains China's only nationwide rock star. He counters Draconian restrictions with a return to the trumpet and a new appreciation of jazz. For many, Cui's songs remain the score of the democracy movement:

> I once kept on asking again and again, 'When would you go with me?'
> But you always laughed at me, saying I have nothing to my name . . .
> I want to give you my pursuit; and my freedom too,
> But all you ever do is laugh at me, 'cause I have nothing to my name

AFTER CHINA OPENED ITS DOORS, Taiwanese and Hong Kong pop music attracted millions of young people like myself. I particularly loved Deng Lijun [Teresa Teng], a Taiwanese singer. When I listened to her songs, I knew they were not the type we Chinese were familiar with: hard, political, and impersonal, songs to serve the 'workers, peasants, and soldiers'. With a sweet and beautiful voice she sang sentimental ballads, in a soft, unique style. At that time, the very beginning of the eighties, periodic government campaigns opposed 'bourgeois liberalism', and her songs were among the targets. Rebellious as I was, it made me like them even more. Yet after a while, I realized her songs were still not exactly the music I was looking for.

It was around then that I first picked up the guitar. I had grown disinterested in playing the trumpet: I had never been a confident player; more importantly, I felt I couldn't express my emotions freely (now, after dropping it for so long, I've become very fond of the trumpet again). As I was practising guitar, I began to sing, basically to amuse myself. After one late performance in 1983, I was drinking beer with friends when I suddenly picked up my guitar and sang with passion, 'Mama, do you remember the old straw hat you gave me?' Everyone went quiet. The song was from a hit Japanese film *Witness*, where a half-black, half-Japanese American came to Japan to look for his mother, only to die at her hands as she feared he would damage her success. It was a very human film, showing people's longing for maternal love. The song could always strike a responsive chord among young people with all their questions. My friends' reaction encouraged me.

I was a keen listener too. I bought whatever reached the market, at first American country music like John Denver, Kenny Rogers, and Andy Williams, then, with more variety, I became fascinated by rock and roll. I indulged myself listening to the Beatles, Rolling Stones, Bob Dylan, Police, Talking Heads . . . . I can't explain what in rock music excited me so much, but it touched the bottom of my heart. First of all, it is very personal. When I listened to rock music, I felt it brought me closer to music. When I sang, I felt I sang words from the heart; and I sang for myself, not anyone else, even if I sang other people's works. With rock, I could express myself freely and directly. Some of the lyrics were so simple, almost like conversation, that I thought why didn't I compose myself? One of my early rock songs went: 'I didn't know what it was to be broad-minded before. Then, I didn't know there were so many strange things in this world. I had the illusion the future cannot be like today. Now it seems clear what the future will be. It's not that I don't understand. It's the world which moves too fast.'

The event that changed my life was the concert held at the Beijing Workers' Stadium in May 1986, when 100 singers were invited to mark the International Year of Peace, but less than thirty could sing solo numbers. I chose a newly finished song, 'Nothing to My Name'. Many people later asked how I created it. Nothing extraordinary, really. I remember I composed it at home, very quickly and easily in one go. If you force me to give a better answer, I'd say it was written by the 'hand of God.' The whole event was organized by Wang Kun, a veteran musician from the Oriental Song and Dance Ensemble. Through friends' introduction, I handed her my song. 'Not bad. Did you compose it yourself?' After attending a rehearsal, she agreed to let this small potato perform a solo.

I had no idea whether the audience would like it, nor did I ever expect my song could make such a splash. I came onstage wearing a set of *magua*, Qing dynasty-style clothes with one trouser leg longer than the other. I swear I didn't do it deliberately. At that time, I only knew what I didn't like—the fancy gold and silver outfits worn by Hong Kong and Taiwanese singers. So I borrowed the *magua* from a friend's father. I just wanted something different, though it didn't really suit me, and I never wore it again. On that day, people must have thought, 'Who is this guy in his funny *magua*?' I was nervous facing such a large audience but told myself to keep cool and sing loudly. When I finished, to my amazement, thunderous applause burst out!

I was lucky because there was no other such music at the time. China had just opened up, and young people, tired of dull political songs, wanted something new and different. Even the songs we sang as children were full of political content, such as 'I Love Tiananmen', 'Great Leader Chairman Mao Leads Us Forward', and 'Red Star Shining'. People wanted to sing something that could move them, something they felt belonged to themselves. We were probably the first bunch of musicians to provide such music. Shortly afterwards, I spotted a boy in the street trying to copy the way I danced, jumping and moving around in a funny and naïve way. I was very amused, since I was far from famous. The live tape of the concert spread 'Nothing to My Name' throughout China; critics even refer to it as 'the song that made Chinese rock history'!

It was certainly a turning-point in my personal history. From that day onwards, I no longer had to worry about money. Before, I had to go to other people for gigs. From that day on, people came to me. In spring 1988, I signed a contract to record my first solo album; it turned out to be the first rock album in China. I took an outrageously long time, rehearsing again and again till I felt each song was perfect: 'Nothing to My Name', 'It's Not That I Don't Understand', 'Greenhouse Girl', 'Phony Monk', and others. When it eventually came out, in early 1989, it was an instant hit.

During that year's democracy movement, the students at Tiananmen Square adopted 'Nothing to My Name'. I was very surprised at first. Then I thought, 'Well, if they didn't sing that, what else could they sing?' The dissatisfied youth wanted to have a good yell, but the song was no longer mine. They interpreted it in their own way, with new meanings. In this sense, the song was indeed written by the 'hand of God'. Some students wrote new lyrics, so it became a song of democracy. Others even substituted sexual lyrics to make it pornographic. There were at least ten versions of 'Nothing to My Name', as far as I know.

Some people insist my songs are politically charged, and the fact students sang them on the square only entrenched their views. Actually, I don't think I'm a political person. I had no political intentions when I wrote my songs. 'A Piece of Red Cloth', another song favoured by the students, is actually a love song. On the other hand, politics is an important part of life. Nothing can go beyond politics, especially for a highly politicized society like China. Some say my songs are getting *more* political, probably because I pay more attention to social issues. I want to sing about matters that have some weight in real life, matters that others do not or dare not sing about.

Compared to before, artists nowadays have much more freedom. In my father's time, art had to serve the Party and the great masses. It was a joke. I feel more and more strongly that modern society is a individualized society. Everything is for the individual. People have to admit it. Yet there are many limitations. In many people's eyes, rock and roll is still associated with spiritual pollution and bourgeois decadence. In 1990, we made a tour to raise money for the Asian Olympic Games in Beijing. After we performed in Sichuan, I remember one local cadre telephoned the central government to complain: 'Forget about the Asian Games if you don't have the money. There's no need to let mad dogs like Cui Jian out to beg for it!'

After 1989, the authorities intensified control over rock and roll. It can't be shown on TV, nor can it be advertised. We can't stage large-scale performances. There are no films about rock and roll. Well, there's no written rule that rock music is strictly banned: you can *apply* for permission to perform; whether you ever obtain it is another matter, and even if you do, who will sponsor you without advertising? I really don't understand why the government wants to suppress it. Rock and roll is only music, after all. Maybe in a corrupt society, anything uncontrollable is politics; anything successful is a mistake.

Some people say that Chinese people are not suited to rock and roll. That's totally unfair because we haven't been given the chance. I shouldn't complain, because I am a beneficiary of this society. I have no money worries, I drive my own car, live in a flat I bought, and hire people to do things I no longer bother to do myself. Yet maybe I am not truly successful because I have failed to reach my ultimate goal—to have the freedom needed by an artist to do what I want, say what I think, and perform as I wish.

I'm talking about an ideal situation, but the reality is not too bad. When we get permission to play, my band Ado have given great performances in various parts of China, and the audience is always enthusiastic. We've even toured Europe, America, and many Asian countries. My fourth solo album, *The Power of the Powerless*, came out last year. It's not been selling like hot cakes, I'm afraid, but I refuse to believe I'm going downhill. True, I'm not as romantic as before, but technically I'm improving and maturing. Nowadays, people have more choices, all kinds of music from abroad and many more varieties from

China itself, which of course is great. Luckily, we can still gig at bars and pubs. That's so important to me, almost like a physical need. Just as people have to eat and shower, I have to sing and play my guitar. One of the most enjoyable moments in my life is just after each performance. My whole body is soaked through with sweat. Exhausted but satisfied, I sit down on a sofa, drinking beer and chatting with friends. Oh, it's just divine! Isn't life wonderful? I wish I could live forever, and rock and roll forever!

Zhou Peikun

A Peddler's Pride

The conspicuous success of the overseas Chinese diaspora has entrenched Western views of the Chinese as a highly commercial people. Yet merchants have been officially frowned upon within China ever since Confucius opined on their lowly social status back in the sixth century BC. The Communist Revolution went even further, systematically abolishing the private sector in a bid to provide wealth for all. When Deng Xiaoping's economic revolution in the early 1980s launched a generation of *getihu*, this new class was widely spurned. The term itself—literally, 'individual household'—reflects a highly political and stratified society where collectives and other state-owned work units represented respectability and the 'iron rice-bowl' of cradle-to-grave social security.

Zhou Peikun was on target for such security, until the Cultural Revolution broke and swept the 21-year-old factory worker into its turmoil. He joined a workers' rebel group in his hometown Nanjing, capital of eastern China's Jiangsu province. Perhaps it was his suspect background that drove Zhou's desire to prove his revolutionary credentials: his father once served as a Nationalist county chief. Zhou swiftly rose to head a provincial rebel group and led a bloody fight against another rebel faction near the seat of the municipal government. Several deaths resulted. In 1970, Zhou and other leaders were jailed for twenty years.

Without city residence permits, vital for food and other rations, his wife and three young children returned to her poverty-stricken birthplace in Anhui. Their privations spurred Zhou's dream of providing his family with a comfortable life, after his 'early' release in 1984 for good behaviour. How China had changed: class struggle had given way to a rush to reform. Rural and urban markets were booming again, peddlers worked the streets, private restaurants mushroomed. With his customary zeal, Zhou created a business from nothing, becoming a 'model' *getihu* in 1988, and later board member of the national *getihu* association. He is unlikely to squander his new-found wealth: a yuan-millionaire he may be, but Zhou takes no holidays and travels across Nanjing by public bus.

Zhou embodies the entrepreneurial spirit that the Party tried in vain to eradicate over the course of three decades. After twenty years of reforms, his story is now commonplace, as millions have overcome the prejudice and obstacles of a semi-planned economy to succeed through sheer hard work. A few go on to national fame, and global ambition, such as Liu Yonghao, but most remain the heads of small family businesses like Zhou's, proud of their achievements. Together with township and village enterprises, the private economy creates badly needed employment and competition for the state sector. *Getihu* is no longer such a dirty word.

I MIGHT NOT HAVE BECOME a *getihu* if my work unit had taken me back when I came out of jail in 1984. Unsurprisingly, they didn't. I might have landed a job somewhere else, but the pay would be pretty bad. I desperately needed money. The first thing I did after my release was to bring my wife and three children back to Nanjing from the countryside, even though we had to live with my parents, brother, and sister in a tiny 23-square-metre flat. For years, our family had relied on my father's miserable salary. Now, there was no way he could support us all. I was terribly sorry for the hardships I brought to them. When trapped in prison, all I could do was save and send home my 1.5 yuan monthly allowance. It was high time to do something for them. The only way out was business.

It wasn't easy to start one. We didn't have any money, and we were so poor nobody dared lend us any. A colleague of my father finally lent 400 yuan, on strict condition it was repaid within one month, plus 10 per cent interest. It was something to start with, so we quickly agreed. We decided to sell 'hatched eggs', where the chick does not emerge successfully. In some places they are thrown away, but Nanjing people love them like a delicacy. I got up at midnight and rode a borrowed tricycle 50 kilometres to a chicken farm on the north bank of the Yangtze. At midnight the next day, I reached home again with 500 *jin* of eggs. We sold a third to peddlers for a small margin, then boiled and sold the rest at a busy junction. My wife and two younger children all helped out. Three days was a round, buying and selling, then another began; we spun like machines without rest, under pressure to return the money.

We only ate our own eggs if they had gone bad; throwing them away meant throwing money away.

The lump and scar on my middle finger is a reminder of that bitter month. Riding the tricycle home in the small hours after selling the last egg, I was so tired I fell asleep and crashed into a tree. I could see my finger bone, but I didn't want to waste money on a hospital. I applied some incense ash from a nearby temple to stop the bleeding and carried on as usual. It took three months to heal properly. When I first sold eggs on the street, I felt embarrassed, and lowered my head if I saw people I knew. Before the nightmare of the Cultural Revolution began, I was a promising young worker at a large enterprise. But I fell to an egg-seller in the street. Gradually, I overcame the feeling. I was making clean money with my own two hands; there was nothing shameful about it.

From each *jin* of eggs, we made 20 cents profit. In one month, we made just over 1,000 yuan, no small amount for the time! The loan, and interest, were returned. But the egg business was too exhausting after fifteen years' imprisonment. I'd become a skeleton. From egg profits, we bought a sugar-cane crusher for 120 yuan. It looks insignificant, but selling sugar-cane juice was quite lucrative. One *jin* of cane made two cups of juice that sold for 30 cents, but the sugar-cane cost only 6 cents per *jin*. Again, that 24-cent profit required lots of work to locate, buy, transport, wash, peel, and chop the cane. My wife knew the rural suburbs, so we always found cheap, good-quality suppliers.

Eight months later we expanded into the fruit business, which needed more capital and space. By the time I set up shop in Nanjing's Fuzimiao (Confucius Temple) district, all the good sites had been taken. I found only a little corner in front of somebody's door, but the family objected. I pleaded with the man to let me to stay, explaining my background and how my whole family's survival depended on this money. Moved by my confession, he agreed. I was very careful not to leave a mess and always offered his children juice when they returned from school.

I wasn't a 'proper' *getihu* yet, as I didn't have a licence. But to get a licence, you need a 'proper' place. Madam Huang from the local *getihu* association collected administration fees from guerrilla peddlers like me. She and her family had also suffered badly in the Cultural

Revolution; a mutual acquaintance had been a rebel leader. As the only one who learned the full story of my shameful past, she was understanding and sympathetic. When there was a campaign to expel peddlers from outside town, she helped me get a site, more or less where I was. I became a proper *getihu*, licensed to sell fruit, in spring 1985.

My younger brother, newly employed at a large state-owned enterprise, tried to stop me. So did my friends. A *getihu* was not a well-respected profession; even wealth didn't win him social status. Few people would give up 'decent' jobs to become one. To be fair, the overall quality of *getihu* at that time *was* poor. Many were jobless, rejected by companies, sent down to the countryside, or ex-prisoners like myself, disowned by their work units. I was often reminded of the *getihu*'s low position. In arguments with customers, people always assume it's the *getihu*'s fault (some *getihu* do try to cheat). Once, I spilt sugar-cane juice on a man I vaguely knew. I humbly apologized, but he was furious. 'You ex-prisoner! You only deserve to be a low and dirty *getihu*!'

I was too angry for words, and greatly humiliated; few people knew about my past. He was so mean to broadcast it in public, without explaining *how* I got into prison. When my fellow peddlers asked, I had to tell them the truth. No one would connect me with prison: I was not a rapist, or a thief—when I ransacked people's houses, there were plenty of valuable items around, but I never stole anything. For days, I couldn't sleep. I felt my old scar was reopened. In that man's view, a *getihu* is no better than a prisoner. But actually I'm doing fine as a *getihu*. I should learn to respect my own job, without caring what others think about it. It's time to walk out of the shadow of the past.

By the time I applied for a licence, I already felt more comfortable about being a *getihu*. It was my choice, not desperation. Our monthly income from sugar-cane juice was 700 or 800 yuan, much more than a skilled worker at a state-owned enterprise, though we had to work harder. Selling fruit was even more demanding. The fruit comes from different locations and you have to be so careful about quantity. Too little wastes time and energy; too much and it goes bad. I used to sell the bad ones at cheaper prices to move them quickly. Presentation was important. I always kept myself busy cleaning and polishing the fruit, lining them up nicely. These rules sound so simple, but not everyone follows them.

State-owned shops never stayed open as late as us, and nor could you choose fruit yourself. We let customers choose themselves, as many shoppers worried they would be cheated by *getihu* salesmen. I put up a big red banner in front of our stand: 'Feel free to pick your own fruit: If you find you are one gram short we will compensate you by one kilogram!' Our banner, hardly seen elsewhere, attracted lots of buyers. There's a scale at Fuzimao's administration office where you can weigh your purchases if you have any doubts. We did our best to provide good service, even offering home and hospital deliveries.

Fuzimiao was ideal for fruit, as it's surrounded by residential areas. It was a prosperous commercial centre in Ming and Qing times, and in the 1980s the old architecture was rebuilt. It became a tourist spot throughout China. Competition was intense. To stand out, I was always the first to introduce the season's new fruits, and at very high prices. Water melon was my favourite, popular and long-lasting. To be the earliest buyer, I slept in the melon fields far from Nanjing. Mosquito bites covered my whole body. On the bumpy return journey, I tied myself to the side of the truck and slept on top of the melons. In the hot season, we sold all night long. For several years, I rarely slept at home as I had to guard my fruit stand, even on New Year's Eve, when families enjoy reunions. Festivals are the busiest time for us. One New Year's Eve, it snowed as I slept in the open. I was cold, lonely, and miserable. But the money was great. Later we hired a migrant worker for night duty.

In autumn 1990, I made another big move. We had saved 300,000 yuan, so I gave the fruit business to my daughter and her husband while I rented a counter in a new shopping centre. My new business was underwear, fashion, and fashion accessories, more profitable and less labour-intensive than fruit. When I had enough capital, I moved from retail to wholesale. Funny, when you have that much money, you don't need it to run a business. People know I'm reliable, and how deep my pocket is, so they let me to take goods without payment.

I've no regrets about the path I chose. How much can my former colleagues at the factory earn now? Perhaps 700 to 800 yuan per month, maximum 1,000 for the most skilled workers. In our profession, people like to play down their wealth, for tax reasons among others. Let me boast just once: I've got a million yuan in my hands. Nowadays, it's not so bad to be a *getihu*. Twenty years' reform and opening up have changed people's concepts—they care more about money and less about social status. You can even find university students among *getihu*. Many old colleagues have been laid off and are struggling to find work, even as *getihu*. Honestly, it's not as easy as it used to be to make money as a *getihu*. The tax is about 100 times heavier than when I started, and there are many different fees to pay.

Both my younger children are *getihu* and doing well. My second daughter had a poor education in the countryside, and I must take some responsibility. Partly sponsored by me, her boy studies at the private Nanjing International Boarding School, known as the 'noble school', where they learn English from year one. She and her husband live in a new flat, but my wife and I live in the same old place. We're better off now, but by no means ostentatious. My wife's from a peasant background and hates to waste money on clothes, make-up, or anything fancy. The only valuable thing she owns is the gold necklace I gave as her fiftieth birthday present. She liked it very much but complained it was too expensive.

I work long hours every day, seven days a week, 365 days a year. Our children suggested several times that my wife and I take a tour to Thailand, the fashionable thing for well-to-do people. I calculated: not working for a week, we'd lose a few thousand yuan, and the trip costs over 10,000 yuan. Put the two together and it's more than I'm willing to lose. We're just small business people with no ambition or ability to be worldly entrepreneurs. Saving hard is the only way to accumulate wealth.

People ask me if I'm grateful to Deng Xiaoping and his reforms. In public places, I know the right thing to say. But deep in my heart, I don't feel I need to be grateful. Before China was just not normal. Now, China *is* more or less normal, where people get rewarded for their hard work. And I have no worries about a change in policy. Of course, I benefit from market economy policies. But how about the government who sits there and collects good money from us business people? About a third of Fuzimiao tax revenue is collected from private business people. In towns like Wuxi, where there are well-developed township enterprises, the proportion is as high as 50 per cent. Why would they want to give up such easy money? I think my future as a *getihu* is pretty safe.

Dai Qing
Yangtze! Yangtze!

During China's first decade of boom-and-bust economic reform, few stopped to consider the environmental cost. Yet the race to catch up lost years has compounded the mountain-moving devastation of the first three decades of Communist power. Air pollution causes 26 per cent of all deaths in China, compared to 2–3 per cent in the United States. Without favourable winds, the visitor to Beijing is smothered in smog, yet the capital pales beside cities like Benxi in Liaoning, hidden from satellite photos by coal and industry haze. As desertification eats up good land, mass logging strips hillsides and floods rivers toxic black with industrial waste. In Lanzhou, a mountain is literally being moved in the desperate hope that a through-wind will clear the clouds and let the sun shine again.

Such is the state that transformed a guided-missile engineer, with impeccable revolutionary credentials, into an environmental activist and historian of liberal Chinese thought. Dai Qing was born in 1941 in the wartime capital, Chongqing. After her father died a revolutionary martyr, Dai was raised by Ye Jianying, one of China's Ten Marshals, and entered military college, where she also joined the Communist Party. Sent down to the countryside in 1969, Dai gained firsthand experience at ravaging the land. Her first attempt at writing, a 1979 story of Cultural Revolution suffering, drew a sympathetic response from *Guangming Daily* readers. Three years later she joined the paper. Ground-breaking work on the terrible 1988 Daxing'anling forest fire was followed by the opposition to the Three Gorges Dam project on the Yangtze, for which Dai has become most widely known.

The dream of a dam on the Yangtze has fascinated generations of Chinese nation-builders. The 'father of modern China', Dr Sun Yatsen, proposed the plan in 1919. In the 1950s, Chairman Mao's poem 'Build a Stone Wall in the River' spurred forty years of feasibility studies until Deng Xiaoping finally took the plunge. The 1989 bill to dam the river at Sandouping in Hubei drew the first negative votes ever cast at the normally compliant National People's Congress. Critics charge that official arguments—citing

improved flood control, access to hydropower, and ease of navigation—
do not hold water. But the country that built the Great Wall does not
shirk the grandiose: construction began in 1994 to complete by 2009 a
2.08-kilometre, 187-metre high dam, flooding 1,000 of the river's 6,300-
kilometre length.

Yangtze! Yangtze!, a book of protest edited by Dai Qing, saw her thrown
in jail after Tiananmen, together with the same democracy activists who
had criticized her calls for them to retreat from the square before they fell
victim to the Party power struggle. Banished from Mainland journalism,
Dai turned to the international Green movement. Her 1997 study, *The
River Dragon Has Come*, revealed details of the 'secret' 1975 Henan
disaster, when crumbling dams drowned perhaps 230,000 people. While
Dai hopes to focus on her organic farm outside Beijing, few expect this
lively campaigner to retire quietly.

The Yangtze dam provides a concrete lesson in the power of a one-
party state, where free debate remains intolerable. Dai's environmental
passions lend her insight into the persecuted intellectuals on whom she
writes, for the Chinese government still fears thinkers who put country
before Party. If the West has polluted the world to date, its future rests in
Chinese hands: in the first decades of the twenty-first century, China will
replace the United States as the leading global warmer and source of acid
rain. While poverty and population pressure ensure the first concern of
most Chinese is a meal and security, increasing protests at polluting
enterprises hint at the birth of a civil society.

I'M NOT REALLY AN ENVIRONMENTALIST. I became involved in the Three
Gorges Dam project, or rather against the Three Gorges Dam project,
because of my deep belief in the freedom of speech. I am a journalist.
If I can't speak the truth, what kind of journalism is that?

Yet I wasn't trained as a journalist either. I studied missile technology
at Harbin Military Engineering College—as a patriotic youth, I wanted
to learn something useful to serve my country. And useful it was: I
became a guided-missile engineer for the People's Liberation Army! It
was a joke that led me to a writing career, back in 1979. We were talking
about new books, when I criticized one novel, typical of the 'wounded'

literature of the time. My colleague challenged me: 'Could you write better?!' 'Surely I can!' So I began to write and just couldn't stop. To the amazement of my colleague, I didn't do badly at all, even becoming a member of China's writers association.

Having said I'm no environmentalist, I've loved nature and outdoor activities ever since I was a little child. It broke my heart to see my beloved nature being destroyed, so I became one of the first to focus on environmental issues, when fast economic growth began exacting a high price. As early as 1982, I wrote a story 'Calling for the Birds' on the conservation project by the Beijing Botanical Garden. The numbers of birds in the Xishan area outside Beijing grew fewer and fewer as people killed them for food or fun, combined with a worsening environment. To kill the increasing numbers of insects, people used pesticides, which killed even more birds. In the end, the whole mountain looked so bleak.

I first became aware of the Three Gorges Dam project in 1985 through a family friend and prominent member of the CPPCC. When he and other delegates returned from an investigative tour, they were quietly ignored, with no press conference or other way to express their concern. Any report opposing the project was strictly forbidden. But he invited me to an internal meeting, where I learned about the potential ecological and archaeological nightmares. I remember when I entered the huge CPPCC hall, a small crowd at the front rose to applaud: 'Welcome a journalist from *Guangming Daily*!' The report I submitted to the paper was, of course, rejected. I warned my editors: 'At least in the future, when you praise the project, exercise restraint.'

I'll never forget my shock at seeing all the dam coverage in the Hong Kong media during a brief trip there three years later. Many reporters questioned if the project was sensible. I asked myself, 'Why are we Mainland journalists so numb?' Our Hong Kong colleagues were so concerned about a matter which ought to be a concern for all Chinese. I was ashamed. After that, a friend in Hong Kong kept feeding me the local newspaper reports. Now I knew the hard truth, I could no longer remain silent.

I mobilized my journalist friends, all top reporters in major newspapers nationwide, to interview experts with doubts about the project—there were more than enough stories about how wonderful it would be. We tried to get them published in newspapers, magazines, journals, or wherever, but all attempts failed. By early 1989, I became desperate, as I knew the dam would be discussed at the March National People's Congress (NPC). If I didn't do something right now, I would miss the opportunity forever. In the end, I turned to the last resort—to publish a book, the only loophole I could find. At that time, one could print a book with one's own money. So, in a record fifteen days' time, the book of our interviews was published as *Yangtze, Yangtze: Controversy Over the Three Gorges Dam Project*.

In China, it is extremely difficult to express any view on paper which is not totally in line with the government's. Journalists are controlled by their newspaper bosses, who in turn are controlled by the Party's propaganda department. Yet it was not the first time we did such a thing. In 1987, I united several journalists to compile *Eyewitness of the Heilongjiang Forest Fire*. After the shock, we began to question the real causes of the ecological disaster. Publication of a book of that nature was unprecedented.

Generally speaking, a book is the least effective way to publicize an idea. But we believed our Yangtze book played an important role. Its impact was greater than we expected, for when the NPC voted on the Three Gorges Dam project in 1989, one-third of the delegates decided against. It was really a miracle! Ordinarily, NPC approval ratings are 95, if not 100, per cent. If the situation had been handled fairly, there would have been more negative votes, for some NPC members were denied an opportunity to voice their views against the project. Of course, if there was real democracy, and everyone was granted access to free information, I am confident the majority would have opposed the proposal. There would have been no need for me.

Sadly, the Yangtze book was banned after June Fourth, an event which also changed my life forever. On that day, I declared I was giving up my Party membership. I cut off my ties with the Communists, for whom my parents had devoted their whole lives. My father died for the cause and my mother, from a well-established, rich family, could have lived a much more comfortable life. But I rejected their path. In doing so, I also cut off ties with many powerful figures whom I had called 'brother' or 'sister' when I was young.

Afterwards, I was put in Qincheng prison for ten months, without trial, for my role as an 'instigator of the turmoil', despite the fact that, ever since April, I had actually been trying to persuade the students to return to university. I know the real reasons were my liberal articles and involvement with the dam, which annoyed conservatives in the leadership. The propaganda department instructed the police to arrest me. After my release, I couldn't go back to work for *Guangming Daily*, who indeed had publicly denounced me. So now I have no job, no salary, no work unit, medical care, or pension. All I retain is a citizen's rights, which I am going to make good use of.

Everyone asks, 'Why do you hate the project so much?' There are many reasons, such as the budget of RMB600 billion (US$72 billion), which China can't really afford. Over 1.3 million people have to be relocated to already densely populated areas, creating enormous potential for social problems. Sand and silt in the reservoir will cause navigation difficulties, while evidence indicates the flood-control ability is less than the authorities claim. Factories, mines, cities, and towns will be inundated, but the worst aspect is permanent ecological damage. Up to 115,000 acres of very fertile land will be flooded. Peasants will have to cultivate less-fertile slopes and hillsides, which will lead to land erosion. Rare wildlife and riverlife will be destroyed. Over 1,000

unexcavated 'priority-level' cultural sites and their ancient treasures will be submerged. The beauty of the Three Gorges will be spoiled.

The authorities criticize me, advising people not to listen—Dai Qing is neither an expert, nor an hydraulic engineer. True, I am neither. But the people I interviewed *are* real experts. I want people to hear their views, not mine, yet that is impossible. If there were freedom of speech, the experts would have spoken out publicly. Again, there would be no need for me. In China, we are paying a 2 per cent electricity tax because of the dam, but the ordinary people don't know.

How could such a project, threatening such hazards, take place at all? In my view, it is simply a political game. Because this was the project desired by Sun Yatsen, by Mao Zedong, by Deng Xiaoping, and now by Jiang Zemin. Because we want to show the world that only socialist China can conquer nature, mobilizing a nation's resources and manpower to build the largest dam in the world, and its most incredible engineering project!

I believe the Communist Party has inflicted two major forms of damage on China; one is to her people—so many innocent people suffered under the series of political movements; the other is to her environment—in Mao's time, in the name of political campaigns, how many trees were felled to feed the 'backyard furnaces', how many rivers and lakes were filled for rice fields? I worked on these projects in Hunan during the Cultural Revolution. I knew how many lakes disappeared, and why the area is now plagued by annual floods. In Deng Xiaoping's era, too many people are too obsessed with making money to care about the environmental pollution they cause. To recover from both types of damage will take a long, long time.

On the other hand, I have to consider myself very lucky. The very fact that I am still alive shows China has improved. People with so-called ideology problems back in the fifties and sixties, like the persecuted writer Hu Feng, faced life sentences or death. I would have died nine times over. I do acknowledge the change: for example, numerous newspaper articles tackle environmental disasters, calling on people to protect nature. There are environmental NGOs [non-governmental organizations] doing wonderful work in educating people, improving environmental consciousness, and other 'green' activities. But there is a limit. It is okay for these NGOs to do good work, as long as they do not offend the authorities. Therefore, I am not satisfied with the change. That is why I am fighting for the freedom of speech and democracy I believe in.

Some of my friends feel sorry for me. As a writer, I've been unable to publish anything in mainland China since 1989. It's a shame, as I feel many readers would appreciate my works, but I can still write and be published outside China, and I've been fortunate to receive fellowships abroad. After my current study in the US ends, I will go to live on the farm my family and friends have contracted in the outskirts of Beijing to grow organic vegetables. I've grown increasingly frustrated with the grim city life, full of business-minded people, pollution, and traffic noise. I just want to escape to the countryside, where the fresh air, trees, animals, and honest farmers delight me. But whenever people need me in some way, I am always ready to stand out.

Na Han

Blood on the Square

The watching world called it a massacre, the first chapter of China's long revolution to be broadcast live on global news. A decade later, the Chinese government still called the June Fourth Incident of 1989 a 'counter-revolutionary rebellion', led by a 'handful of conspirators whose goal was to negate the leadership of the Communist Party'. At its height, the handful numbered a million people per day, who flocked to Tiananmen Square in support of peaceful demonstrations for more open and honest government. Na Han, a student from a city in northern China, was typical.

Na joined a sea of protesters that conjured up images of the Red Guard rallies of the Cultural Revolution, but these young Chinese danced to nobody's tune. They proudly recalled the Tiananmen protests of the 1919 May Fourth Movement for science and democracy. More immediate clues abound in Democracy Wall of the late 1970s, and most pointedly in the student protests held in Anhui, Shanghai, and elsewhere in the mid-eighties.

Party Secretary-General Hu Yaobang, forced to resign over the 1987 protests, became the posthumous genesis of the 1989 movement. Students sought to commemorate his death on 15 April by laying wreaths at Tiananmen, in conscious echo of events following Zhou Enlai's death in 1976. While the latter mourners opposed the Gang of Four, the targets of the 1989 protesters suggested a deeper malaise. Na Han, a history major, inherited a keen interest in politics from his father, who had joined the Party at a young age, before serving many years in army and industry. His son shared the widespread discontent at government corruption and nepotism that expanded into catch-all calls for greater democracy and freedom. As student hunger strikes began in mid-May, the arrival of Mikhail Gorbachev, the first Soviet leader to visit in thirty years, catalyzed demands for political liberalization.

The Beijing Spring of 1989 flowered with hope and idealism for just fifty days. It produced astonishing confrontations—such as pyjama-clad students, at a televised meeting, berating Premier Li Peng for ignoring their requests—but in retrospect the die was cast by 19 May, when Hu's reformist successor Zhao Ziyang paid a tearful dawn visit to the hunger-strikers and stated, 'I have come too late.' Martial law was declared on 20 May. Party hard-liners would no longer condone this massive affront to their authority.

If the massacre rudely demonstrated the Party's utter loss of any remaining Mandate of Heaven, subsequent repression left little doubt of its monopoly on power, or its willingness to sacrifice people's lives to preserve it. Student leaders were hounded across the country, while the Party reserved the harshest sentences for certain political scientists and labour activists whom it feared could rouse the wider populace. It took two years and the consolidation of Deng Xiaoping's position to transform the 1976 Tiananmen Incident from 'counter-revolutionary' to 'entirely revolutionary'. Na Han and the rest of his generation still await a similar reversal of the verdict on June Fourth.

Eyewitness accounts of June 1989 have been published by foreign journalists or Chinese who now live abroad. Na Han is a pseudonym for someone who, like the majority of participants, had little chance of fleeing into exile and now faces the daily dilemma of defending his principles without risking liberty and livelihood—a restaurant he manages in his hometown. The need for a pseudonym is a reminder of the Chinese government's vigilance towards the democracy movement in general, and June Fourth in particular.

IT HAS BEEN TEN YEARS since the 1989 student movement. I took part in it, I'm proud to say, and I still remember every detail. It's one of the few events in your life that will not fade away with the years. Hu Yaobang's death triggered everything. I was already at university, where a group of us followed the television news. It was exciting to watch students march in the rain to Tiananmen Square. We talked about it late into the night, shouting, 'Rehabilitate Hu!' and beating our wash-basins with chopsticks, but we didn't organize any demonstrations ourselves.

As the protests continued in Beijing, I became increasingly restless. On 28 April three friends and I travelled to Beijing, just missing the big protest against the *People's Daily* editorial that called the student movement a 'planned conspiracy and turmoil'. I stayed with friends in the university district in the north-west. Through their introduction I met leaders from the Autonomous Union of Beijing Students. As a representative of students from other provinces, I took part in delivering the petition on 2 May. It was actually an ultimatum, demanding that the authorities agree to our terms for talks, or there would be another mass demonstration on 4 May. Dozens of us cycled all the way to the Great Hall of People. We waited half an hour until an official from the National People's Congress received our petition. I felt delighted to be part of the movement instead of watching from afar.

Of course, the terms were rejected, and the demonstration went ahead, on the seventieth anniversary of the [beginning of the] May Fourth Movement. I remember that morning so clearly. More and more students turned up at Beijing Normal University, from inside the campus and elsewhere. At eight o'clock we set out on foot. The authorities knew about the demonstration, as there were many policemen outside the gate, and barricades on the main road, but we just pushed on. Some clashed with the police, but since there were so many of us, we went through fairly easily. Many onlookers cheered as we continued our march. Students from different universities formed one line of procession headed south for Tiananmen Square. There were more attempts by the police to stop us, but none succeeded. The human stream was just unstoppable.

Along the 15-kilometre walk, we were warmly greeted by the locals, who sometimes chanted with us: 'Down with corruption!', 'Long live democracy!' Peddlers and strangers gave us ice cream and water, all free of charge. When we reached the square at 11am, after three hours' marching, we were tired and hungry. Again, people offered us bread rolls, dumplings, and rice boxes. During the whole movement, the support shown by the people of Beijing was overwhelming. Later, when I was developing rolls of film, the shop assistant refused any payment when he knew I had come to support the Beijing students. I was very moved.

When I looked around, I was surprised how many students had come from all over the country, except remote places like Tibet. Everyone sincerely believed we were carrying on the unfulfilled mission of our forefathers seventy years ago. We were proud to participate, and though our spirits were high, we were cool and disciplined on the square. Students sat in neat lines with their own university. Before the passionate speeches began, we sang the national anthem and the Internationale, loudly and solemnly. There was no fighting with the police and by four or five o'clock, we gradually left the square. We had achieved our purpose.

I left Beijing the next day. Our friends at university awaited our description of events in the capital. The leaflets, photos, and tapes we had recorded aroused great interest. Though we were circumspect, the university authorities still found out, yet did nothing at first, as the nature of the movement was still so uncertain. By mid-May, when the Beijing students launched the hunger strike, we could no longer sit back and watch. Three major universities in town organized a three-day demonstration. We wanted to show our support and held debates and fund-raising activities, earning enough for the loudspeaker system we installed on campus to broadcast the latest news.

As the movement showed no sign of calming down, we began sending students to Beijing—over 150 made the trip, funded by money we raised in the street. The first group left around 24 May, four days after Li Peng declared martial law. I had been too busy organizing others to go, but from returned students and foreign radio, I understood the situation was growing more tense. On 2 June, three friends and I boarded a train to Beijing.

When we reached the square at 11pm, the atmosphere was fairly calm. Having spotted our flag, we weaved through the maze of tents to join students from our university. Exhausted from the journey, we lay down to sleep but were soon disturbed by noise. News came that army troops were trying to break in at the Dongdan junction, under 2 kilometres east of the square. Wide awake now, I rushed there with many others. Two public buses were stationed as barricades. To the east were a couple of thousand soldiers. On the west were students streaming from the square. Some sat on top of the bus, trying to persuade the soldiers to go home. But without an order, they couldn't do so. Pushing and shoving soon escalated into more violent skirmishes. Assisted by local Beijingers, the students gained the upper hand and the soldiers withdrew, abandoning their belongings.

I was tired but exhilarated by action so soon after our arrival. We returned to the square with our trophies: guns, walkie-talkies, and food rations. The student leaders reacted quickly, broadcasting warnings not to give the authorities an excuse to attack. It was a wise decision: stealing arms could easily bring charges of counter-revolution. The next morning, we took the soldiers' belongings to Zhongnanhai. In front of Xinhua Gate, student leaders wanted to see a government leader to make two points: firstly, we returned the items we found; secondly, how could you tackle unarmed students with real guns? Since no one came to address us after the goods were unloaded, some students began a sit-down protest.

I returned to the square to erect the tent I had been given by the logistics section under the Autonomous Union of Beijing Students. In the daylight, I could see 5,000 to 6,000 students stationed there. The flags on their tents showed the majority were from outside Beijing. During the day, another 5,000 or 6,000 students came. With all the locals and journalists, the square was always crowded. The logistics section provided free lunch, but it wasn't enough. Luckily, many local citizens brought us food.

As we ate, alarming news came that large numbers of soldiers were emerging from a secret tunnel under the Great Hall of the People. The union leaders urged us to stop them taking the square. We encountered them outside the west gate and decided to block the junction before Tiananmen. Some students went to the main road and brought back public buses—or rather they were driven back by their willing drivers. So many soldiers kept turning up from the Great Hall of the People, maybe two thousand or more. The atmosphere was tense, but the two sides exercised restraint at first. The soldiers sang: 'We are the people's soldiers who love the people.' The students sang back, telling them to go home if they were indeed the people's soldiers.

I was on the top of a bus, waving a flag while conducting my 'propaganda' work: 'The student movement is not turmoil. Go home, you are being used.' I almost felt sorry for the soldiers. They were all so young, around 20, like me. They looked tired, confused, and helpless. They said they had only been called up the day before. They didn't know what was happening. Suddenly, a squad of anti-riot police turned up with sticks and shields. More aggressive than the army, the police began to push around and hit the students. The soldiers sandwiched in the middle were caught up in the skirmish. People threw whatever they could pick up—beer bottles and stones. Again, we had the advantage of numbers. Without a warning, tear gas was thrown at the students, causing more chaos and panic. As some students began to bleed, others grew angry and fought back fiercely. The soldiers eventually withdrew.

The afternoon was fairly calm. I was woken from a nap by three teachers, who had come all the way to Beijing to take us home. They had heard there would be a bloody crack-down and pleaded with us to return. Most of their sixty students agreed to leave. Only eight of us, all male classmates, chose to stay. We just didn't believe the government would use force against students.

After their departure, we went out to discover what was going on. The news was bad. It looked like the army truly intended to clear the square. The student leaders held an emergency meeting, but they themselves were unsure what was the best move. One moment, they broadcast a message telling us to prepare to leave; the next, they said we must guard the square with our lives. When they suggested we prepare ourselves for the fight, we began to search for weapons, but there was barely a stone on the square. I found a bamboo flag-pole, then another broadcast announced we must leave everything, since there was no chance we could possibly fight against armed soldiers and police.

Around 11:30pm, we were startled by the first audible gunshot from the western end of Changan Avenue. Eventually, the army had opened fire, though we didn't know then that the shots were aimed at people. By 12am, the gunfire intensified from all directions. As we were far from the shooting, the shots sounded like roasting soya beans, but we could see the red blaze in the sky. None of us young students had any experience of war; we could not comprehend what all this meant. We were nervous and anxious, but I was not really frightened yet. Even at this late stage, I still naïvely believed the government would never open fire on unarmed students conducting a peaceful demonstration. At midnight, some kind civilians brought us food and pleaded with us to leave: 'Go now! We heard the soldiers have opened fire and killed people. ' We stubbornly remained. Naturally, we didn't sleep. We listened to broadcasts urging us to stay calm. They became less assertive and frequent.

At 4am, the lights on the square suddenly went off. Panic struck in the total darkness. The loudspeakers called on us to move to the Monument of the People's Heroes. By this time, there were only the final four-thousand students there. Standing in the darkness, we sang the Internationale to encourage ourselves. About half an hour later, when the lights came back on, we were stupefied by what we saw: we were surrounded by troops! Looking north, I saw many soldiers, in white shirts, steel helmets, and combat boots. I turned around and was amazed that men dressed in camouflage and carrying rifles were already at the monument. They must have come from behind Mao's mausoleum. Amid the chaos, loudspeakers urged people to move out of the tents. Tanks had already reached the square. They rolled over the tents; then soldiers set them ablaze. Rumours claimed students were still sleeping in them, but I doubt anyone could sleep under such extraordinary circumstances.

What I was about to see was the most terrifying moment of my life: thousands of soldiers were running towards us. I couldn't see their weapons at first. Suddenly, one man in authority raised up a wooden stave 1.5 metres long. Immediately they all did the same and marched at us aggressively. The frightened students at the front tried to run back to the monument, as some inside tried to rush out. There was pandemonium, all manner of crying, yelling, cursing, and the sounds of gunshots. Even the monument was fired at, though I didn't know why. I was pushed into the hedgerows at its base. As more students fell on top of me, I felt I was going to die. I held out a hand, shouting for help. I never got to thank the man who kindly stopped to pull me up.

It was a hair-raising escape. I followed the stream rushing out of the square. We ran between approaching tanks as soldiers chased students and beat them ruthlessly. Those at the edges suffered most. I myself was badly hit on the back. Some protesters became outraged, tried to fight back empty-handed, and were hurt even more. I didn't see anyone shot dead on the square, but I am sure some were beaten to death in this way. I saw with my own eyes one slim little girl, crying and cursing angrily. One soldier kicked her in the stomach so heavily she lay motionless. I was pushed away by the stream of people. There was simply no chance for me to help her.

I lost all sense of direction. Somehow I managed to exit the square and reach a side street east of Tiananmen leading to the Beijing Public

Security Bureau. Sympathetic onlookers told us to get away as soon as possible, since police and soldiers were everywhere. Other students ended up in the same street. In front of me, a girl held her boyfriend bleeding from a head wound. He told her not to cry. 'How can I not cry? These people are animals. How could they do such things to unarmed students?' She sobbed uncontrollably, setting off all those nearby. I ran into a classmate wearing only one shoe. He was crying, too. We hugged each other like brothers and cried together. 'Good, you didn't die!' 'Nor did you!' Shaken and angry, we felt lucky to be alive.

Even in the backstreets, we were not clear of danger. When soldiers carrying rifles soon turned up, we fled for our lives as shots were fired from behind us. At one point, we hid in a doorway as my classmate couldn't run fast in one shoe. A granny took us to her home. 'Come in, you poor child. My grandson is also a university student. Let me give you a pair of shoes.' We were running towards the train station, like many students from outside town. A helicopter tracked the large crowd. We ran and hid, ran and hid. The train station was under 1.5 kilometres away, but that short, nerve-racking journey took us hours.

We eventually reached the station around 7am. Soldiers were busy checking IDs, so we dared not approach the ticket windows ourselves. A middle-aged man bought us tickets for the 8:30 train. Before boarding the train, we hid nervously in the toilet. Back at our university, we gave speeches to student gatherings, describing the nightmare we witnessed. One classmate's shirt, stained with the blood of an injured student, was used as evidence of the violence in Beijing. Somehow, the local police found out, and the blood-stained shirt was used as evidence of our participation in the 'turmoil'. All eight of us were interrogated and forced to write detailed accounts of what we did in Beijing, and what we knew about others. My involvement was marked in my personal file, leaving a permanent black mark. Even I myself don't know the verdict they wrote in my file.

I was given a demerit as punishment. Worse still, when I graduated, they refused to give me a graduation certificate. I was so angry, as I had excellent academic records. I stopped the Party secretary when he came out of his office. I threatened him: 'Give me my graduation certificate, or you may regret what I am going to do.' They already knew I was a troublemaker, so they gave in, but I was allocated the worst possible job among my classmates: a teaching position at a remote and backward island.

The democracy movement *was* inevitable, just like Deng Xiaoping said. It was determined by the political and social environment of the time. Without Hu Yaobang's death, it would have been triggered by something else. The students played a leading role, and outstanding intellectuals like Fang Lizhi and Wang Ruowang offered theoretical guidance, but without the massive support of people from all walks of life, the movement might not have developed to that scale. There was growing dissatisfaction at the widening inequality in society; there was unfair competition in the marketplace, as those in power traded it for money, while their children exploited their connections for huge profits. The people strongly supported the students' calls to end corruption, while intellectuals and journalists wanted more speech and press freedom. People simply wanted more breathing space. For despite improvements, ordinary citizens still resented the controls over their daily lives, such as restrictions on city residence that could mean separation from loved ones.

What was not inevitable was its tragic ending. China is a country ruled by man. At the time, Deng Xiaoping had the ultimate power to decide what to do. He must take some responsibility, though emotionally I didn't blame him totally. He did so much for China, and was so old by that time. The information he was fed might not have reflected the true picture. As for the students, they performed several provocative acts, since they were so inexperienced with political movements. The involvement of some older people, even with good intentions, just complicated the situation—the behaviour of some of Zhao Ziyang's political advisers left his position awkward.

I have never regretted what I did then. It was a great student movement which can be compared to the May Fourth Movement. In both cases, students were injured and killed, but the blood and lives they sacrificed will never be in vain. After the 1911 Revolution, May Fourth proved an important force advancing democracy and freedom. June Fourth had the same significance, so many were enlightened and inspired by it. Ten or twenty years down the road, participants will explain to their children the concepts of democracy and freedom they learned. For those promoted to high office, their June Fourth experience will influence policy-making and ultimately benefit the cause of democracy.

Though it was hardly mentioned, the movement had significant impact on the economy. At the time, students opposed official involvement in business; later, the issue was actually addressed, and now private enterprises and the market play a greater role. So too does the rule of law, for which some credit should be given to the movement. I am confident our student movement will be rehabilitated and go down in history as a glorious page. Every single Chinese I know agrees with me on this. It may be difficult at present, since Jiang Zemin assumed power because of 1989, but it is only a matter of time.

The eight hard-core protesters who stayed behind on the square are now teachers, academics, or in business like myself. We are not democracy activists or dissidents, just ordinary people who get on with ordinary lives. But if a movement like 1989 happens again, I will take part just like before, if a little more cautiously so I can protect myself better. I know my former classmates will do the same.

Entering the World

1990–1999

Just as Mao felt betrayed by his two designated successors, Liu Shaoqi and Lin Biao, Deng had now removed both of his favourites, Hu Yaobang and Zhao Ziyang. Pundits predicted a similar fate for the Party's new General Secretary, Shanghai party boss Jiang Zemin. Although democratic protest across China had been crushed in June 1989, it soon swept Eastern Europe in triumph. The execution of Romanian dictator Nicolae Ceausescu in December horrified the Chinese Communist leadership.

When Deng resigned his last party post in November, his only title was Honorary Chairman of the Chinese Bridge Association. But he would remain China's paramount leader until his death, lending Jiang and the reform movement crucial backing. After the shock of 1989, the 'go-slow' faction, headed by Zhou Enlai's adopted son, Premier Li Peng, called for moderation. Investment slowly recovered as overseas Chinese led the charge back into China, but caution was the political watchword—a campaign against pornography was heralded 'a struggle between socialist and capitalist ideology'.

While Chinese diplomats worked hard to soften China's pariah status, the lure of a billion consumers did most to dissolve Western threats of sanctions. In 1990, McDonalds opened its first outlet in China and the new Pudong development zone in Shanghai promised investors access to the vibrant Yangtze River delta. Continued political repression did not preclude economic reform. After forty years of being reviled as the ultimate symbol of capitalism, the Shanghai Stock Exchange reopened at the end of 1990. This was how the Party would cope with the crisis of Communism—by channelling the people's energies into making money. Even the collapse of the Soviet Union in 1991 was harnessed to the cause: 'In the past, only socialism could save China, now only China can save socialism.' As the heirs to the Bolshevik Revolution sank into disorder and economic dislocation, Chinese state media drew on traditional fears of instability to confirm the wisdom of undertaking economic before political reform.

As the economy picked up, few noticed in 1991 when Mao's widow Jiang Qing, imprisoned for her activities in the Cultural Revolution, committed suicide. Most Chinese were more interested in rising grain prices and a survey that showed China was now home to 500 dollar-millionaires. Deng, however, was far from satisfied. Since the last boom cycle in 1988, conservative opponents had slowed the reform process that Deng considered the Party's best hope against Soviet-like collapse. In January 1992, he toured southern China to rally support. Nowhere provided a better backdrop for his message than Shenzhen, the showcase special economic zone bordering Hong Kong. Where once tourists had travelled to the border lookout at Lok Ma Chau to gaze on tranquil rice paddies, now they saw a boom town reaching skywards.

Deng's 'southern tour' set China firmly back on a reformist path. Entrepreneurs, officials, and academics were persuaded to 'jump into the sea' of business and trust his 'socialist market economy'. The money-making fervour sparked riots in August in Shenzhen, home of China's second exchange, when thousands of potential investors were denied lottery tickets for a new share issue. At the Fourteenth Party Congress in October, Jiang Zemin agreed that 'reform is a revolution . . . to liberate productive forces', while at the same time affirming China's rejection of a Western-style parliamentary system. The nation's GDP in 1992 jumped 11 per cent on the strength of Deng's efforts. Key to his success was investment by the non-state sector of town and village enterprises, private Chinese enterprises, and foreign investors. Driven by these small-scale, flexible operations, southern coastal provinces, including Guangdong, Jiangsu, and Fujian, soon outpaced the state-run heavy industrial belt of the north-east. These small enterprises were increasingly staffed by rural migrants, whose number exceeded 100 million by 1992. Pressured by floods and barren land, or simply drawn by the promise of prosperity, this 'floating population' provided a cheap labour force, as well as scapegoats for rising urban crime.

The downside of the reforms was exposed in 1993 in Daqiuzhuang, China's richest village, where peasants built luxury houses and ran factories with outside labour. Daqiuzhuang eclipsed spartan Dazhai as a model for rural China, until the corruption and brutality that built it became a national scandal. For most of the year, China was transfixed by Beijing's bid for the Year 2000 Olympic Games, and, by extension, global forgiveness for June 1989. Desperate to curry favour with the International Olympic Committee, the Party even released China's foremost dissident, Wei Jingsheng, after fourteen years in jail. Sydney scraped by in the vote, but there seemed little doubt Beijing would host a future games. With similar dedication to the former eastern bloc, the

Chinese government recognized the value of sport as both national propaganda and a release for its citizens, eager for new heroes in the post-Mao age.

Spurred on by cheap credit and a lax banking system, inflation, the bane of pre-Communist China, reared its head as the economy bubbled upward. For the first time in the reform era, Deng was absent during a major crisis. Bar a television appearance at Chinese New Year in February 1994, he stayed hidden, too ill to participate. When his daughter disclosed his ill health early in 1995, the Hong Kong stock market plunged, and a conservative agenda dominated Chinese politics. The burden of righting the economy fell on Vice-Premier Zhu Rongji, one of the few members of China's 'collective leadership' who grasped modern economics. Zhu implemented strict credit control and closed scores of economic zones. While inflation was reined in, corruption, according to Premier Li Peng, remained 'a matter of life and death' for China. Beijing's vice-mayor Wang Baosen quickly chose the latter, by a gunshot to the head, to avoid the graft investigation that netted the Beijing Party chief, Chen Xitong. As the decade closed, corruption was still rampant, despite official determination to stamp it out.

Zhu's success in engineering a temporary 'soft landing' for the breakneck economy became clear in 1996. But so too did the dire situation of many state-owned enterprises, backbone of the planned economy since the 1950s. Crippled by outdated ideology, facilities, and massive intracompany debts, almost 50 per cent of state firms floundered in the red throughout the decade. Despite the low efficiency of their bloated payrolls, the government was reluctant to enforce mass redundancies for fear of social unrest—a problem that continued to plague the party as the fiftieth anniversary of Liberation approached.

After four years, and endless false alarms, the Deng Xiaoping death-watch concluded on 12 February 1997. As the 'Great Architect' of China's reforms would have hoped, his passing aged 92 was an anticlimax. Two decades of 'economics in command' had achieved social and economic transformation as profound as the vicissitudes of Mao's 'politics in command', but far more welcome. By disbanding the communes, Deng toppled the sacred pillar of Maoist economics and emancipated the peasants. By encouraging private enterprise, he spurred economic growth and forced the state-owned sector to compete. While he conceded little ground on political reform, and dealt harshly with dissent, China under Deng became a more open society, its citizens at greater liberty to make the key choices in life.

Deng's remarkable career was denied the finale he treasured: presiding over Hong Kong's return to the motherland on 1 July 1997, a source of great national pride for all mainland Chinese. It was left to Jiang Zemin to lay to rest the shame of the opium wars over 150 years earlier. If successful in Hong Kong, China hoped Deng's 'one country, two systems' formula might forestall Taiwanese attempts at independence. At the Fifteenth Party Congress in September, Jiang finally took centre stage, the 'core of the collective leadership of the third generation'. Under the banner of Deng Xiaoping Theory, the Party endorsed private ownership of enterprises and urged the restructuring of the state-owned sector.

By the end of 1997, both the Yangtze and Yellow rivers had been diverted as part of massive and controversial water-control projects. Summer flooding in 1998, the worst since 1954, highlighted the need for better flood control, though some analysts doubted if either dam would help. Nature's ravages were more than complemented by the environmental degradation of mass campaigns under Mao, and commercial greed under Deng. The challenge of feeding, clothing, housing, educating, employing, and policing some 22 per cent of humanity, on just 7 per cent of the world's arable land, presented an administrative burden unique in history. At least in Zhu Rongji, appointed premier in March 1998, China had a committed economic reformer. By and large Zhu has kept his promises to slash government bureaucracy and turn round the loss-making state-owned sector, despite the Asian financial crisis that has emphasized the dangers inherent in China's banking system.

In an anniversary-conscious country like the PRC, 1999 offered something for everyone: eighty years since May Fourth (1919), fifty since Liberation (1 October 1949), and ten since June Fourth (1989). The memories stretch from early idealism, through to the victory of the PLA and national unification under Communism, to the day the PLA turned its guns on the people. Yet the only event to provoke marching in the streets was the bombing in May of the Chinese embassy in Belgrade by warplanes of the NATO alliance. Ten years after students raised the Goddess of Democracy in Tiananmen Square, their successors were burning the Stars and Stripes after state media insisted the bombing was deliberate. There could be little doubt of the Party's successful trade-off: the economic freedoms that sponsor rising standards of living, in exchange for its continued monopoly on power. In strident nationalism, the Party found a useful, if perilous, way of deflecting attention from domestic ills, like the worker and peasant unrest that has it fighting fires nationwide.

'Without contradiction, nothing would exist', Mao wrote in 1937. There are few more startling contradictions than the 'socialist market economy' created by his successors. Redrafts to the Constitution in 1999 enshrined Deng Xiaoping Theory, the role of private business and the agricultural responsibility system, anathema to past regimes, while efforts were also made to solidify the rule of law, not man, to ensure that disasters like the Cultural Revolution would never happen again. Economic pluralism within a one-party state has opened a world of temptation and corruption and it is no longer enough to extol the selfless example of revolutionary heroes like Lei Feng. The Chinese are individualists again. Yet strong, impartial government institutions are essential to the continued success of market reforms. The search is on for a Chinese way to supervise the administration and economy, just as democracy provides the checks and balances in the West.

After fifty years of the PRC, perhaps the greatest triumph is that the 1.3 billion Chinese people, no longer bullied by annual campaigns, can finally get on with their lives in peace. They can focus on material gain without fear of denouncement. The family, albeit a one-child version, is once more the basic unit of society and economy—communes are a bad and distant memory. No longer are people obliged to inform on their relatives, spy on their neighbours, and struggle against their colleagues. Political study sessions are rare, like the need to queue for poorly made products, or pickle cabbages to supplement a montonous winter diet. While Mao would have abhorred the end of collectivized agriculture, and China's neon communion with Western capitalism, he would surely have admired his successors' Leninist grip on internal dissent, for fighting peaceful evolution and securing the return of Hong Kong. China has been kept waiting on entrance to the World Trade Organization, the last major club for it to join, but elsewhere Chinese foreign policy has been increasingly assertive. Macau's return to the fold in 1999 leaves Taiwan as the only unfinished business from the 1949 Revolution. Its integration, peaceful or otherwise, should prove a major test of China's next fifty years.

Liu Yonghao

To Get Rich is Glorious

As Deng Xiaoping said, let some of the people 'get rich first' as examples for others to follow. He would have delighted in the success of the four Brothers Liu, fellow Sichuanese who have pushed to the limits the reforms Deng set in motion. While the lure of China's numbers has been the undoing of many foreign investors, they were clearly in the Liu family's favour: Sichuan's 106 million people raised 64 million pigs in 1988. The pig-feed mill the brothers founded that year is now the Hope Group, China's largest private enterprise, with over 100 subsidiaries and 16,000 employees. The youngest brother, Liu Yonghao, is Communist China's first Renminbi-billionaire.

Mixing with the rich and powerful at the World Economic Forum, Liu has come a long way from the village to which he was sent down as an 18-year-old in 1969, though his customer base remains there. While others left the countryside after one or two years, a poor class background condemned Liu to almost five. He spent the time acquiring skills for the future, like raising pigs that slept under his bed. By selling puffed rice from dawn to midnight one Chinese New Year, Liu cleared daily profits of 100 yuan that dwarfed his usual 27 cents. His first encounter with market economics had left a sweet taste in his mouth.

The Liu Brothers were ideally located to cash in on Deng's revolution. In the late 1970s and early 1980s, Sichuan's crowded, fertile basin was the site of pioneering rural and urban reform driven by the provincial Party secretary, and Deng protégé, Zhao Ziyang. The Lius' quail-egg business stretched from their Xinjin country home as far as remote Xinjiang before they took the road to becoming China's 'feed kings'. Liu Yonghao has scored impressive firsts ever since: in 1996, he co-founded the Minsheng Bank, the first bank set up by and for private entrepreneurs. In 1998, his New Hope Group became the first private company to list on one of the country's two stock markets.

China's shift away from the traditional 'leading power' of public ownership marks a sea change in economic policy. The non-state sector now supplies two-thirds of industrial output and employs 200 million people, 70 million of them in almost 30 million private firms. Despite residual distrust in some quarters, there is now constitutional recognition of the private economy as a vital engine of growth, compared to China's loss-making state-owned enterprises. Spearheaded by men like Liu Yonghao, the private sector is lobbying ever louder for equal access to loans and capital markets. For his part, Liu is anxious to engage the authorities in what remains a highly political economy. In due recognition of years of charitable work, he was elected in 1998 as a standing committee member of the CPPCC, the only private enterpreneur to hold such a position. Liu Yonghao is the acceptable face of capitalism.

AT THE END OF 1982, when we started from scratch, we didn't even dare dream that one day we would have millions to play with. Great changes were taking place in China, as reforms began in the countryside where peasants raised their own animals, while in the cities some people emerged as small private businessmen. My three brothers and I watched all the changes with great interest. I subscribed to even more newspapers than the library of the school where I taught! Few people with government jobs thought about business, but we four were restless and grabbed the opportunity to start our own, in the hope of a better life than our meagre salaries could afford. We chose quails eggs, as these 'delicacies' were selling well in the cities, a sure sign that living standards were improving. To raise the 1,000 yuan seed money, we had to sell our watches, our bicycles, all our personal belongings.

I was responsible for sales and marketing, which later became my specialty. I carried quails eggs in baskets on a shoulder pole to sell in Chengdu's backstreets and markets. Other teachers might have felt embarrassed, but experience as a 'puffed-rice man' had thickened my cheeks. Deng Xiaoping said, 'To get rich is glorious', and I was making money through hard work. What is wrong with that? I didn't resign from the school at first, or the whole family would have to vacate my flat. When business grew, I set up wholesale stations and expanded into neighbouring cities. Taking a peasant as my assistant, we boarded the train to Chongqing with baskets and baskets of eggs. We began to

Liu Yonghao with the foundation of his success

sell at dawn and slept overnight at the market. Gradually, wholesale stations sprung up in other cities and provinces, forming a sales network throughout China.

My second brother, Liu Yongxing, and third brother, Chen Yuxin, looked after production at our headquarters in Xinjin county, not only home to Yuxin's foster parents, but also where I laboured as a youth. We knew the place like the back of our hands. Eldest brother Liu Yongyan was always good at electronics, so he took charge of technical matters— quails need the right temperature, you know. As competition intensified, we sold not only eggs, but a series of services, like quails for breeding and quail feed—we added amino acids, fish powder, worms, and other ingredients to chicken feed, which proved very effective. We developed much, much faster than we ever anticipated. By the end of the eighties, Xinjin had become the largest quail base in the world with over 10 million quails and a daily yield of about 10 million eggs! Unsurprisingly, the market became saturated, with so many copycats around, and sales slowed. We had to change direction.

The idea came quite by accident. On a sales trip to Shenzhen in 1987, I noticed a long, long queue in front of a factory, the first feed mill established on the Mainland by Thailand's CP Group. People told me, 'It's magic! If you give 1 kilogram to a piglet, it will grow by 1 kilogram!' I was amazed—the feed was even more expensive than rice, yet customers waited for days to buy it. I asked around and found a fellow from Sichuan who was working at the mill and took me inside to have a look. The feed was pellet-shaped, yellowish, and with a nice, biscuit-like smell. But the basic ingredients were more or less the same as ours.

I was inspired. When I returned home, my brothers all agreed to start a pig-feed business. It made lots of sense: Sichuan, a densely populated agricultural province, was a major base for pig-raising. But pigs were bred only on a diet of grass and leftovers. The potential feed market was enormous. We began it as a sideline, but went full-time after CP established a mill in Chengdu. Despite high prices, their feed sold like hot cakes, soon dominating the market. We killed the remaining quails for meat and with our 10 million yuan in savings built a mill and feed-research institute. The government was organizing experts to devise effective feed to match foreign-made feeds like CP. In the end, our own researcher, coupled with our market experience, produced a feed we could boast was equal to the imports. A national award-winner, we named it Hope No. 1.

When we started, I am sure CP paid no attention to this small, obscure feed mill with an uncertain future. We worked hard on name-building with advertising refrains like, 'If you hope your pigs will grow, let Hope help you' and 'One kilogram of Hope feed makes your pig grow by one kilogram'. We were truly small potatoes, yet with our own advantages— investing in a factory cost us US$1 million against CP's US$6–7 million. We had very tight management and cheap labour; CP managers were foreigners with salaries 50 times more than our workers. As natives, we knew where to buy high-quality materials at low prices. These were the reasons we could win the price war.

Wisely, we had no intention to challenge the high-end market, CP's stronghold. We emphasized mid-range feeds most appealing to ordinary Chinese consumers. When sales reached 20 to 30 tonnes a day, CP began to notice us, since they stopped raising prices. As we continued to grow, they cut prices by 20 yuan per tonne. We responded likewise and sales reached 50 to 60 tonnes a day. CP cut another 30 yuan, and so did we; we could comfortably afford it. Later CP slashed prices by

100 yuan, while three of us four brothers were in Australia. During an emergency call from home, we calculated that even an 120 yuan reduction would leave us a small profit. Monthly sales grew from 100 tonnes to 1,000, 3,000 to 5,000, 10,000, and then 15,000. We rose to become number one in Chengdu, Sichuan, and all south-west China!

After the 1989 political turmoil, the atmosphere somewhat changed in China. Conservative forces, which didn't approve of the private economy, became quite strong. There was all kind of talk about rich business people and their businesses. Numerous private enterprises went bankrupt or shut down. No one was sure what direction China would take next. As a large private enterprise, we faced tremendous pressure, particularly Chen Yuxin, general manager of our Hope feed mill. We were fairly well known by then, especially in Chengdu and the south-west. Some of the attacks were driven by jealousy. Once, Yuxin received a letter, demanding 50,000 yuan be delivered to a park at a certain time, or our whole family would be in danger. He reported it to the police who caught the blackmailer at the park, but the incident was typical of the difficulties and troubles we endured in the early 1990s. Yuxin stepped down through illness, but we agreed to keep going, for agriculture was a safe field of business, strongly supported by the government, and we had already gained rich experience.

We didn't have to worry for long. The year 1992 started with Deng Xiaoping's southern tour. China's economy boomed after his speeches encouraging a daring move towards the market economy. In autumn that year, we brothers had a meeting to restructure the company. Taking advantage of the more open environment, we formed our strategy: firstly, to keep feed as our mainstay; secondly, to take a step forward from our successful mill by forming a group. Shortly before the meeting, a trip to America to understand other business enterprises was a real eye-opener for us. Why couldn't we establish our own group?

I was confident we had the capacity and feasibility to expand. Feed is a low-profit business, so the distance from factory to market should not be far. I suggested opening up factories elsewhere. Yongxing supported my idea; thus we joined hands. Yongyan, the high-tech enthusiast, set up an electronics company with his share—all four brothers had an equal share of the mother company, plus a small share held by our younger sister, the chief company accountant. After his recovery, Yuxin set up a real-estate company with Yongyan. Many have heard about the later restructuring in 1996, commonly known as the 'split' among us four brothers. In fact, this was an equally important landmark in the company's history.

I took the difficult task of getting our Hope Group Co. Ltd. officially approved. When I went to the provincial industry and commerce bureau, I was told, 'I have never heard that a private enterprise can be a group.' 'Well, let's start the trend.' When I went to the State Administration of Industry and Commerce in Beijing, I heard the same response. I am not saying it was easy, but, overall, the officials showed quite a good attitude in dealing with our unprecedented case. After a year's continuous effort, we eventually obtained the approval!

At the March 1993 CPPCC session, as a newly elected member, I gave a speech called, 'Private Enterprises Are Full of Hope', on the promising aspects of cooperation between the state-owned and private sectors. State-owned enterprises usually have sites, facilities, and skilled workers, whereas private enterprises are usually more flexible and experienced in the market. The two sectors can supplement each other wonderfully. I know not all CPPCC members agreed with me. With Hope's still limited resources, we couldn't afford to start all our new factories from scratch. As soon as the CPPCC meeting was over, Yongxing and I explored three provinces in a single week and bought four state-owned mills. After merging with Hope, all four are doing very well.

Yet our first attempt at cooperation with a state-owned enterprise had ended in failure. For three continuous years, a feed mill in Neijiang, Sichuan, recorded losses with huge debts and unpaid workers. Aware of Hope's good reputation, the mill leaders approached us, and ultimately we agreed to buy a 70 per cent share. The union between the private and state-owned sector even won the consent of the local government, but a higher authority strongly opposed it: 'How could a private enterprise buy a state-owned one?' Maybe, in some people's minds, a private enterprise is somehow inferior. The mill leaders insisted: 'Our workers need to eat. A merger is the only way out.' So the authorities promised, 'Fine, we will let you merge', before finding a Hong Kong businessman to undertake it.

The event was given massive coverage in the media. One article asked, 'Why favour foreign businessman instead of fellow countrymen?' We were the losers but won overwhelming sympathy. Undaunted, we tried again with a collectively owned rubber plant in Mianyan. Its situation was identical to the first plant, but as soon as we took over it turned a profit. Now, it's an important part of a listed company in Shenzhen. By October last year [1998], we already had 107 factories under our control, scattered all over mainland China, bar Qinghai and Tibet. Our earnings in 1997 jumped to 6.5 million yuan, compared to 300,000 yuan in 1992. In that year, our net assets were 2.5 billion yuan, or 2.5 million times more than when we started!

In the early days, policies were not as tolerant as today. We had no loans or whatever, so our assets belonged totally to ourselves. We were among the first to enter the market economy when China was still more or less a planned economy. We learned the rules of the market as we went along: how to sell products and adjust them to market needs. When the business was small, problems like who should be in charge were not obvious, but the situation changed as we expanded. By dividing the Hope Group, we can pursue the projects that suit our interests. Of course, we are still brothers, and all are under the same Hope Group umbrella.

Looking back, we should be very pleased with ourselves. But being too pleased with yourself could be a negative force to pull you down. When I gave a lecture at Beijing University on how to be a successful businessman, I told the young students, 'There are two important things to remember. One is not to get depressed during difficult times; the other is to remain cool-headed when victory comes.' It is essential one looks beyond the flowers and praise at such a time. I've been fortunate to go abroad to see some truly successful enterprises and entrepreneurs, which made me realize the gap between us.

One of the reasons I wanted to list in Shenzhen was to generate new pressure on ourselves. Some reports stated Hope was the first private enterprise to be listed on the stock market, but that was not totally true. The lack of policy, and difficulty of approval, meant some private enterprises attach themselves to the state-owned sector. Hope Agriculture was the first open listing of a private group. There were false rumours we had tried to list in Hong Kong, but we felt we were still small, with little international market experience, and had better concentrate on the domestic market. Other than pressure, we naturally expected some profit from the stock market, and the listed vehicle is a good publicity tool too. On the other hand, as it only accounts for 5 per cent of Hope Group assets, it is no big deal or risk.

Our future is full of plans and promise. Feed will remain our core business, but it is high time for us to diversify and move into neighbouring countries. We've been genuinely lucky to live in the era of reform and opening up, and I am deeply grateful to Deng Xiaoping. We grew together with his reforms and were among the first to 'dive into the sea of business', so we made money earlier than other people. As Chinese care more about their quality of life, the demand for meat, and thus the demand for feed, can only rise, particularly in a country where food culture is dominant. Among the four Project Hope schools I have built, one was at Deng's hometown in Guangan county. Due to him, China has become a much richer, better, and stronger country. Just as I am confident about my own company, I am confident about our country's future. Once China is opened up, nothing can change it. I can't imagine *I'd* be happy to go back to the old life, when my salary was only 38.5 yuan per month.

Xiao Liangyu

Rubbish Man

'Surrounding the cities with the countryside' was Mao's tactic in late 1940s battles with the Nationalists' armies. His strategy is now being revisited in a manner he could never have foreseen, as the forces of guerrilla migration, China's peasants, overcome the odds to seek work and a better life amid the bright city lights. Where Mao kept peasants tied to their communal plots, Deng's reforms opened the doors of urban opportunity to farming masses long confined by the socialist revolution. With up to 140 million rural workers now surplus to requirements, a 'floating population' of 80 million migrants is driving China's transition from an agricultural to an industrial economy, and from a rural to an urban society.

No Beijinger gives Xiao Liangyu a second glance, as the rubbish man combs the streets on his tricycle-cum-warehouse, stacked with cardboard, polystyrene, and strings of cans and bottles. Yet back in his southern Anhui village, this Everyman of the new Chinese revolution enjoys hero status for breaking out of rural poverty and into a new life in China's capital. From the mid-eighties, China's uneven development began to reveal glaring disparities between the southern coastal cities and the poorer hinterland, as well as a growing rural–urban income gap. The demands of economic growth meant rural migrants were at first welcomed with open arms. The special economic zones were hungry for factory workers, whose meagre salaries, still several times village earnings, compensated for long hours and harsh conditions.

Thirty-year-old Xiao began his foray into the new China on a construction site, the classic migrant destination. Doing the dirty jobs increasingly spurned by white-collar city dwellers, Liangyu and fellow migrants send up to 50 per cent of their earnings home: by 1996, some 30 per cent of rural incomes in Anhui, Jiangxi, and Sichuan provinces came from absent relatives. Yet despite their contributions to the economy, migrant workers have become the scapegoat for government fears of social instability and urban discontent at rising crime and unemployment. As the number of workers laid off by the state swells, local authorities protect their interests by expelling migrants, banning them from certain jobs and razing their inner-city ghettoes. Xiao and his family have themselves been forced to flee Beijing's 'Anhui village'.

Even with close to 40 per cent unemployment among agricultural workers, China remains a rigorously rural economy. While Deng abolished internal travel restrictions, social mobility is inhibited by a residence-permit system that ties health, education, and housing to employment in a state enterprise. Despite its 1.2 billion people, China has just eleven cities with populations above 2 million people, and only 17 per cent of the country's total population lives in cities with over 500,000 people. Yet frustration with agriculture's stagnating returns, mandatory grain levies, and heavy taxation could force millions more into the cities. To stay the human tide, the government is compelling migrants to cease their perambulations at small cities under 200,000 people, despite global experience that wider macroeconomic forces mean big is beautiful.

Efficient rural–urban migration may prove essential to the successful modernization of China's economy. If discriminatory policies persist, rich cities will continue to be encircled by poor villages. Analysts predict the typical Chinese in 2020 will not be tilling his own land but working on a (terminable) contract in industry or services. As long as income gaps remain, rural residents will always try to squeeze in. Recycling the detritus of success, Xiao Liangyu rides the urban dream.

I AM ONE OF BEIJING'S 3 million 'floating population', migrant workers from outside the city. We might be second-class citizens here, yet life is much better than back in the village. Mine is called Xiaocun in Anhui, where most people share my family name Xiao. It's a beautiful place encircled by rivers and hills. Now I don't live there, I often talk fondly about my village, though the reality is that it's very poor. We grow rice, cotton, and rape, but even though Deng's reforms made us work harder, you can never make good money from farming. It's damn hard sweat. You sell the grain for a small profit, but then the fertilizers are more expensive, taxes are higher, and 'voluntary work' is ordered for countless excuses. Worst of all, you sometimes get a piece of paper for your grain, an IOU, just a promise of money instead of cash. Such a phenomenon is rarer now, but it was common practice in Anhui in the 1980s.

I always hated 'repairing the earth', though farming is the only profession my family has done for generations. I became a full-time farmer when I dropped out of school aged 16, yet I was the lucky one— on and off, I had four years' education. My wife and two sisters never reached the school gate; even my elder brother only got two years. At that time, a few daring lads from the village had already ventured out to the cities. Gradually they sent money home. The only families that began to build new houses with white china tiles were those with family members who worked as migrants. I began to ponder the idea of going away myself. When I told my family, I met strong resentment: 'Who do you know in the city? What are you going to do? What skills do you have?' I had no answers to the questions and was criticized for being too restless. Yes, I was restless.

I still remember the moment I finally made up my mind. On a scorching summer day in 1987, I was coming home from a distant hillside, with a load of firewood on my back, when sweat blurred my vision and I fell. Sitting on the hot ground, in pain, I decided, 'That's it! I'm going to the city to work! Why should I suffer here?' I was 18 that year. I asked around the village, and through the friend of a friend got work as a builder in neighbouring Henan province. The job was no easier than my usual toil in the fields—we worked up to twelve hours a day, eating and sleeping in harsh conditions at the building site. That wasn't much of a life, but the pay was much better than farming. After four years there, I saved enough money to return home to marry my childhood playmate at Chinese New Year 1992.

I stayed at home for a while after the wedding, but soon became restless again. The wedding banquet ate most of my savings—it's just the tradition of our village that you throw a lavish banquet no matter how poor you are. I wanted to go out to work again, but I had had quite enough of building. A cousin who had 'made it' suggested I try my luck in the capital, so I took my new wife to Beijing. At first, we stayed with him in a cramped room in the north-west suburbs, where many universities are. Then, we rented a tiny room for ourselves in the same neighbourhood, Lanqiying. So many migrants from Anhui settled there it's also known as Anhui village.

We opened a foodstall selling *youtiao* [fried doughsticks] for breakfast at a busy junction near Qinghua University. Before long, I learned that many fellow Anhui workers were in a more lucrative line: the rubbish business. With help from friends and costly gifts that smoothed the way, I earned a very desirable position as a rubbish man in Qinghua's residential area. You see, not every rubbish man can just turn up inside the compound where there are plenty of newspapers and cans and the well-educated residents do not bargain so hard over minimal sums. You need a pass to get inside and the head of security oversees the rubbish team, about a dozen of us, divided into two shifts. I can only work every even day of the month. If I turn up on the wrong day or go beyond the proper university area, I could be fined or even lose my job.

Let me clarify what I do. Though called a rubbish man, I don't actually pick up rubbish at dumping places. I only buy and sell old or discarded household goods for recycling. Every even day of the month, I ride my tricycle across the university's residential area, singing out loudly, 'Collecting reeee-jects! Any old books, newspapers for sale? Bottles, caaardboard?' I change the melody every few houses. Some items have a fixed price, such as aluminium cans, and I bargain for the rest. I think I've become quite good at it. I would say: 'Look, older sister,'—I always address them respectably—'10 cents or 50 cents doesn't mean much to you, but it makes a big difference for poor little people like me.' My humble attitude usually works well.

At the end of the day, I pedal my purchases home, where I go through them like a soldier counting war trophies. I must say I enjoy that part very much. You never know what kind of stuff people want to sell. I spent 40 yuan to buy a black-and-white TV set we still watch today. I got a lot of our furniture this way. On odd days of the month, I load my tricycle with refuse and take it to sell at a recycling centre. When I get itchy, I sometimes venture out to other residential areas to collect rejects, but there's a risk of being caught and heavily fined by the police. However, if people stop me for business on the way to and back from the rubbish centre, I'm not going to say no.

Honestly, no local would like to be a rubbish man. My clothes are shabby, hair messy and dusty, and my hands often bleed from cuts. But it's actually not a bad business. I buy plastic bottles for 5 cents and sell for 7.5 cents, and make 5 to 10 cents from each aluminium can.

Small profit, but it all adds up, and I can sell big items like stoves or washing-machines for 50 per cent more than I paid. I earn something between 1,000 to 1,500 yuan every month, deducting the 50-yuan administration fee I have to pay to the university. I dare say my income is more than many urban workers.

Ever since we had our son Baobao in autumn 1994, my wife gave up her job as maid for a Beijing family. I make enough to support us and we watch every penny. Our rent is only 200 yuan, and apart from the money I send home to my parents, we've managed to save quite a bit, mostly for the future of our boy. You know, people like us without proper Beijing residence have to pay a lot more to get a kindergarten or school place. But I'm determined to do it. Some migrants leave their children behind at home and others don't bother with education at all. I'll do my best to give him a good education, so he can find a decent job. If you have money and education, who dares to look down on you?

I know the people here look down on me. If I get into a row with taxi drivers on the busy roads, they shout rudely, 'You stupid country bumpkin!' They can always tell you're not one of them. 'Looking for trouble? Go home!' I have no intention of going home yet, even if I only hold a temporary residence permit. Honestly, I won't be able to put up with the hardship in the countryside any more. I knew that for sure when we made a visit home to show off the baby during Spring Festival in 1995. I'm nobody in the city, but back home I was welcomed like a hero. Of course, I wasn't in my rubbish-man outfit, but a woollen coat with a fur collar. Most of the young and capable youths in the village have some experience working as a migrants, though few have made it to the capital in years.

As for those who stayed behind, their lives were just the same. And it won't be easy if they do want to leave now, as it's getting more difficult for migrants to find jobs or residence permits. Luckily, we made the move early. Even for myself, it's harder now to make good money as a rubbish man and I'm looking at other possibilities. I heard we migrants are now allowed to learn to drive. One friend vaguely promised me a job as a truck driver if I had a licence, so I'm going to enroll at a driving school. My dream is to drive a Liberation-model truck, in a pair of clean white gloves. The salary may not be much higher, but a truck driver sounds much better than a rubbish man!

Wang Xingjuan

Holding Up Half the Sky

Throughout the 1960s and 1970s, the slogan 'Women hold up half the sky' signified the progress China's better half had made under Communist Party rule. The Cultural Revolution pushed gender equality to the extreme: women no longer had special interests but only common class interests with men. Even the party's own Women's Federation was abolished, as its existence served to 'divide the proletariat'. Across China, women were exhorted to copy the Iron Maidens of Dazhai, robust peasant girls whose farming exploits rivalled any male production team. Visiting US President Nixon was treated to the rifle-wielding ballerinas of the revolutionary opera, *The Red Detachment of Women*. In a Mao-suited nation, gender neutrality seemed the goal.

Only in the reform era of the eighties and nineties has the tenacity of male chauvinism and discrimination become apparent. China's social revolution had burdened women with male roles without lightening household and family responsibilities. In the cities, women's emancipation encouraged widespread labour participation, among the highest in the world, but mostly into low-skilled, low-paid jobs that are prime targets for restructuring. Rural women have faced the restoration of traditional labour patterns just as clampdowns on childbirth reduce available manpower and increase pressure to bear sons. The many challenges of a modernizing economy have created new problems and threaten some of the gains made since 1949. Fighting to improve women's status and spread awareness of their rights are activists like Wang Xingjuan.

Born in Shanghai in 1931, Wang heeded the new government's call in 1949 to abandon her literature studies in Nanjing for a career as a journalist and later the editor of a publishing house. After publishing over two million characters, including a biography of Mao's second wife He Zizhen, Wang took up the cause of her fellow Chinese women in the late 1980s. Old social evils such as prostitution, pornography, and wife-beating have resurged, while women remain second-class citizens in education, employment, and career promotion. Wang's own happy family—a loving husband and two children—leaves her very sympathetic to those suffering marital problems. Unofficial figures suggest divorce rates as high as 25 per cent in some Chinese cities.

Women and children still comprise the majority of China's poverty-stricken and illiterate population. Alarmingly, surveys have indicated almost 57 per cent of all female suicides worldwide take place in China, home to only 21 per cent of the global female population. Most victims are young women from the rural areas hardest hit by reforms: women now perform up to 70 per cent of China's agricultural work, while their men labour in the cities as migrant workers for much-needed cash. Abortions of female infants have raised fears of a generation of bachelors roaming the Chinese countryside looking for brides. The forced abduction of women for marriage or sale, banned under the stricter regime of Mao's China, is an increasing concern. Apart from the lack of marriageable women, the cost of dowry gifts drive some peasants to the slave traders—it is cheaper to buy a wife than marry one.

The growth of NGOs, such as Wang's Women's Research Institute, is an encouraging sign of China's budding civil society. Given the Communist monopoly on political power and the media, NGOs are often at the cutting edge of what is permissible. Those with a more political agenda established in the late 1980s were shut after June Fourth, but self-help citizens' groups are increasingly tolerated. Wang and her colleagues concentrate on empowering their fellow women. Since direct confrontation would serve no purpose, China's women are experiencing more freedom than ever before, yet complete emancipation remains a distant dream.

BEFORE 1949, WOMEN HELD a very low position in Chinese society. A women's role was confined to the home, yet even there she was a subordinate figure, expected to help her husband and bear their children. Only after the Qing dynasty was overthrown were women allowed to go out to receive some education, though educated women remained a minority, as they had never been encouraged to learn. Confucius said, 'Women with no talent are moral', and tradition laid down the rules of conduct: three obediences (to father before marriage, to husband after marriage, and to eldest son after husband's death) and four virtues (morality, proper speech, modest manner, and diligent work). Bound and deformed feet were considered beautiful, called the 'golden lotus', and the smaller, the better. Why was that? Because men wanted women to be totally dependent on them.

After 1949, the first law issued by the new government was not the Constitution, but the Marriage Law that granted women equal rights to men and showed how seriously the authorities regarded the gender issue. Women were given the right to vote, and received the same amount of land as men—that was why so many land-reform activists were women. Women went out to work and gained an economic independence vital to their position at home. I am deeply grateful to the Communist Party for liberating Chinese women, or I would have followed my mother's footsteps to become a housewife and child-bearing machine. As his first wife was barren, my father, a small businessman, bought a young concubine from Guangdong, a poor illiterate girl who followed him to Shanghai. She gave birth to nine children. I was number four.

For many years, I worked in large governmental organizations where women's positions were not bad and we were treated quite reasonably, so I didn't see women's problems at all. My interest began almost by accident. In the early eighties, as I researched the book *Must Reading for Young Girls*, I discovered the high suicide rate among teenage girls. For various reasons, clever and talented girls were taking their own lives. I thought back to my own childhood. It was not a happy time, growing up in Shanghai with little attention and care. As a young girl I remember feeling lonely, confused, and depressed. When I read these girls' sad life stories, I felt great sympathy for them and in my book offered advice on coping with loneliness, building confidence, and looking good. There were few such publications in those days. After it became a best seller and won a national award, I wrote two more books for women of different age groups.

I reached a turning-point on retiring in 1988. I could continue writing, through which I might find wealth and success, or pursue research into women's issues. One might expect women's position in society to improve as time goes by, but it's not necessarily the case. The reforms of the previous ten years had offered women opportunities they never enjoyed before, particularly well-educated and capable women. Some from low backgrounds rose to become respectable white-collar workers, even rich and powerful entrepreneurs. But the pressures of change have also caused many set-backs to Chinese women. Ever since the reforms of state-owned enterprises began, women were the first victims to lose their jobs. Female students have more difficulty finding work after graduation; some young girls end up as concubines or even prostitutes. These less fortunate women have to ask: is the sacrifice by women the price we have to pay for social progress?

If they ask 'Why are there so few women in the top leadership?', the simple answer is that China remains a man's world. So many traditional values persist, particularly in the countryside, where most parents still prefer boys. It is understandable in some ways: men are better at working in the fields, while girls leave their parents' house once they marry. Although baby girls are abandoned less frequently now, though that still happens, the more common phenomenon is for women to abort the baby once ultrasound tests show it is a girl. The imbalance ratio is already very clear, more pronounced in some areas than others, and the result is that some Chinese men will never have wives.

Back in 1988, besides a feminism research centre in Henan University, there was not a single individual or group in the whole country investigating the practical difficulties faced by women. So why not establish an NGO to research women's issues and promote equal rights for women? We attached ourselves to the China Academy of Management Science, a non-governmental scientific institute, and on 7 October 1988 held the inaugural meeting of our Women's Research Institute. After our supporters, social celebrities, Women's Federation officials, and other guests had gone, we were left to face the harsh reality in a tiny rented room just big enough for two desks. We couldn't afford heating in winter, and when it poured outside, it drizzled inside too. We had to raise a RMB20,000 registration fee among four and a half staff, with 50 per cent from my own pocket. Money problems haunted us for a long time, as without funding we could do no research. We tried to make money through various schemes, like selling women's clothes, but all ended in failure.

Finally, we gave up business and turned to what we enjoyed and were good at: training women cadres. Previously, a certain percentage of female government officials were guaranteed, especially in the higher ranks. Since contested internal elections began in the late eighties, however, many women lost their posts. The proportion of female cadres at different levels shrank nationwide. Our courses aimed to improve the quality of female cadres, increase their concept of competition, and boost their confidence. We taught them management science, the art of being a leader, and how to overcome psychological barriers. We earned enough to keep going and benefited many women, while the trainees were simultaneously our research subjects.

Our next topic was prostitution. It had been wiped out by the Communists after Liberation but was resurgent in the reform era. I dare say we were among the first to research this sensitive phenomenon through a national symposium and surveys of prostitutes in three major cities. We discovered many prostitutes are young, even adolescent, migrant girls from rural areas. With little sex education, many suffered abuse before falling into the trade. I gave lectures to girls held in reform-through-labour institutions as we tried to help them develop new lives.

We had always hoped to provide a direct service for women. Articles and books are not enough. When a woman feels lost or depressed, even a

few sensible suggestions and kind words can really warm her heart. Our women's hotline, the first for all China, started on 1 September 1992 and soon became widely popular. There are few counselling services in China, yet in some situations a woman simply cannot discuss her problems with her colleagues or neighbours. But she will open her heart to our hotline. Many callers ask: 'After the reforms and opening up to the world, has the position of women gone up or down?' When women have lost their jobs, they also feel the loss of social and economic status. Even former model workers couldn't escape being laid off. They went home and became housewives. They had to start from the beginning again. No wonder they were puzzled by what had befallen them.

Other women complain about trouble at home. Changes in social and economic position create changes in the family too. Traditionally, men worked outside the house and women inside, but ever since Liberation, Chinese women have always worked. Men have no concept of being the sole breadwinner: their wives came with their own rice coupons. Working women in China still do a lot of the housework, but many Chinese men now share it. Shanghai husbands are even known as 'apron men'. Some women thought even if they lost their jobs, they could come home to look after their husbands and children and still have a bowl of rice to eat. But some husbands, expecting their wives both to look after them *and* make money, would not let them in peace. In families with laid-off women, conflicts between couples have multiplied.

Marriage, divorce, dating, and similar family-related matters remain the number-one issue, nearly half of all calls. The majority concern divorce, often provoked by extramarital affairs. The general advice we offer is simply the four selfs: self-respect, self-confidence, self-reliance, and self-importance. One middle-aged caller announced she didn't want to live anymore because her husband wanted a divorce. She said they lived happily together for many years until the husband 'jumped into the sea of business', grew successful, and began an affair with his young secretary, whom he insisted on marrying. 'If I'd known earlier, I would rather stick to our poor and simple life!' she cried. We suggested she talk frankly with her husband and convey her true feelings to him. If he had already made up his mind, she just had to let him go. There was no point in trying to insult him or her, let alone kill herself. We encouraged her to be strong and positive, to do something to make her feel proud of herself. She hated the divorce, not only because she loved her husband, but also because she could not bear the humiliation. Traditionally, the family is the centre of a woman's life. If something goes wrong there, she thinks the whole world has collapsed.

Due to the success of the first hotline, we opened a second—the women's expert's hotline—in 1993. We choose a specific topic every day, like law on Mondays, marriage and family on Tuesdays, maternal issues and child-care on Wednesdays, sex counselling on Thursdays, and general women's issues on Fridays. It has worked well. Our hotlines are now our main operating arm, manned by trained volunteers with higher education and profound knowledge in their professions. In 1995, we published a popular series based on callers' questions and our answers. One interesting development is that 20 per cent of calls are sex-related and increasingly from female callers, which indicates greater sexual openness and awareness. Women ask about orgasms and how to achieve them, the kind of question that was unimaginable before. We are no longer merely reproductive tools. Women want to enjoy a better sex life too. Before, under the influence of the ultra-leftist line, women dressed like men. Thankfully, things have long changed, as living standards rise and women become ever more fashionable with jewellery and make-up. It is no problem for a modern, independent-minded woman to have a feminine image. All Chinese women have long admired Song Qiling [widow of Sun Yatsen and honorary president of China] for her wonderful work, intelligence, grace, and beauty. Now many are fond of Hillary Clinton, who showed such understanding and support to her husband when he was in trouble, and is a highly successful career woman herself. He could not have survived without her.

The most common problems we handle are still marriage crises. The divorce rate grows steadily, as marriages prove less stable than before. Partners care more about the quality of their marriage, and there are more temptations now. As a result, the situation is often far more difficult for divorced women. Men always prefer younger women. It is difficult for middle-aged women to find new partners, and even more difficult for middle-aged women with children. Besides research, we organize social activities, like the 'Single People's Weekend Club' for educated people in Beijing. The social circle of Chinese women and men is often limited, so we offer them a chance to meet. We noticed that educated urban women, particularly aged over 30, have difficulty finding spouses, perhaps because men and women have different expectations. Women seek men with higher education than themselves and better jobs, whereas men simply prefer younger women. In 1998, we established the Ark Family Centre, a club for single parents, as more divorces mean more broken families. Every Sunday, single parents, mostly mothers, get together for a chat, a chance to vent some bitterness and to learn how others cope with similar problems. We also provide counselling and organize seminars for them. One woman told me, 'When I first came here, my tears flowed whenever I opened my mouth. After three months, I feel much better. My situation is not that bad after all.'

We were active participants in the Fourth World Conference on Women held in Beijing in September 1995. It was a wonderful, eye-opening experience, as we learned so much from our sisters around the world about coping with women-related problems. Our own efforts were also much appreciated and encouraged, which meant a great deal to us. After the conference, the Women's Federation has claimed there are 5,800 women's NGOs in China. Many are women's groups attached to universities—in China, an NGO must be attached to a work unit or an organization. It is very difficult to establish a completely independent NGO.

Our battle continues. We must keep finding and funding new projects. Our survey on domestic violence uncovered a serious problem, worsening in recent years and possibly linked to the pressures brought by reform. Unlike in the West, there are no shelters for battered women in our country. For a number of reasons, we realize it is not practical to establish one, but we propose setting up a neighbourhood committee-type scheme handling domestic violence in Pinggu county, a poor and backward area outside Beijing. Farmers there treat their wives as goods to be beaten whenever they please, while women quietly endure it—like the Chinese saying, 'Marry a dog, stay with a dog; marry a rooster, stay with a rooster.' We must educate both men and women that wife-beating is wrong and illegal.

I don't think Chinese women have ever held up half the sky, but we have come a long way. It may still be some time before China has a female prime minister, but that day will come. Why does a retired, 70-year-old grandmother like me spend an hour and a half coming to work by crowded public bus on a rainy day like today? Because I want to help less-privileged sisters in villages and cities who are lagging behind China's fast-changing society. I am optimistic about the future. There are more and more people like me working to overcome the problems. We will keep fighting till the end to achieve real equality for Chinese women.

Allan Yuan

Opiate of the People

Each December, China's major cities wear an increasingly festive veneer of Christmas lights and decorations—and with good reason: China is the world's largest producer of such goods. While these remain chiefly for export, from a country whose government equated religion with superstition, estimates of Chinese Christians now range from 15 to 100 million. China traditionally worships a Sinicized Buddhism and follows indigenous Confucian and Daoist rites, not to mention a plethora of local and ancestral gods. Yet none currently matches Christianity for rapid growth and an historical resonance that causes the Party to detain an octogenarian pastor and his wife each time a senior political or religious figure visits Beijing. For many missionaries covertly proselytizing in the Mainland, China is the future of Christianity.

Tension and violence have haunted over four centuries of missionary efforts in China, from the Jesuits resident in the Qing court to the Christian schools, hospitals, and orphanages spread nationwide in the nineteenth and early twentieth centuries. The challenge to Confucian orthodoxy was heightened by fears the Western powers were subverting China with their opium of the people. Religious rebellions like that of the Taiping (1851–64), whose leader's claim to be Jesus' brother was sparked by missionary tracts, ensure fears of unrest remain prevalent today, prompting strict controls and isolation from foreign influences.

Pastor Allan Yuan, a peace-loving man bearing no grudges after twenty-one years' wrongful imprisonment, does not appear so threatening. But as founder of the largest 'house church' in northern China, for worshippers who refuse to acknowledge their first allegiance is to the Party, he represents the kind of independent organization the government abhors, particularly in the business of hearts and minds where the Party once held sway. Born in Guangzhou at the outbreak of the First World War, Allan's conversion to Christ came with a revelation as an 18-year-old, after which he entered a Beijing bible school, to the disappointment of his parents, and performed missionary work in the countryside. In 1946, Allan set up his own church, one of over sixty in the capital. Undeterred by the initial lack of a congregation, he beat a drum to attract onlookers and preached in the streets.

With echoes of the Boxer Rebellion, the Communist take-over targetted missionaries and their followers. During the Cultural Revolution, all religious believers were persecuted and their places of worship ransacked. Monks and nuns were forced to marry and Muslims to eat pork, as churches and mosques became factories and warehouses. Greater tolerance over the past two decades has swelled congregations, with Chinese searching to fill the void left by the retreat from Maoism to materialism. Buddhism and Daoism pose less-obvious threats, but Islam worries authorities anxious over some 8 million Uyghurs in China's north-west, now surrounded by independent Muslim neighbours. Thanks to the dedication of people like Allan Yuan, the underground Christian church movement also booms within its confines. Besides the major religions, traditional cults, millenarian sects, and resurgent secret societies have become an increasing concern. In July 1999, the *qigong* sect Falungong, whose followers are said to number 100 million, was outlawed by a nervous Communist Party.

EVERYONE CALLS ME 'PASTOR YUAN'; actually, I am only a preacher, a humble servant of God. Everyone else is my brother or sister. Bringing God's gospel to people is the greatest joy in life. I only obey Him, never any organization or government. This is the principle I stick to, whatever the cost.

Just before Christmas 1979, I walked away from my prison in Heilongjiang where I had spent twenty-one years and eight months. Thank God, that was a wonderful Christmas gift, though I remained on probation. I went into jail in 1958 on a life sentence, leaving my wife with six young children and an aging mother. When I emerged, all my children had grown up and my mother had passed away. I was never informed about her death, though I suspected it. I'll never forget when I eventually made my way to our little home near the White Pagoda in western Beijing. My wife, who shouldered the heaviest responsibility and suffered incredible misery, looked old, but she was in good spirits. What a miracle!

As soon as I returned, people came to my home almost daily. Friends came to ask about my health, some were lost lambs, others God's servants who simply wanted to share Jesus with me. My wife cooked all day long, entertaining streams of visitors. Our finances were already tight, but somehow we always managed. I was so happy in those days; finally I was with my family, and finally I could read the Bible and talk about Jesus again. We soon set up a bible-study group. Our little house church gradually attracted more and more people, not just from Beijing, but all over China and even overseas. I made some teaching and preaching tapes when the Bible was not available in China. We gave away hundreds of audio and video cassettes. Our situation further improved when foreign friends supplied many bibles that were smuggled into China. Even though China now prints its own bibles, we still get free supplies. After Christianity had been suppressed for so long, I found people were eager to know more about Jesus.

Running a house church might not have been the wisest thing for me to do at the time. There are two kinds of house churches in China: those registered with the authorities, and unregistered 'underground churches'. We fall into the latter category, though we do everything very openly. For ten years after my release, I was on probation without a citizen's rights. I wasn't even allowed to travel outside Beijing, and to this day I still wear a counter-revolutionary 'hat'. More pragmatic friends kindly suggested I embrace the government-run Three-Self church, like they did after their release. They are now well-treated, with a job, salary, and house. I would then be granted a citizen's rights and could ask for rehabilitation. My children wouldn't have to bear the black mark of being 'counter-revolutionary offspring'.

But there is no way I will ever join the Three-Self. Back in 1949, when the Communists took power, all foreign missionaries were forced to flee, leaving behind considerable church property, hospitals, and schools. What was to be done with them? Wu Yaozong, the YMCA's chief-secretary, came to Beijing from Shanghai to hold a long talk with Premier Zhou Enlai. They decided the Chinese church must cut off all connections with foreign 'imperialists' and establish our own self-supporting, self-governing, and self-propagating church. The Three-Self Patriotic Movement quickly swept across China.

Almost all of Beijing's churches that received foreign aid joined the Three-Self church. Under the movement, the church became an instrument of the government, led by the Party and the Religious Affairs Bureau. All those at the YMCA, like Mr Wu, were modernists, not evangelists. Only eleven people, including the well-known preacher Wang Mingdao and myself, refused to join. I am a servant of God, *not* the state, and I believe that politics and religion should be separated. My 'gospel hall' church *was* independent and self-sufficient without foreign funds. Our refusal, and our belief, cost all of us our freedom.

It was bitterly cold in the labour farm in Heilongjiang, near the Russian border. I was so fragile and thin I was convinced I would die a martyr. I saw so many die or commit suicide when the physical and mental torture became too much to bear. We worked in the fields nine hours a day, yet I hardly fell ill. Indeed, my health somehow improved. I had no bible to read, but sang hymns to encourage myself. During the midday break, when others stopped to smoke, I would sing out loud 'The Old Rugged Cross' and draw strength from the hymn. During my entire imprisonment, I only met four Catholic fathers, two of whom didn't make it, and no other Protestants, though I did convert two inmates.

When Deng assumed power, religious policies, like many other areas, grew more relaxed. They released people aged over 60 who had served over twenty years, like me and Wang Mingdao. Maybe they thought twenty years' imprisonment was enough to transform one's mind to the 'correct path'. However, my belief has not changed in the slightest and Christianity has grown steadily more popular. As people became more commercial and money-oriented, they began to feel empty inside. Money cannot fill one's spiritual needs. After the June Fourth Incident in 1989, the popularity of Communism decreased sharply. There was a jump in Christian converts. Having lost their faith in Marxism-Leninism, they felt disappointed, confused, and frustrated. So they turned to Christianity. Christianity gives people love and teaches people to love. One young man came to us shortly after the crack-down. He had been very active in the movement, but now had lost all hope. By listening to God's words, he found peace with himself again. In the early nineties, we christened about 200 people a year in our little church.

Christianity is new compared to China's other religions. The government pays it more attention due to its past association with imperialism, and the Chinese people do associate it with developed Western countries and Western culture. One of the reasons for its popularity is that people had little previous opportunity to get to know Western culture, in which Christianity plays such an important part. In 1995, [the American evangelist] Billy Graham visited China, where he was very well treated. We say he has three faces, trying to please the government, the official church, and the unofficial church. I refused when he tried to persuade me to work together with the official church. A month later, I was honoured to be invited to the White House for morning prayer, but I had to decline, as I did not want to attend together with 'official' church representatives.

In 1996, there was a crack-down on house churches. One hot day in July, officials from the Religious Affairs Bureau came to our house, demanding we register. We replied that since ours is only a residential home, I am not an ordained priest, and we have no organization or system, we don't qualify to register as a house church. Their reply was an ultimatum: 'Many people come to this place. Register, or we'll shut it down.' We knew of crack-downs in other cities and the countryside, where house-church organizers have been hassled, fined, and even arrested. If we ignored their warning and continued to hold gatherings, the same fate might befall us. It was a painful decision to stop. When we told our congregation, many wept.

But people simply kept coming back. At first, just a few devout folk at a time. Well, we can't have a 'gathering', but no one can stop a few friends getting together. In the same way that we started, the congregation gradually grew from a dozen to a few hundred. In a few months' time, everything returned to normal. We have three services a week, though we are more careful—we no longer use the microphone, and try not to sing our hymns so loudly. Can you believe our little home of 19 square meters can hold over eighty people? On busy days, those who come late have to sit or stand outside in the narrow lane.

Most of the time, the authorities leave us alone. Only on special occasions, like a party congress or a presidential visit, are we forced to close and my wife and I are 'invited' to spend time elsewhere. During the Hong Kong hand-over in 1997, we were taken by car every morning to an air-conditioned room in the district government building, where we spent the whole day watching videos and eating banquets! I know they are only doing their jobs.

You'll find all kinds of people among our faithful lambs; the young and the old, migrant girls and city professors. A Hebei businessman recently came to see us. He was unhappy, as he felt the world was cold, empty, and heartless. Business people cheat each other; government officials are corrupt and greedy; everyone seems obsessed with money. But here he found a different world, where people are kind, warm, and giving. He became a believer, and brought along his friend, a disabled man who is treated equally.

According to some groups in Hong Kong, 9 per cent of Chinese now believe in Christianity. It is not the case that 'religion' is more popular, and the government has relaxed controls. It is simply the power of God. The difference between humans and animals is that we are religious beings. Christianity has been suppressed by the atheist government for fifty years, yet has grown in the face of persecution, and the numbers still climb. In Hong Kong and Taiwan, believers total 2.5 per cent, and even less in Japan, where people have everything. Yet China's vast and poor rural area is a rich breeding ground for Christianity. They have nothing but a desperate need to grab onto and believe in something. You cannot imagine how many believers there are in the countryside. Sometimes, the whole village or even the whole township are Christians.

Although Chinese law forbids foreign missionaries, they come as English teachers, business people, and engineers. Others give money to build schools and hospitals, then preach to and convert those around them. Sometimes, the authorities know their true purpose, but rarely bother them as their skills and money are badly needed. I gather they have been quite successful and sometimes they invite me to baptize their converts. As for the Chinese, each converted Christian is a missionary. In August 1998, we hired a swimming-pool from the No. 3 State Textile Factory to christen 316 people. We baptized another 100 in bathtubs, or out in the countryside in rivers or grain vats. The day after the factory christening, officials criticized me for engaging in religious activities in a non-religious place. This year we may use the Ming Tombs reservoir!

Ever since I found my Lord, he has guided and helped me through life's ups and downs. Now, praise be to God, I have a large and happy family of twenty-nine people. Two of my sons have retired! I am in remarkable health for an 85-year-old. We Christians are ordinary people who believe in God. Apart from that, we are like the rest of society. We don't want to form a social force or any organization, as the government would then insist we join the Three-Self. We do not oppose the government, or the Party, for we are all patriotic, law-abiding people. We just want to separate religion from politics.

Chen Liyan & Yue Xiuying

End of the Iron Rice-Bowl

For decades, the 'iron rice-bowl' signified the cradle-to-grave social welfare that a benevolent Chinese government bestowed, regardless of employee performance, upon a workforce faithfully implementing the central plan. The Soviet Union had shown the young PRC how the road to socialism meant a command economy and heavy industry. In the early 1980s, as Deng Xiaoping's reforms got underway, the planning system still dominated 90 per cent of China's economy. Giants such as Beijing's Capital Iron and Steel Works commanded an army of 230,000 workers. Yet the zeal for zero unemployment, shared by worker paradises everywhere, hid gross inefficiency encouraged by generous state subsidies.

With the passing of the 1990s has come reluctant acceptance that China's ailing industrial dinosaurs must be put down or invigorated by radical treatment like mass redundancies. Only by smashing the iron rice-bowl can struggling state-owned enterprises—almost half of whom languish in debt—hope to survive the transition to a 'socialist market economy'. As outright dismissal sparks official nightmares of social unrest, the preferred method is *xiagang*, laying off workers who stay at home on a small payroll and off unemployment lists. *Xiagang*, whose ranks are some 20 million strong, has become a buzzword of the nineties.

Women undoubtedly face the greater challenges from such reforms. The majority of laid-off workers are low-skilled women from sectors like textiles that were ripe for consolidation. Chen Liyan and Yue Xiuying were born to ordinary worker's families in Shenyang, Liaoning, in 1958. Like the rest of their generation, the Cultural Revolution cut short their education: both were among the last batch to be sent down to the countryside in 1976 and 1977. Where once Liaoning was a bulwark of the planned economy, proudly known as 'Liao Laoda' (Elder Brother Liaoning) for the heavy industry introduced by the Japanese, and boosted by successive five-year plans, today it is the epitome of the north-eastern 'rust belt'. It was no coincidence that a Shenyang factory, in September 1986, became the first to be declared bankrupt in China since 1949.

The Chinese Communist Party, veteran of industrial disputes in Shanghai and other commercial centres prior to 1949, is fully conscious of the tinder-box that is labour unrest. Ever more daring protests by laid-off workers countrywide currently focus on basic demands—desire for the money and security a job provides, not to overthrow the nervous powers that be. Once the ringleaders are arrested, the people's demands are often accommodated. Fearful of the development of union movements such as Poland's Solidarity, the Party oversees all labour organizations through the All-China Federation of Trade Unions.

Adapting state-owned enterprises to run on competitive, commercial principles is one of the sternest tests of China's resolve and ability to tackle the painful legacy of the command economy. Chen and Yue represent the human cost, survivors of China's often bitter Marxist experiment, now exposed to the equally raw lessons of capitalism. Besides their limited education and skill base, women face family burdens, supporting children at school and aging parents, while new employers prefer men to women, and younger women to middle-aged. Government retraining efforts can only ready part of China's workforce to meet the new challenges. A robust economy and the kind of determination Yue demonstrates are just as important. China must find work for these heirs of the Revolution, or they will demand change with louder and more disruptive methods.

CHEN LIYAN

ALL OF A SUDDEN, I became a laid-off worker. Life around the factory had seemed normal, as we were paid every month, unlike many other factories. I even enjoyed free lunches there until the very day I left. It was late November 1997, when we were summoned to a meeting and heard that all those aged above 37 must take *tuiyang*, a kind of early retirement. Those aged between 37 and 42 could receive 55 per cent of their salaries, those above 42 years old 65 per cent. I was shocked, as everyone knew it meant permanent *xiagang*. At first I tried to refuse to sign a form we were asked to complete. Then, I heard those who were laid off later might receive no money at all. So, I handed in the form like everyone else in my age group. Two weeks later, all the procedures were complete and we were sent home. So quickly, everything was over!

Staying at home that winter was the worst time I ever experienced. I had always worked, and for the same factory for nearly twenty years. In its sixties heyday, the Shenyang Textile Factory had nearly 100,000 employees, and there were still half that when I joined. I was not highly skilled, but I did my best. For many years, I worked all three shifts, standing in front of the spindles to connect the broken threads. Only in the last few years, when I was too old for the laborious work, was I moved to the weaving section, where I only worked day shifts. But that was it. Twenty years before the normal retirement age and I was stuck at home, so stressed that my health suffered for a long time.

Shortly after I was laid off, my husband, a plumber at Shenyang Silk Textile Factory, was also *xiagang* for a few months, during which he was not paid at all. Suffering from both depression and bad moods, we were always arguing, and often fighting. I accused him of being unmanly, for failing to provide his family with a comfortable life. He laughed at me, saying I was 'absolutely *xiagang*', and thus in no position to say anything. I heard the divorce rate in families of laid-off workers is rising sharply.

I looked around for a job, but it was far from easy. I went to a job fair, but women over 35 years old without any particular skill and low education simply had no chance. I don't mean to be choosy, but some jobs are just not suitable. Some people suggested I deliver newspapers, but I can't cycle very well; another told me a family needed a nanny for a 1-year-old baby, but I declined, as it was too much responsibility. There was a chance to look after an old couple, but I would have to stay overnight at their home far away, and I have to cook for my son in the evenings. In March, one relative eventually found me a job washing clothes at a laundry. I liked the job, as the 300-yuan

salary was not bad with regular working hours. But the business went bust in July. I had to start all over again.

Luckily, it only took me a month to find another job, though not as good as the last one. I was hired by the neighbourhood committee to patrol Ningbo Road. Wearing a green armband with 'City Administration Supervision', my job is to tell peddlers selling goods on Ningbo Road to move to the nearby central market. It's an effort to keep the street tidy, and the market can also charge administration fees. My salary is only 200 yuan and the working hours are 8am to 5pm, every single day of the week. If I want the weekend off, the salary is only 150 yuan! The salary is all I get now. When I worked at the factory, apart from enjoying free lunch, medical care, and a monthly bonus, we were even subsidized for showers, haircuts, and things like that.

It's cold standing in the streets all day long. Sometimes I even run into trouble. When I told a young man selling children's clothes to leave, he replied, 'If you dare to keep hassling me, I'll break your legs!' Another time, an old man hawking bike seat-covers threatened to throw himself under a truck if I insisted on expelling him. The worst aspect is that the job is only for six months. I don't know what's going to happen then.

I daren't think about the future. My husband could be made redundant at any time. He is not very capable, so I daren't rely on him. My son is in his last year of primary school. When he moves to middle school, I've heard every student has to pay a 9,000-yuan 'school construction fee' on top of his tuition. I don't know how we can manage that. I've been paid 170 yuan per month by my factory so far, but for how long, I have no idea. I have no other connection with the factory. In a way, I was lucky to be among the first group of about 1,000 workers to go. The second batch, laid off only two months after us, didn't receive any money, just as the rumour predicted, nor did the third. The saddest case was that of several members of the same family who all lost their jobs at the same time. The factory has now moved to its branch in the outskirts, after the land was sold to a Hong Kong businessman. Dumb as I am, I hope it is good news for our factory.

Falling to this degree, I don't know who to blame, except myself for being unlucky. Before, I was a victim of the *xiaxiang* policy [going down to the countryside]; now, I'm a victim of *xiagang*. Sometimes, when I watch TV dramas about laid-off workers, how they became more successful in their new careers after overcoming the depression of being laid off, I wish it could happen in my life. But I know it's impossible.

YUE XIUYING

I CAN'T REMEMBER how many jobs I've done. When I returned to the city from the countryside in 1980, I was hired by a collectively owned truck-repair plant under the Shenyang Transportation Company, where my father worked all his life. I worked as moulder, welder, and assistant to the top mechanic. My salary was not high, usually around 200 yuan, depending on work volume. The firm went downhill from 1990 until most of the eighty staff were sent home in 1993. *Xiagang* is not a new term for me, though nobody knew it as such at the time.

I tried to find piecemeal work here and there, like selling flour in a grain shop. Luckily, another subsidiary of the transportation company needed someone to control the grinding mill making magnetic discs for medical treatment. When I went for the interview, they asked, 'Can a woman like you cope with the job?' I said I could take anything. It was a tough job—I stood before the mill all day long, my hands soaked in cold water—yet I was grateful to have a job at all. I was also happy with the salary, which came up to 330 yuan including the bonus, one-child fee, and other benefits.

I don't know exactly why the plant turned for the worse. The overall economic situation was poor, but bad management and corruption played a role. I am sure secret deals kept plenty of money in the leaders' pockets. At one stage, the firm was even contracted to private business people, who didn't care at all about the workers' interests. By the turn of 1997, we were not paid for months on end, regardless of whether there was work to do, and no one explained what was happening. To this day, I am still owed two months' salary.

In August 1997, fed up with being 'half dead and half alive', a female colleague and I decided to investigate the labour market. One morning, we visited the temporary job market in the city centre, where migrants from the countryside carried wooden boards saying carpenter, electrician, and so on. Conscious of their 'face', some urban laid-off workers are too embarrassed to visit such places. I didn't care; I was looking for work, just like the migrants. When a guy asked us what

kind of jobs we wanted, and we replied 'Anything!', he took us to clean up a restaurant he was about to contract. Within a few hours, we had finished and received 25 yuan each as promised. Delighted by our first day's success, we returned to the labour market and spent 5 yuan on permits to seek jobs legally there. But we didn't find any more work. Through a relative's friend, I was hired to transport goods by bicycle from shop to buyer. Half a month later, I gave up this laborious job when I was temporarily called back to our plant. After that assignment, the situation remained the same and we had to look after ourselves.

My husband is a builder on a low income, and we have a teenage boy at school to support. I was obliged to come onto the street again to work. I tried to sell pancakes and sweetcorn, then picked up the fruit business from a kind neighbour. This was going well. We bought boxes of fruits from a wholesale market miles outside town, and sold them from a cart in the street. But I suffered from abnormal menstruation after a couple of stressful months in the cold winter. My padded trousers would be soaked with blood after just one hour. My mother forced me to stop.

In January 1998, the plant wanted me to sign a contract, saying 'I would be willingly laid off', or something like that. I didn't even read it carefully. If I signed I would receive 179 yuan a month for the first year, and 120 for the second year. That was it! I might have secured a delay but I decided to sign. The heartfelt truth is that I *would* have stayed if given a choice. I'd love to work in a stable work unit instead of piecemeal work here and there. I miss my colleagues and friends at the plant, but I had lost all hope the plant might improve. Secondly, I hated the bad practices there—if you didn't want to be laid off, you had to bribe the leader with gifts and money. Just disgusting! Still, I felt sad when I signed the contract, which basically terminated my relationship with the plant. From that point onwards, I had no work unit to count on. I was totally on my own.

Another reason I signed was my job delivering the *Liaoshen Evening News*. In December, I heard the newspaper was looking for staff and went to try my luck. I could never expect it would turn into such a wonderful opportunity. They warned me how tiring it would be climbing many flights of stairs. I said 'No problem', and they gave me twenty newspapers as a trial. The newspaper had recently offered a new service delivering to people's homes, free of charge, to attract more subscribers. They also install a little red box in front of each subscriber's door. Not every family has a letter-box and, sometimes, mail and papers get lost in the communal letter-box downstairs. Bringing the paper to one's door was an attractive idea. The newspaper hired many people, mostly laid-off women workers, so we are known as *baosao*, newspaper aunties, though men deliver too. For each delivery, we are paid 10 cents, no matter how high the floor.

In the first month, I felt exhausted just reaching the fourth floor, as I've always lived in a simple bungalow. But thinking of the 10 cents, I forced myself on. It took about an hour to deliver twenty papers. Asking for more papers, I earned 200 yuan the first month, and 250 the second. In March 1998, the paper launched a subscription campaign—we were given a monthly quota of thirteen new subscribers. For each order above quota, we earned 5 yuan; each order under quota cost us 3 yuan. After delivering newspapers in the morning, we went out into the streets in the afternoon. Under a banner with *Liaoshen Evening News* in red characters, we propagandized through a loudspeaker to passers-by on the wonders of the paper and free delivery. It was such a novelty, drawing great attention and many orders, I easily met my quota. My salary jumped to over 400 yuan; in the best months, I earned well over 1,000! I had never earned so much in a single month, yet some did even better. One laid-off cadre is so used to persuading people that one month she earned nearly 3,000 yuan! That peak has passed, though the number of subscribers still grows. In 1998, we *baosao* found

130,000 new subscribers. I don't know the precise number; I guess there are now nearly 1,000 of us.

A typical day starts at 4:30am, when I get up to cook breakfast for my family. Then I bicycle half an hour to our little newspaper station, where I sort out 200 papers for delivery—10 times my initial volume. I wear a red waistcoat with big characters: *Liaoshen Evening News*. The area I cover is spread out, with many subscribers high up in buildings without lifts. But I've got used to climbing stairs. It is around 9:30 when I finish. If I'm lucky to land a new subscriber—I always have the forms to hand—I return to the station to get the letter-box and hammer, and install it. Otherwise, I stay at the station, drinking tea, knitting, or chatting with the other thirty people at our station. Usually, I help out answering calls or with paperwork. Of course, this work is all voluntary. I have now been made a deputy head of the station. I want to do as much as I can.

I am so grateful to the newspaper, who actually saved me. After all my work troubles, I really feel I have a proper job with a decent income. The station has become my home. In the afternoon, I help to weigh and transport the old newspapers collected for recycling—that's another new policy at the paper. If we persuade readers to recycle the newspaper, they are paid for the old papers, and we get a tiny commission. Any extra cash is welcome to me, however little it is. On weekends and holidays, I go to the street with a loudspeaker to attract new subscribers. I am often joined by my husband and our son, who also help me with delivery whenever they can.

Not everyone likes to work as a *baosao*. Two of my friends resigned, as they could not bear the pressure to find new subscribers or to get up so early. I am proud to work for the newspaper, a much more decent organization than my old work unit. I heard they might buy insurance for us *baosao* who have worked here long enough. That would be wonderful if true; at the moment, I have to pay for my own medical care. On the other hand, I have been toughened by my experience and earned back my self-respect. If the newspaper makes me a laid-off worker again, I am confident I won't starve. In this 'socialist market economy' nothing will be easy for little people like us, but with hard work and will power, I believe the market is big enough for all of us.

Yang Yonghe
The Election Campaign

As the Constitution proclaims, all power in the People's Republic of China belongs, appropriately, to the people, who exercise that power through delegates to the national and local people's congresses. This political system is supported by the key administrative organs, the State Council and local people's governments. And above all is the primacy of the Communist Party, a self-perpetuating oligarchy with parallel structures to the state bodies and the ultimate say in all matters. The Party's fear of democratic opposition condemned the protesters of Tiananmen Square, yet since that time a grand experiment in rural democracy has quietly spread nationwide.

Like the rest of the population, China's peasants have for centuries been accustomed to authoritarian rule. Under the PRC, rapacious landlords soon gave way to dictatorial commune leaders, as the Party confiscated the fruits of land reform. The abolition of the people's communes in 1983 led to village committees, the lowest level of political organization in China and initially appointed by higher authorities. Despite official arguments that the poor education of China's peasant masses makes Western-style democracy unsuitable, since 1988 direct elections for village committees have been finally realizing the people's constitutional right to vote and stand for election. Peasants like Yang Yonghe have grasped it with a vengeance.

The fourth of six children, Yang was born in 1964 to an ordinary farming family in Anyang county, Henan province. He enjoyed a good school record until his father's death forced him to take up carpentry to provide for the family. Every year, when not busy on the land or making furniture for other villagers, he leaves his wife and son to work on construction sites in the provincial capital, Zhengzhou, or further afield. His exposure to the changes sweeping China encouraged him to contest the first free election in the village's history.

By February 1999, all of China's provinces, and over half of its 930,000 villages, had given their farmers a taste of democracy. Village committees enjoy considerable autonomy over issues like irrigation and housing that matter more to villagers than the macroeconomy of distant Beijing. In campaign speeches, candidates offer villagers promises of higher incomes and reduced burdens. While irregularities are commonplace, if not inevitable, China has been happy to show off its achievements: on his visit in 1998, US President Bill Clinton witnessed a local election in progress.

Encouraged by Party and state leaders paying lip-service to the virtues of village democracy, some of China's townships, the first formal rung of China's administrative ladder, have surprised authorities with direct elections. The leaders of China's 45,000 townships, groups of at least ten villages and up to 20,000 people, should still be appointed by county Party officials. No official timetable has been offered for expanding the experiment to the township level, once village elections have been 'standardized'.

By seeking better, popular administrators to handle the day-to-day issues that affect the majority of its citizens, the Chinese government is relying on them to preserve social stability through economic growth. While the elections act as safety valves for local discontent, the authorities retain sufficient legal and covert means to influence ballots and appease nervous conservatives. Few observers believe village elections are accelerating political reform in China, yet limited representation at the very bottom of society does comprise a step towards liberalization, and a solid foundation for the future. Only time will tell if China's 'rice-roots' democracy fuels demands for accountability further up the power structure.

IF YOU TRACE BACK EIGHT GENERATIONS of my ancestors, you won't find any in a position of authority. But so what?! As a carpenter, a 'commoner', I too now have the right to be elected village leader. The idea to contest for the leadership got into my head in spring 1998, watching the *In Focus* programme after the national news. I always watch both, for I like to know what is going on. Farmers in the north-west were fiercely competing for the village committee through democratic elections. I thought to myself, Premier Zhu Rongji is launching a campaign to fight corruption, yet our own village leaders are so corrupt. Why don't I give it a good shot when I have the chance? I'm fairly educated and not stupid.

I didn't have to wait long. In early October, we were told that on the twenty-eighth there would be an election for the new village-committee chairman and two committee members. For the first time, it would be a direct election by secret ballot, open to all voters. I was very excited; it meant a more democratic election, and more opportunity for a commoner like me. I must admit I have never served as a cadre in the village. There were supposedly two elections before, but I only remember one half a dozen years ago. Even though I was over 18, I had nothing to do with that election, and only a few representatives cast votes. To be honest, most people didn't even care at that time, as they assumed, 'The candidates were nominated by the authorities, so that's it!' Some hold such views even today.

All villagers here in Shangzhuang are divided into twelve groups. The head of ours was Mr Yang, a relative of mine—up to 90 per cent of the villagers share the family name Yang and many are related. One day, he showed me a piece of paper with three names on it. 'Do you agree that these three will be our representatives?' I asked what for and he couldn't even give me a clear answer. Most people just agreed without asking. I then found out these representatives were the important people who would decide the candidates for the election. The old village committee nominated three representatives from each group, supposedly with the consent of villagers.

I immediately threw myself into the election campaign. I told my fellow villagers, and particularly the representatives, that I wished to run for village-committee chairman. On the twenty-second, the day before voting for preliminary candidates, I put up three big-character posters in which I declared my administrative programmes if elected. I concentrated on three issues: firstly, I want to solve the old problem of village chiefs spending public funds on lavish banquets; secondly, I want to deal with the distribution of land for housing in a just and fair way; finally, I plan to set up a service company to engage in various businesses. My poster roused a big stir. Such behaviour was unheard of! Some appreciated my efforts, some said I just wanted to satisfy my thirst for power, and others thought I was crazy. Anyway, probably with the help of my posters, I got myself elected as one of six preliminary candidates. I was the odd one out: the other five previously held positions in the production team, and all are Party members.

On 25 October, three days before the real election, the names for the final candidates were decided according to election procedure. As expected, I failed. Yang Yanqing, the old village-committee chairman, and Yang Shukuan, the cadre in charge of family planning, would compete for the chairman's position, as they achieved the highest votes. The other three names announced were candidates for two committee seats. Disappointed, I did not want give up yet. The day before polling, I put up another poster, signed by five respected old Party members, in which I urged people to cherish their sacred ballots and elect someone they really trust. This caused more gossip, and some criticized my 'Cultural Revolution style'. I argued that I didn't ask people to vote for me, only to vote carefully.

That same night, our Party secretary called on me. By the way, the Party secretary is appointed, not democratically elected, yet he is just as powerful as the village-committee chairman, if not more so. He asked me what all the fuss was about. I explained I did not mean to make trouble, but to take part in the election sincerely. I asked if he could talk to the election work team and let me give a speech, even a very short one, as I knew candidates may make campaign speeches if they wish. He refused at first, but I begged him, and he eventually agreed to speak to them, but made no promises.

On 28 October, election day, I got up early, anxious and excited. That morning, my younger brother, the village electrician, set up a loudspeaker at the primary school where polling would take place. How I wished I could use that loudspeaker! When he returned, he brought back a message, saying the election work team wanted to see me. I found the team in a classroom. Made up of rank-and-file villagers, they were very polite but soon came to the point: did I have any intention of making speech. I replied, 'Yes'. They first praised my enthusiasm but suggested I forget the idea, as they were under pressure to ensure the election was carried out smoothly. 'You have no chance anyway,' they pointed out, 'why make things difficult for everyone?' That was my weak point: I knew I had little chance, and, after hesitation, I agreed.

I felt so depressed at that moment, but I remained civil. I heard in other villages, when people were unhappy with elections for some reason, they burnt the ballot boxes and boycotted elections. Walking out of the classroom, I met some friends and confessed my agreement not to speak. 'Silly man!' they replied, 'why don't you try?! You have lots of good ideas.' I began to regret I had given up so readily.

At 10am, the election began, accompanied by the national anthem. The chairperson announced the election procedures and rules. Just as people were about to cast their ballots, on impulse I threw myself to the ground. Kneeling in front of the podium, I pleaded, 'Please give me a chance! I want to say a few words.' Kneeling down is a traditional way to beg from the authorities. The people who sat high on the podium immediately jumped up, while I was encircled by curious and excited crowds. 'What's happening?' they wondered. I had caused a big scene, and was taken away to a quiet classroom by an election-team member.

The civil affairs officer who came to supervise the election explained that only formal candidates have the right to deliver campaign speeches. Others added that if everyone wanted to give a speech, there would be chaos. It was indeed getting chaotic, as more and more people entered the room to have a look or shout 'give him a chance to speak!' I was too excited for words and hot tears rolled down my face. 'A real man does not shed tears easily.' I didn't know why I cried. As the situation was getting out of control, the election team decided to let me speak. There was no other way for the election to continue.

Yang Yonghe gives his election speech, Henan, 1998

Overjoyed, I went up to the podium and made a passionate speech, the only one of my life, in front of my fellow villagers. I basically summarized my administrative programme. When I finished twenty minutes later, I was greeted with loud applause. I thought people would like my points. We all hate to see village leaders entertain their bosses from the township or higher authority with expensive banquets, or find all kinds of excuses to treat themselves. True, this is a common problem in China's countryside, but our place is poor: our average annual income was RMB1,600 in 1998.

Another major complaint concerned land for housing, as the government in recent years has restricted non-farming land usage, to protect shrinking arable land. As it grew more and more difficult to get permission to build new houses, the village committee took advantage by letting people bid for plots of land. Prices soared, from RMB2,000 to a record of RMB36,500, and that doesn't include the actual construction cost. I believe such a practice is illegal.

Finally, I don't think the village committee tried hard at all in leading the villagers to get rich. I frequently go out to work as a temporary migrant worker and see changes happening everywhere. How about us? There are a couple of iron mines which started back in Chairman Mao's time, plus profit from house-bidding, and limited farming income. That's all we have. There are no rural enterprises or any other kind of business. The idea of my service company is to provide farmers with more business opportunities, such as raising animals, or some kind of processing industry, to help people get rich.

The results came out in the afternoon: there were 1,230 villagers qualified to vote, but I am not sure how many votes were valid. The two official candidates Yang Yanqing and Yang Shukuan won 337 and 150 respectively, and I myself 197. If it had been explained properly how to vote for unlisted candidates, I believe I might have won 100 more. Voters needed to cross out the listed candidates and add my name, but many did not cross them out, or circled them *and* added my name. Since none of us received more than half of all votes, the election was declared a failure. Another one will have to be held.

My life changed completely after the election. I was shunned by village leaders as well as their families. On the other hand, I won sympathy from people who felt that I had said what they wanted to say. When they asked, 'Why did you do it?' I always answered, 'It's not important that I get elected or not. I just hope that the democratically elected leader will feel the pressure and responsibility, and therefore do his best to serve the village during the three-year term.' That's the whole point about this system. I am sure it will push forward not only democracy, but also the development of rural China. Many problems remain, and some villagers are still not interested, while others don't even know how to vote. But once they see they can make a difference, they will vote carefully. Some people may try get elected through bribery, but when the people see he does not want to serve them, they won't give him a second term.

I don't know when the new election will be. Of course, I will contest it again, but I'm not going to waste my time waiting. I've just invested in a new type of sweet potato which is said to give higher yields and has better resistance to pests. If it's successful, I will introduce it to my fellow villagers, as I want to have more to offer them when I am village leader. I don't mean to promise miracles—I am no miracle worker with three heads and six arms. What I *can* promise is a clean chief keen to work for their interests.

I don't know much about Western democracy, but I'm confident about China's grass-roots version. I heard about President Clinton's sex scandal from the television. In their system, there are incredible events like putting the president on trial. I'm not sure we want that kind of democracy. But as China develops, maybe one day we will have a democratically elected president too.

Sherry Liu

Coming Home

Hundreds of thousands of Chinese were persuaded to return to rebuild their devastated motherland in the 1950s. Maoist controls prevented most from leaving again, until Deng Xiaoping opened China's door to foreign investment and technology. In the last two decades, over 300,000 of China's top students have viewed that door as an exit sign through which few would return. One who did was Beijinger Sherry Liu. After ten years realizing the American dream, Sherry (born Xiaohong, 'Little Red') returned in 1995 as Motorola's legal director for Greater China, a mediator between two very different worlds increasingly bound up in the global economy.

'We set no value on objects strange or ingenious, and have no use for your country's manufactures.' In 1793, the Qing emperor Qianlong thus dismissed the fruits of the Industrial Revolution brought by the British Macartney mission. Two centuries later, Chinese passion for ingenious objects and the rest of the high-tech revolution makes the PRC the key market worldwide for multinationals like Motorola. Once the Qing was cajoled into accepting foreign participation, Confucian reformers espoused the formula, 'Chinese learning for the essence, Western learning for the function'. The principle still applies today, for the protectionist measures and many idiosyncrasies of China business mean that bridge-builders like Sherry Liu are highly prized.

Fighting a deluge of emails, her mobile phone rarely silent, it is Sherry's duty to steer Motorola through a country where the rule of man has long held sway over the rule of law. Building that rule of law, enshrined in the 1999 state constitution, has become a key slogan of the current regime. It is a trend that would have horrified the PRC's founding fathers, as it ultimately challenges the Party's monopoly on power. The growing appreciation that individuals can take their grievances against each other or the government to court, and occasionally win, is a vital foundation to developing civil society in China.

Deng had hoped Chinese who studied overseas would return as the vanguard driving through his reforms. Beyond the products and services they sell, the returned Chinese are exerting a subtle influence on local society through the transmission of Western concepts of business, law, and politics. In a few years, US-trained officials will outnumber the technocrats educated in the Soviet Union in the 1950s who still dominate the government. Sherry represents this new breed of Chinese, boasting international outlooks, transferable skills, and falling outside the authorities' usual control mechanisms. Despite her demanding job, she writes poetry, paints, and travels widely.

Fifty years ago, the dream of peaceful unification and an end to civil strife galvanized the enthusiasm of Chinese in and outside China. Fifty years on, the problems facing China may be different, but no less significant if the government is to ensure continuing development and a stable, prosperous foundation for the fresh challenges of the twenty-first century. To overcome them, and give all the Chinese people the standard of living they deserve, the PRC must nurture and keep the brightest and the best.

I DIDN'T WANT TO BECOME a lawyer. Back in 1980, filling out my university application, I was obsessed with James Bond 007 and badly wanted to be a spy. Yet it was my last wish, China's Political Science and Law University, that took me. Six years later I went to America. Unlike most of the ambitious young people who wanted to study or find work, I left China to follow the man I loved. It was a miracle I got the visa, and we decided to marry almost as soon as I landed in the United States. At the registry office, neither of us understood what was going on. A friend told us to say 'yes' and 'yes', so we did.

Sadly, our marriage didn't work out, though I gained in other ways. I had hoped to change careers by studying art, but as law was the only free course on offer I enrolled at law school as a visiting scholar and mastered English by attending class. In my first few years in America, I faced an identity and value crisis. America seemed so much more civilized than China, with a greater material life. Many mainland Chinese felt looked down upon—some even put on Hong Kong or Taiwanese accents. Though I never bothered, I sometimes wished I had been born there. I wished I were an American: these people have so many privileges and opportunities when people from the Communist world have almost nothing. I grew up in a Communist society that only appraised altruistic value.

To own nothing, to envy no one's success, in fact not even to desire to be better off than any other fellow comrade, these are the greatest virtues one should have. Here in this capitalist and egotistic world, everything seemed the opposite and people seemed to be happier. How do we maintain our dignity and ideals in a materialistic world when we've got nothing but our ideals? God dammit, I sometimes thought, why wasn't *I* born blond with blue eyes?! Fellow Chinese envied my success—I was the first female Chinese lawyer in Phoenix, and the first Chinese to pass Arizona's bar exam—but I knew I never had the opportunity to work on major cases. Well, between an American Harvard graduate, and a Chinese from an ordinary law school with a 'funny accent', which would you prefer?

I sound ungrateful, as the firm was extremely good to me, but by working only as an American lawyer, I felt half my brain was asleep. I wrote many poems to express my bitter struggle with identity. I thought I loved my own country, but its society was so mismanaged, I had to stay abroad. Gradually, I became reconciled with myself and the world, though for a long time my ego prevented me from handling China-related projects. I wanted to prove to myself I could survive anywhere. My father always said, 'Whatever you do, do not disgrace our ancestors.' That family pressure, the desire to 'return to one's hometown in silken robes', drives many Chinese. When Motorola knocked on my door in 1995, I had been away from China for ten years, but my friends persuaded me it makes sense to use one's best strength. They were right. I make decisions all the time. The decision to work in China might be the best I ever made.

A few weeks after my return, my American boss handed me all the documents on our marathon negotiations with a Chinese partner for a pager joint venture in Shanghai: 'Here, you take care of this.' I was left on my own, under pressure to reach a deal before a deadline that meant millions of dollars in tax breaks. Each side had different agendas, and for two days and nights we worked around the clock. I gave advice spontaneously on dozens of issues, updated working drafts, and summarized the main points after each round of negotiations. At dawn on the third day, we reached an acceptable consensus just in time. Motorola gave me the general counsel award, its top award for a company lawyer.

I soon realized that knowing how to function in China is in my blood. I feel like a mediator bridging the two cultures, or 'a fish in water', as the Chinese say. It's a misconception that lawyers should remember every item of the law. What's important is to know where the law is coming from, to understand the language and culture, and make sound judgements with common sense and tact. Every day is a challenge, exciting and fulfilling—that's why I love my job. Now I am making a contribution and feel part of China again. Motorola's challenge is to benefit both the company and China over the long term. Its China strategy is heavy long-term investment, technology transfer, localization, and partnership with the Chinese. We reinvest all the money made here. One reward was being among the first and most successful foreign companies permitted wholly owned operations.

China is a socialist country, meaning the government is heavily involved in almost everything. In the West, you largely do business on your own. But anything you do here, from setting up a company to sacking people, requires lobbying the government. It's a constant battle to discover laws and regulations that are often neither published nor binding nationwide. The best resource is word of mouth. The lack of transparency is worse when no one is definitive: interpretation depends on who and where you ask.

One reason Chinese companies operate more easily here is simply that many don't care. It's not that they *want* to violate the rules, rather a mentality of 'if I'm not caught, I'm okay'. But if I tell my clients, 'just ignore the law, it's not clear', I'd be fired on the spot. Western multi-nationals are extremely legalistic, with a higher level of business ethics and integrity. Without clear instruction, they hesitate to go ahead. 'Don't panic!' I tell them. 'If you demand 100 per cent certainty, go home now, as there is no perfect solution. Make an informed decision and sleep with it.' By explaining the pros and cons from a different cultural angle we can find a compromise solution and move cautiously. A giant like Motorola, committed to a market with huge potential and intense competition, cannot afford to stand around and wait. I believe foreign investment does have a positive impact in China, because foreign companies foster a legal environment with greater transparency, meaning no closed-door decisions or judgements.

To be fair, tremendous progress *has* been made in China's legal system, though there is a long way to go. Despite the fact that judges, and many others who make important decisions for society, are paid so little, the chances of getting a fair trial *are* increasing. Many new laws have been published, including criminal procedure law and commercial and financial legislation. Foreign investment regulations are already more sophisticated than most of China's legal canon, and people in this sector *are* trying harder, probably thanks to higher publicity. China may even have enough laws. The problems are consistency, interpretation, and enforcement. Court verdicts should be based on right and wrong, not who knows who, or offers the bigger bribe. There is a medicine to cure the disease—an independent and open judicial system—but it is still too strong for the authorities to take.

I usually come over as a patriot, since people often say that I always try to defend China. In China, people call those who come back from abroad 'returnees'. Yet in a sense, a great comfort and realization that has come to me over the past few years in China is the feeling that I'm not really Chinese, nor American, but a global citizen, comfortable in any culture. Despite the frustrations of living and working here, I see China in a better light, as I remember what its past was like. We only need to look at ourselves, fifteen or twenty years ago, and how poor our lives were, how little personal freedom we had in choosing the job or lifestyle we wanted.

If we look further back, we can hardly believe what the Chinese people have gone through. Many old people seem so ordinary, yet have extraordinary stories to tell. My parents describe events not so distant in time yet so foreign to me. When people have suffered so badly— from division by foreign powers, famine, and civil war—they are likely to be instigated by someone offering utopian dreams of a better life, and willing to accept more suffering, or even totalitarianism, in pursuit of that goal. During the Anti-Japanese War, my father escaped his Japanese-run school aged 11 and walked for a month at night through the blockade to reach a Nationalist base area, and then joined the PLA. He was still fighting in Yunnan in 1950; he walked all year across the country bearing food and arms as heavy as himself. Later, aged 18, he commanded 100 soldiers and rode a white horse. In the Great Leap Forward, he returned to my grandmother's village where he witnessed and survived the terrible famine.

I was 3 when he was locked up in 1966 at the start of the Cultural Revolution. By then he was propaganda minister at a top military academy. Three years later, we were exiled with my mother for re-education in the Ningxia desert, while my father was sent to a different camp. All the exiles from the academy basically built their own prison. Some former Nationalist generals and Communists like my father were put in the same village. They hated each other at first but in time became friends and together made the desert bloom. My parents were such loyal Communists—people could have escaped from the camp, but everyone sincerely wanted to re-educate themselves. Yet the pressure of reform through labour proved too much for many inmates, who committed suicide.

My earliest memories are chasing the mice around the horse stable that was our home for a few years. The greatest fears of my childhood were bandits, floods, and Soviet attack—though our camp was in the desert, we, like the rest of the country, dug tunnels and practiced emergency evacuation. I remember a big furnace was lit in 1971 to celebrate Lin Biao's death and burn all the documents that incriminated camp residents. Everyone was so emotional, for it meant we were spared the planned transfer to Maoergai swamp, equivalent to a death sentence, where many Red Army comrades had died on the Long March.

When I went to college in the early 1980s, my father would still underline political rhetoric in the newspapers for my sister and me, to ensure we took the correct party line. But gradually my parents changed, until they have become more pro-reform and right-wing than me. 'How could people change like that?' an American colleague once asked me. She had visited China in the seventies, and again in the nineties. In the isolated environment of Mao's China, we may have appeared a dumb army of identical blue suits. But give people greater freedom to think and access to the outside world, and they will think and act differently.

Now people are more concerned about money, careers, and individual success than the road to Marxism. It would be hard for me to give up this life and become a guerrilla fighter for utopia. Yet if I had returned to live like an ordinary Chinese in a state-owned enterprise, I doubt I'd be so content. I can't blame the millions of Chinese in America who don't want to come back. It is only human nature to seek a better life. If China can't provide equivalent living standards, challenging employment, and the freedom they enjoy abroad, why would they want to come back? Fortunately, as China opens up and gradually enters the world family, there will be more opportunities here. I didn't see it so clearly until my own return.

I am proud of China's achievements over the last fifty years—look where we have come from, when no one took China seriously. Now people think, 'How will China react?' I'm proud too of the pace and direction of change—we are achieving in decades the progress other countries took centuries to accomplish—and cautiously confident in China's future. Political struggles are decreasing, as we are a more 'normal' country now and increasingly prosperous. Yet as Marx said, 'The economic foundation determines the upper structures.' The Chinese leadership knows its priority is getting the economy right—if the people have enough to eat, they won't cause trouble. We were so confident two years ago, before the Asian financial crisis hit, and the dangers are still there. Mao warned 'a single spark can start a prairie fire'. The rise of unemployed rural, urban, and government workers is just one issue that could trigger instability.

I have read that if you test laboratory mice by changing their environment once, they try to adapt; twice, and they are confused; but change it too many times, and they go crazy. Look at us, we have been confused countless times and are still more or less sane! The Chinese have an old curse, 'May you live in interesting times', yet ultimately I believe these times of change have made the Chinese soul more beautiful. Those who have suffered pain and loss appreciate life more intensely. Through war, famine, and ideological struggle, we have retained a human quality and become even more real.

Maybe I have died hundreds and thousands of times.
Maybe I will be crushed, buried, and completely forgotten.
Yet I will always accept the circumstances I live within.
And still will I hold a passionate faith
in the ultimate triumph of ordinary men.
[From 'The Uncertain Faith', by Sherry Liu]